'Some have suggested that victimology boundaries; this book shows how it is done. A valuable field, which will captivate students and scholars alike.'

Robert Elias, *Professor of Politics & Legal Studies,
University of San Francisco, USA*

'This book is something new under the sun: a lively, politically astute study aimed at widening the compass of victimology to include an emergent cultural victimology and victimology of collectivities. It is the most interesting victimology text I have seen in a long while.'

Nicole Rafter, *Professor of Criminology, Northeastern
University, USA*

'*Victims: Trauma, testimony and justice* exposes how the processes of victimization are as much cultural, structural and social as they are personal and emotional. It reinserts the real and symbolic human, historical and social dimensions of victimisation back into victimology. It takes a radically innovative approach that engages the reader through case studies that illustrate the complexity of victims' experience of trauma, justice, suffering and resilience. *Victims: Trauma, testimony and justice* is essential reading for a wide range of professionals in the justice sector, as well as students and academics of criminology, victimology, sociology, social work, psychology, law and gender.'

Kerry Carrington, *Head of School of Justice, Faculty of Law,
Queensland University of Technology, Australia*

'Victimology has recently undergone a dramatic transformation within criminology linked to the increasing social recognition of victims, who had long been objects of suspicion. Accounting for this moral inversion and defending a qualitative approach, Ross McGarry and Sandra Walklate propose a renewed perspective on the field through case studies on trauma, testimony, and justice. Their valuable endeavor thus paves the way for a long-awaited dialogue between criminologists and the other social scientists who have explored the ambiguous emergence of the figure of the victim.'

Didier Fassin, *Professor of Social Science, Institute for
Advanced Study, Princeton, USA*

Victims

The study of victims of crime is a central concern for criminologists around the world. In recent years, some victimologists have become increasingly engaged in positivist debates on the differences between victims and non-victims, how these differences can be measured and what could be done to improve the victims' experience of the criminal justice system. Written by experts in the field, this book embraces a much wider understanding of social harms and asks which victims' voices are heard and why.

McGarry and Walklate break new ground with this innovative and accessible book; it offers a broad discussion of social harms, the role of the victim in society and the inter-relationship between trauma, testimony and justice and asks:

- How has harm been understood and under what circumstances have those harms been recognised?
- How and under what circumstances are those harms articulated?
- How and under what circumstances are the voices of those who have been harmed listened to?

Each chapter draws on case studies posing a range of questions designed to assist in reflection and critical engagement. This book is perfect reading for students taking courses on victimology, victims and society, victims' rights and criminal justice.

Ross McGarry is Lecturer in Criminology within the Department of Sociology, Social Policy and Criminology at the University of Liverpool. He has written widely in international journals on criminology, victimology and military sociology. He is the co-editor (with Sandra Walklate) of other forthcoming texts, including *Criminology and War: Transgressing the Borders* from Routledge, and the *Palgrave Handbook on Criminology and War*.

Sandra Walklate is Eleanor Rathbone Chair of Sociology at the University of Liverpool and is internationally recognised for her work in and around criminal victimization, particularly the fear of crime. She has written extensively with Ross McGarry and Gabe Mythen on risk, resilience and cultural victimology and in 2014 received the British Society of Criminology's award for outstanding achievement.

Victims

Trauma, testimony and justice

Ross McGarry and Sandra Walklate

Routledge
Taylor & Francis Group

LONDON AND NEW YORK

First published 2015
by Routledge
2 Park Square, Milton Park, Abingdon, Oxon, OX14 4RN

and by Routledge
711 Third Avenue, New York, NY 10017

Routledge is an imprint of the Taylor & Francis Group, an informa business

© 2015 Ross McGarry and Sandra Walklate

The right of Ross McGarry and Sandra Walklate to be identified as authors of
this work has been asserted by them in accordance with sections 77 and 78 of
the Copyright, Designs and Patents Act 1988.

All rights reserved. No part of this book may be reprinted or reproduced or
utilised in any form or by any electronic, mechanical, or other means, now
known or hereafter invented, including photocopying and recording, or in any
information storage or retrieval system, without permission in writing from
the publishers.

Trademark notice: Product or corporate names may be trademarks or
registered trademarks, and are used only for identification and explanation
without intent to infringe.

British Library Cataloguing in Publication Data
A catalogue record for this book is available from the British Library

Library of Congress Cataloging in Publication Data
McGarry, Ross.
Victims : trauma, testimony and justice / Ross McGarry and Sandra Walklate.
pages cm
ISBN 978-0-415-85633-1 (hardback) -- ISBN 978-0-415-85634-8
(paperback) -- ISBN 978-0-203-72737-9 (ebook) 1. Victims of crimes.
I. Walklate, Sandra. II. Title.
HV6250.25.M395 2015
362.88--dc23
2015001024

ISBN: 978-0-415-85633-1 (hbk)
ISBN: 978-0-415-85634-8 (pbk)
ISBN: 978-0-203-72737-9 (ebk)

Typeset in Bembo
by Taylor & Francis Books
Printed in Great Britain by Ashford Colour Press Ltd.

MIX
Paper from
responsible sources
FSC
www.fsc.org   FSC® C011748

Contents

List of figures

Preface and acknowledgements

The contents of this book represent a different personal journey for each of the authors. Its focus has been generated through many conversations both formally and much more informally between us, from the classroom to the coffee shop.

Sandra would like to acknowledge the importance of the opportunity presented to her by George Murphy, a probation officer on Merseyside, who opened the door of Victim Support to me in the early 1980s and set me off on this journey with 'victims' all those years ago. I was engaged with victim support (and Rape Crisis) throughout the 1980s and the early 1990s and I witnessed the growth, development, and influence of those organisations (Victim Support in particular) on the changing face of the policy process. I also had a great deal of fun! Changing occupational circumstances took me in a different direction, one that more squarely addressed the efficacy of policing responses to domestic violence. Throughout, however, my passion and concern for more general victim–related issues has not diminished. Over the last decade my work with Gabe Mythen (and latterly Ross) has been a joy, as has the willingness of my partner, Ron Wardale, to read and comment on everything I write; even though we do not always agree with one another, it is of huge value to me. More recently conversations with Jon Shute, Lizzie Cook, and Will McGowan have been an important impetus to the work produced here. The faults that remain, however, are my own!

Ross would like to first and foremost acknowledge the support and guidance of Sandra throughout the production of this book, not to mention numerous other publications over the years. In many ways the content of this book represents (for me at least) one long conversation that started between us some time ago and has been influenced and matured by numerous conversations with colleagues and students at Liverpool. Particularly instrumental in shaping my thinking in this way has been our friend and colleague Gabe Mythen, always on hand to offer friendly support, guidance and an intellectual edge to many a conversation; he was, indeed, responsible for the focus of Chapter 5, thanks to a well timed passing comment in the midst of the writing process. I would also like to thank in advance any colleagues and students who pick up this work and endeavour to read it for themselves. If even one person is offered a way to think differently about the discipline of victimology in the ways that I was desperately trying to piece together as a student, then I will consider this book to have served its purpose. On a personal note I would like to thank my soon-to-be wife Amanda, who has patiently listened to numerous iterations of many of the ideas and concepts aired throughout these pages. All of my contributions in this book are dedicated to her as she has, in many ways, written them with me, but of course any inaccuracies are mine and mine alone. Thanks also go to Rex Features for their kind permission to reproduce the image of Anders Breivik in Chapter 7.

Finally, we would both like to thank Heidi Lee from Routledge for her warm and consistent encouragement throughout the production of this book. Bringing a book to print is by no means an easy process and we are once again grateful for the ways in which Heidi has helped us manage this manuscript to completion.

Sandra Walklate and Ross McGarry
Department of Sociology, Social Policy and Criminology
University of Liverpool, January 2015

Introduction

In the *Criminological Imagination*, Jock Young (2011) noted that mainstream criminology is guilty of an over-reliance on statistically driven research that abstracts the experience of crime and bloats the criminological lexicon to the detriment of its own creativity. Following Young's call for a critical and theoretically informed criminology, Walklate and Mythen (2014: 185) have recently averred that,

> this 'fetishism with numbers' not only takes its toll on what is considered to be acceptable criminological work but also rests on unsound assumptions about social reality.

Within this book we position ourselves in a similarly minded way about the discipline of victimology. Following some of the critical and cultural strands outlined by Young, and developing the case for the kind of critical victimology first put forward by Walklate (1990) and Mawby and Walklate (1994), this book picks up where Walklate and Mythen (2014: 185) conclude in observing that, 'The toll taken by the "bogus of positivism" is equally pertinent to victimology'. This 'toll' has indeed impacted upon the discipline of victimology, evidenced by the volume of victimological research that relies upon mass victimisation surveys as its chief means to observe the *occurrence* of criminal victimisation. If this data is taken as constituting *the* view of the (victimising) social world then it can, and does, abstract the lived experience of *being* a victim (qua Spencer, 2010) and pushes the advancement of a more challenging theoretical and empirical agenda to the margins of victimological concern. However this is not to be read as an abandonment of quantitative data sources within victimological research, quite the opposite in fact. Like Young, we advocate for quantitative data to be used critically: to be employed where necessary with healthy scepticism to strengthen theoretical and empirical claims about the social world as experienced by victims. The image on the cover of this book provides a pertinent example of the reasoning here.

A deeper analysis of this image is addressed more fully in the conclusion, but for now it is worth noting that it is a photograph, taken by the first author, of

The All Souls Altar of Remembrance, Trinity Church, Manhattan. The building itself is situated in close proximity to the site of the Twin Towers of the World Trade Center, and remains standing post the terrorist attacks in the US on 11 September 2001 (9/11). The image is indeed striking. It is littered with brief personal testimonies depicting messages of remembrance for lost loved ones. The question it asks is: how does this help us to think critically and creatively about victimology in the ways briefly implied above? From the point of view to be developed here, the practices of recording victimisation associated with mainstream victimology in the aftermath of 9/11 sit in the shadowy backdrop of this image. The deaths of 2,996 civilians in Manhattan on 9/11, in what ostensibly amounts to mass murder, were remarkably not counted in US Uniform Crime Reports for that year. This prevented the skewing of localized victimisation data with a dramatic spike in homicide in 2001 (Leighton, 2002). Agamben (2005) might term this practice as being one of 'exception' in rela-tion to domestic penal processes. Indeed thinking critically about what has been foregrounded by the 9/11 moment (Roach 2011) and what has been simultaneously rendered 'exceptional' is a good place to start for the kind of victimology we want to develop. The starkest illustration of exceptional responses to these events was evidenced by the subsequent invasion and occupation of both Afghanistan and Iraq, in 2001 and 2003 respectively, by Western military forces. These events were said to have been rationalized domestically by the United States government in the appropriation of the 2,996 victims' obituaries, using the 'ordinariness' of their lives to depoliticize and rationalize a brutal military response (Edkins, 2003). However the con-sequences of 9/11 did not just impact upon these direct victims. As we have noted elsewhere,

> the legacy of the trauma associated with 9/11 extends way beyond those that died and their families. It haunts witnesses who are less frequently heard.
>
> (Walklate et al., 2014: 267)

Indeed other embedded experiences of the traumatic effects of 9/11 have played themselves out in multiple forms of primary victimisation in the decade that followed. Alison Young (2010) points out that the wider ramifications of 9/11 were felt far beyond its direct victims, with over 400,000 people within a kilometre of ground zero said to have suffered from PTSD in the aftermath of the attacks. As for the sites of Western retaliation for 9/11, in Afghanistan over 11,000 civilians were killed as a result of the subsequent war and are merely a fraction of the actual number of direct victims there since recording of civilian deaths began in 2007 by the United Nations Assis-tance Mission in Afghanistan. Thus there is potential for scores of what Strobl (2004) describes as 'non-victims' to have gone unnoticed for half of the war's duration. These figures, added to over 149,000 civilian deaths caused as a result of war-related violence in Iraq (Iraq Body Count, 2014), means that the scale of victimisation caused as a result of 9/11 remains indeterminate. Coming to terms with these events as forms of victimisation, and the consequences that they have, is often (with notable exceptions as we shall see) excluded from victimological interests. Yet their undeniable presence demands a critical and cultural engagement for a victimology informed by theory and creativity, not simply quantification.

In the following pages we wish to extend our thoughts about victimology by taking some creative license with the work of Young (2011) and frame our endeavors as the beginnings of a *Victimological Imagination*, a project that we have begun in small ways elsewhere (see McGarry and Walklate, 2011; McGarry, 2012; Walklate et al., 2014). In so doing, three lines of inquiry, that have differently captured victimological interest, are traced through the chapters of this book: trauma, testimony and justice. Each chapter uses a case study embedded in different ways to help exemplify the issues that these lines of inquiry draw our attention to. To be clear, we have purposefully avoided simply placing each case study in a separate box that the reader can easily bypass. Instead we hope to engage the reader with each case study as a heuristic device. They are intended to facilitate the development of our arguments, explore victimological theory, and encourage trespassing into other cognizant areas of study. There is no uniformity to the ways in which each case study has been employed; some are used comparatively, others are used to demonstrate the application of methodology, a number of them are embedded in the chapter as a whole, while others are used as platforms from which to launch broader discussions. So with this in mind it is worth briefly outlining the overarching structure of this book.

Outline of the book

Chapter 1 explores the different ways in which the concept of the 'victim' has been understood. Here the different theoretical perspectives that can be identified within the area of victimology are discussed. These perspectives are routinely identified as positivist, radical and critical victimology. To these a fourth emergent perspective is added that is returned to in the conclusion: cultural victimology. In offering an overview of these perspectives the different emphases each of them give to choice, suffering and power relations are considered. Arguably these are the three key dimensions to understanding who is, and who is not, considered to be a victim. Within this chapter we make use of our first case study, presenting two public inquiries: the *Saville Inquiry* into Bloody Sunday and the *Savile Inquiry* into allegations of historical sexual abuse by the late celebrity Jimmy Savile. This case study is used to offer some appreciation of the relative strengths and weaknesses of these victimological perspectives in relation to victimological theory and victim policy. This opening chapter sets the scene for the exploration of the three themes with which we are concerned: trauma, testimony and justice.

Trauma

Chapter 2 considers the impact of crime by asking questions about the relationship between individual experience of criminal victimisation and the notion of trauma. From fear to post-traumatic stress syndrome to loss of earnings as a result of not being able to go to work, being a victim of crime takes its toll on individuals. This chapter traces the different ways in which the impact of crime has been understood, and in so doing identifies two narratives claiming to make sense of such impact: the victim narrative and the trauma narrative. The convergence of these two narratives poses problems for how responses to individuals might be put together and acted upon, but understanding it affords an important backcloth against which to understand the contemporary policy preoccupations with criminal victimisation. To help articulate this, the second case study is split into two parts between the personal testimonies of Jill Saward's *Rape: My Story* and Doug Beattie's *An Ordinary Soldier*. These help to problematise the nature of individual victimisation and raise the question of gender. Chapter 3 follows by addressing the connection between traumatised individuals and those of collectivities. Two types of victimisation are set out within this chapter as being intimately related: interpersonal violence and the violence experienced as a result of war. To assist in making these claims this chapter is structured around a third case study which also has two elements: the *Murder of Stephen Lawrence* and the *2003 Iraq War*. When situated in the overarching discussion of hate-crime victimisation, it is possible to connect the individual act of murder and mass killing at war (i.e. genocide) with the concept of essentialism. By engaging in and examining the extremes of victimisation that this case study enables us to do, the trauma experienced by collectivities is drawn more squarely into victimological debate.

Testimony

Chapter 4 addresses the question of methodology within victimological work. It is commonly known that victim research has been led by positivist victimology, contingent upon large victimisation surveys that look to abstract the occurrence of being a victim from the experience itself. In the interests of re-engaging victimological research with the subjective experience of being a victim, John Tulloch's personal testimony *One Day in July* is used in this chapter as a fourth case study to demonstrate an alternative way of employing victim 'data' and victimological methods. The practice of 'testimonio' is proposed as a more sensitive and critical approach to allow victims to speak for themselves and on behalf of others with similar experiences of victimisation. Moving on from the testimony of individual victim voices, in Chapter 5 we recognize that the experience of collective victimisation can gather attention from victim movements, often with the intention of pursuing 'justice'. This chapter situates victim movements in the broader problematic context of victim 'needs' and 'rights' to illustrate the ways in which personal testimony can be used as practice to fight for victim restitution and justice. To illustrate this, the fifth case study concentrates on the thirtieth anniversary of the *Bhopal Industrial Disaster* in India and is employed in an extended way throughout the chapter. In doing so we demonstrate that when pitted against corporate victimisation even large victim movements with global recognition struggle to keep blatant victimisation from being subsumed by legalese, obscured from public view, or hidden in plain sight.

Justice

Listening to victims' voices can be manifested in a number of different shapes and forms. Chapter 6 takes a critical look at how this 'listening' is expressed within contemporary criminal-justice policy interventions. Set against the backcloth of therapeutic jurisprudence, this chapter considers the extent to which victim impact statements and restorative justice affords victims effective mechanisms for expressing their feelings about what has happened to them. We provide an exemplar of this by presenting our sixth case study in two parts. In the first we address two victims' personal statements published in the British press, labelled as *Massacre in Flat 12*. In the second we reflect upon the victims' voice in the restorative justice process reported in *Transcending: Reflections of Crime Victims,* a book of portraits and interviews by Howard Zehr (2001). Across both of these cases we argue that these mechanisms raise possibilities for apology and forgiveness, encourage reflection on the potential for justice as therapy, and set the scene for a consideration of justice as reconciliation. Chapter 7 then considers the extent to which the contemporary recourse to international justice can afford the victim in post-conflict situations the opportunity for reconciliation. Our seventh case study takes the form of an image of Anders Breivik, the man guilty of carrying out the *2011 Terrorist Attacks in Oslo and Utoya*. This image is used as a platform to launch a review of the efficacy of international criminal tribunals, truth and reconciliation commissions, and transitional justice. In doing so this chapter develops an appreciation of reconciliation as multilayered and multifaceted, in which there is space for the hierarchy of victimhood to operate. The chapter suggests there is some value in reflecting on these policy interventions as comprising part of a political economy of reconciliation in which the victim's voice can be sometimes muted and sometimes erased.

Finally in Chapter 8 we revisit the issues covered throughout these chapters and look to posit some new ground for victimology to traverse – that of cultural victimology. To help facilitate our intentions we return to the cover image of this book and reflect upon it in our eighth and final case study: the *Victimologist as Witness*.

Our hope is that engaging the reader with what we consider to be marginalised but entirely relevant debates within victimology will make a small contribution in pushing forward a creative and more critical agenda within the discipline. This was indeed the intention of Young (2011: 181), who posited what he saw as two opposing sides of criminology:

> One is the criminology of the imagination; the other frowns on such exuberance and resolutely proclaims the mundane nature of the everyday world. One carefully patrols its borders, shutting out the philosophical, the overly theoretical as too reflective, and carefully excluding war, genocide, state crime, crimes against the environment and so on, as outside its 'scientific focus', while the other views such boundaries as there to be crossed and there to be learnt from.

Within this book our intentions are much the same for expanding the victimological imagination through a theoretical engagement with victimological theory across these three overarching themes: trauma, testimony and justice.

References

Agamben, G. (2005) *State of Exception*. Chicago: University of Chicago Press.

Edkins, J. (2003) 'The rush to memory and the rhetoric of war', *Journal of Political and Military Sociology*, 31(2): 231–50.

Iraq Body Count. (2014) 'Documented civilian deaths from violence'. Available at https://www.iraqbodycount.org/database.

Leighton, P. (2002) 'Decision on 9/11 victims is a crime', *Long Island Newsday*.

Mawby, R. and Walklate, S. (1994) *Critical Victimology*. London: SAGE.

McGarry, R. (2012) 'Developing a victimological imagination: an auto/biographical study of British military veterans', unpublished PhD thesis, Liverpool Hope University.

McGarry, R. and Walklate, S. (2011) 'The solider as victim: peering through the looking glass', *British Journal of Criminology,* 51(6): 900–917.

Roach, K. (2011) *The 9/11 Effect: Comparative Counter-Terrorism*. Cambridge: Cambridge University Press.

Spencer, D. (2010) 'Event and victimisation', *Criminal Law and Philosophy*, 5(1): 39–52.

Strobl, R. (2004) 'Constructing the victim: theoretical reflections and empirical examples', *International Review of Victimology,* 11: 295–311.

Walklate, S. (1990) 'Researching victims of crime: critical victimology', *Social Justice*, 17(3): 25–42.

Walklate, S. and Mythen, G. (2014) *Contradictions in Terrorism: Security, Risk and Resilience*. Oxon: Routledge.

Walklate, S., McGarry, R. and Mythen, G. (2014) 'Trauma, visual victimology, and the poetics of justice', in M. H. Jacobsen (eds) *The Poetics of Crime: Understanding and Researching Crime and Deviance through Creative Sources*. Surrey: Ashgate. pp. 263–83.

Young, A. (2010) *The Scene of Violence: Cinema, Crime, Affect*. London: Glasshouse Books.

Young, J. (2011) *The Criminological Imagination*. Cambridge: Polity.

Zehr, H. (2001) *Transcending: Reflections of Crime Victims*. Intercourse, PA: Good Books.

Chapter 1

Exploring the concept of 'victim'

Introduction

The *Oxford Dictionary of English* offers several interpretations of the word victim:

A person harmed, injured, or killed as a result of a crime, accident, or other event or action: *(for example) victims of domestic violence / earthquake victims.*
A person who is tricked or duped: *(for example) the victim of a hoax.*
A person who has come to feel helpless and passive in the face of misfortune or ill-treatment: *(for example, a victim might say) I saw myself as a victim.*

Soanes and Stevenson (2005: 1963) add to this by including 'A living creature killed as a religious sacrifice'.

From this list it is already possible to discern a number of key, taken for granted, characteristics associated with being a victim. By definition a victim is someone who has suffered (suffering that in itself can be multidimensional and multifaceted), sometimes willingly, sometimes not, as a result of forces more powerful than themselves. Thus suffering, power relations and choice are central to how we understand who is, and who is not, given the label 'victim' and, as a consequence, who acquires or does not acquire victim status. Victimhood is therefore highly contested. It is also important to note that when the word victim is gendered, as in French for example, it becomes inextricably linked with being female. Historically, feminists have consequently objected to the use of this term since it implies that the passivity and powerlessness linked with it are also, by implication, associated with being female. Their preference for the term survivor over victim, and the ideological differences that the adoption of this implies, has resulted in some tensions between feminism and victim-oriented work. Viewed contemporarily, these tensions now appear a little sterile since much recent empirical work points to the value of understanding that being a victim or a survivor are, at a minimum, part of a process (see, for example, Walklate, 2011). In any event, it is the case that an either/or approach to victimhood suggests a rather static, uniform and unifying use of the term victim (or survivor) not borne out by empirical reality.

Dignan (2005) and Furedi (2013) have also indicated that the term victim has only recently become commonly used and intertwined with crime. The more common usage, as illustrated by the dictionary definitions above, is more general and connotes individuals who have experienced misfortune through no fault of their own. Indeed it is important to note that technically, in any criminal justice system, talking of 'victims' is highly problematic given that in such a context it is more usual to refer to complainants. Legally the terms victim and offender are deemed inappropriate since using them potentially assigns guilt and/or innocence to participants in a process in which the outcome has yet to be determined. Such issues notwithstanding, Strobl (2010: 6) suggests four analytical possibilities in the construction of victimhood: the actual victim (someone seen by themselves and others as a victim), the non-victim (not recognised as a victim by themselves or others), the rejected victim (seen by themselves as a victim but not by others), and the designated victim (regarded by others as a victim but not by themselves). So in addition to presumptions of suffering, power relations, choice and gender (as implied by the feminist intervention), Strobl's categorisation centres the importance of process: who is and who is not recognised as a victim, how this happens, and who is involved in this process. By implication, focusing attention on processes of *recognition* of victimhood implicitly connects how victim status is understood and articulated, or not, in policy.

In this first chapter we explore the different ways in which the contested nature of the concept of 'victim' alluded to above has been expressed within the sub-discipline of victimology. We consider the strengths and weaknesses of the different perspectives to be found there, the claims they make for and about the victim, and we examine their usefulness by exploring our first case study. This presents two public inquiries: the *Saville Inquiry* into Bloody Sunday and the *Savile Inquiry* into allegations of historical sexual abuse by the late celebrity Jimmy Savile. In considering these different perspectives in this way it is important to note two things. The influence of each of the perspectives within victimology is variable over and through time. In addition, as debates within victimology have ebbed and flowed, they have paralleled, though not always connected with, developments within the policy sphere addressing the victim of crime. Over time these policy concerns have steadily risen up the policy agenda, both nationally and internationally. This chapter will also offer some comments on these interconnections. But first, how has victimology thought about the 'victim'?

Contesting victimhood

Different commentators attribute the founding of victimology to different people, but there is some common agreement that the work of both Mendelsohn and von Hentig made a significant contribution to this field of enquiry. These men, as émigré lawyer-criminologists, were concerned, as many other intellectuals were from the late 1940s onwards, to try and make sense of the events surrounding the Second World War, particularly the Holocaust. Their interest in the victim, stemming from these wider concerns, generated two key concepts: victim precipitation and victim proneness. Emulating early criminological thought, these writers were concerned to identify what made victims different from non-victims. In order to do this they each produced victim typologies. Mendelsohn's typology centred on the notion of culpability and asked the question: To what extent could the victim be held culpable for what had happened to them? Von Hentig's typology centred on the notion of proneness and asked the question: To what extent did the victim possess characteristics that made them more prone to victimisation than those who were not victimised? In their different ways each of these typologies implicitly dealt with the issue of choice: the extent to which the victim had made or not made a choice in relation to what had happened to them. As has been argued elsewhere (Walklate, 2003) choice was not the only concept implicit in each of these typologies. Both Mendelsohn and von Hentig made assumptions about the non-victim against whom the victim was to be measured.

As has already been intimated, this early work shared with criminology the desire to understand victimhood through differentiating victims from non-victims, and these differences determined the likelihood of their victimisation. In each of these typologies the non-victim was assumed to be the white, heterosexual, middle-class male. These assumptions, by implication, specified who early victimologists thought victims were most likely to be and not to be: the young, the elderly, the disabled and members of ethnic minority groups for von Hentig; those who were least culpable for what had happened to them for Mendelsohn. These assumptions in their respective ways also reflected particular understandings of vulnerability and blame. As a result, men, for example, were not assumed to be vulnerable and did not easily acquire the victim label. In addition, in taking on board notions of culpability, it is easy to see how this work, almost by definition, became occluded with the assignation of victim blaming (Antilla, 1974). Indeed it was this potential for blame that feminists were so concerned to challenge. Taken together, the implicit embrace of culpability and vulnerability within early victimological work became the mechanisms through which victims were 'othered' and pathologised: rendered different.

As some of the comments above imply, victimology mirrors criminology in many ways in its search for explanations, data gathering, and desire to influence the policy agenda. Also, like criminology, it draws together a heady mix of academics, activists and policymakers. This mix results in a number of tensions. Miers (1989: 17) has observed, for example, that 'victimology has too many voices to allow any coherence in its reported understanding of the world' and Rock (1986) has commented on its 'catholic' nature. Some time ago these tensions moved Fattah (1992) to call for the separation of 'humanistic' victimology from 'scientific' victimology and, as has already been noted, there has been an unhappy coexistence between victimology and feminism (see Rock, 1986; Walklate, 2007). This heady mix can produce quite different agendas for victimology which, when overlaid with the politicisation of the victim observed by Miers (1978), it can be difficult to disentangle evidence, from politics, from emotion. Here we shall take the available theoretical perspectives found within victimology as one way to begin to understand how these issues can be differently intermeshed.

Contemporarily it is possible to identify at least four competing perspectives on how to make sense of victimhood: positivist victimology, radical victimology, critical victimology and the emergent strand of cultural victimology. Coexisting, though somewhat separate from these perspectives, it is also important to note the hugely influential impact of feminist-informed work within and outwith victimology, particularly in relation to violence against women. As we shall see, each of these perspectives works with different interpretations as to the centrality of choice, suffering and power relations in their understandings of the nature of victimhood. We shall say something about each of these perspectives in turn.

Positivist victimology

Miers (1989: 3) was one of the first commentators to coin the term 'positivist victimology'. He defined this perspective as being concerned with

> the identification of factors which contribute to a non-random pattern of victimisation, a focus on interpersonal crimes of violence, and a concern to identify victims who may have contributed to their own victimisation.

Others have used different labels to draw attention to work with this kind of focus (for example, Karmen, 1990, talks of conservative victimology and Walklate, 1989, discusses conventional victimology). Whatever label is preferred, this work has, as its bedrock, concepts like victim proneness and lifestyle that have their historical roots in the work of the Founding Fathers of victimology. Empirically these concepts direct attention to the need to understand the regular patterning of criminal victimisation. This is exampled in the work of Hindelang et al. (1978), who developed a lifestyle approach to understanding exposure to criminal victimisation and operationalised this through the increasingly sophisticated refinement of the criminal victimisation survey. (Incidentally, it should be noted that the criminal victimisation survey as a method has also proved to be of significant value to those concerned with violence against women. This is discussed more fully below and alluded to in Chapter 4.) The marriage between this rather conservative conceptual agenda and the survey method centres the production of data about the regular patterning of the kind of criminal victimisation considered to be normal and routine: street crime, burglary and violence against women. Moreover, latterly it should be noted that a version of a criminal victimisation survey has been deployed to measure the nature and extent of crimes against humanity, particularly genocide (see Hagan and Rymond-Richmond, 2009). All of this activity has made its presence felt in the realm of policy. Thus it has to be said that positivist victimology is the version of victimology whose presence has had the most consistent and influential impact on policy debates in relation to a number of different aspects of criminal victimisation. Nonetheless the question remains, what does this version of victimology have to say about choice, suffering and power relations: how does positivist victimology construct and understand the victim?

Positivist victimology is underpinned by the presumption that the term 'victim' is itself non-problematic. The victim is given by the criminal law. This provides the framework for what is understood as the self-evident nature of suffering. Giving pre-eminence to the law in defining victimhood is the means whereby patterns of criminal victimisation can be measured not only nationally but internationally. The law then becomes the arena in which claims can be made to improve conditions for the victim. For example, John Hagan and his colleagues recognised the need for hard, quantitative data in the form of a criminal victimisation survey so that the international criminal court might be encouraged to 'see' the crime of genocide in Darfur (we return to his work in similarly informed ways regarding the war in Iraq in Chapter 3). However, using the law as the frame in which the victim becomes visible (or indeed remains invisible) has consequences. First the experience of the individual (their suffering) can become transposed into a threat to social order (in the recognition of their experience being criminal) and can open the door for greater punitive responses to offenders. Second, and perhaps more importantly for this discussion, is that the *individual* and *collective* voice of the victim is both silenced and co-opted into that (potentially) punitive agenda. Put simply, there is little scope here for an *appreciative* stance towards the victim as an individual, or a group, who has choices and makes choices. Third, taking the law as a definitional entry point for victimology belies an inherently static and functionalist view of society, with consequent implications for its understanding of power and power relationships. Thus Dignan (2005: 33) has commented that,

> both the state itself, through its agencies, and also the legal and penal processes that it sanctions may themselves create new victims and also further victimize those who have already been victimized by an offender.

In this way positivist victimology contributes to the presumption that victims and offenders exist in a zero-sum relationship with one another, denying that they might overlap as experiences or indeed that there might be 'delinquent' victims (Miers, 2007).

In putting the potential role of the state to the fore, as well as the social reality that victims and offenders can be one and the same person, both Dignan and Miers are alluding to the consensual view of power inherent in a functionalist view of society. Such a view of society and the power relations therein restricts the vision of victimhood available to positivist victimology. This version of victimology can only reveal to us the regular patterning of criminal victimisation as given, defined and responded to by the criminal justice process. It has a very limited capacity to help us understand why the patterns take the shape and form that they do, what that looks like for the individuals concerned, and, importantly, what the patterns of victimisation that go on 'behind our backs' look like. Vulnerability to crime and risk from crime are given by the measured patterns of criminal victimisation. In sum, positivist victimology cannot help us understand how victims are produced and reproduced through time and space.

Radical victimology

Belying the radical potential that was clearly evident in the work of Mendelsohn (Rafter and Walklate, 2012), the origins of this strand of thought within victimology are more often than not attributed to the essay written by Quinney published in 1972. In that essay Quinney asked the provocative question: Who is the victim? Quinney (1972: 314) pointed out that 'our conceptions of victims and victimisation are optional, discretionary and are by no means given'. Thus this version of victimology renders visible those made invisible by positivism: victims of state crime, victims of corporate crime, victims of oppression and so on: harm that goes on 'behind our backs'. It is a perspective within victimology that takes a human-rights position, rather than a criminal-law position, in setting an agenda for its subject matter and is one that has been pursued in the work of Elias (1986) and latterly by Kauzlarich et al. (2001) and Rothe and Kauzlarich (2014). So Kauzlarich et al. (2001: 183–89) offer six propositions framing a victimology of state crime that draw on the concepts of power and suffering (for example, victims of state crime tend to be the least powerful social actors whose suffering can be neutralised or for which they can be blamed, as we go on to discuss in the forthcoming chapters). Rothe and Kauzlarich (2014) push this agenda further.

Rather than take either the criminal law, or indeed human rights as their starting point they make a case for thinking about the nature of the harm perpetrated as the entry point for victimology. The chapters in their edited collection illustrate how this might be operationalised: from 'street' children, children in institutional 'care', the 'Mukaradeeb Massacre', the normalisation of civilian bombing, victimisation during and after war, through to Somali piracy and the role of immigration policy in victimising the undocumented alongside displaced persons. All of these substantive topics offer ways in which the victim label could be reasonably and justifiably applied in these different contexts. The themes that seem to tie these issues together are power and power relations, the propagation of systematic violence(s), and vulnerability. In centring the powerful as arbiters of social harm, this version of victimology brings to the agenda a much wider appreciation of who can or cannot be a victim, including those who might be the least likely to acquire such a label (see McGarry and Walklate, 2011). Leaving aside the questions of harm and vulnerability for the moment (both of these issues are discussed more fully in Chapter 2), Box (1983: 17) pointed out some time ago, 'the majority of those suffering from corporate crime remain unaware of their victimisation – either not knowing it has happened to them or viewing their "misfortune" as an accident or "no-one's fault"'. This is referred to by Geis (1973) as 'victim-responsiveness' (which we return to address in Chapter 5). Whilst it might be argued that Box and Geis are alluding to an empirical rather than a conceptual problem, the implied case made for widening conceptions of victimhood is a solid one (see Whyte, 2007). This is especially the case as victimological concerns have increasingly reached into the arena of mass victimisation and atrocity crimes (see for example Letschert et al., 2011). The question remains, however: What sense does this perspective make of power relations, suffering and choice?

Self-evidently, radical victimology centres on power and power relations. Understanding the nature of these relationships and how they set the frame for claims to victimhood are not just central for the radical victimologist, they are given primacy. Whilst the harm done and/or suffering caused by the state and/or 'the powerful' also feature as drivers for radical victimological concerns about who is given a voice and who is not, the state and state power constitute the starting point for analysis, whether or not the suffering caused is attributed to such power relations. So, in privileging the state and state power, individual choice is at best downplayed, if not erased, a process that can raise difficult empirical questions (see for example Rafter and Walklate, 2012). The same might be said in respect of suffering. Whilst suffering (harm) is clearly privileged in terms of its structural dimensions, a dilemma remains in terms of who defines which suffering counts, under what conditions, and how these issues relate to individuals' accounts of their circumstances.

Critical victimology

Critical victimology is a label for a perspective that has been differently interpreted by different people (Holstein and Miller, 1990; Miers, 1990; Fattah, 1992; Mawby and Walklate, 1994). This discussion will focus on that version of critical victimology adopted by Walklate (1990), and developed by Mawby and Walklate (1994) and Spencer and Walklate (forthcoming). Influenced by the questions raised by feminist-informed work and the theorising of Giddens (1984), this approach to victimhood marries the concepts of power, choice and suffering in a different way to that adopted by either positivist or radical victimology. This understanding of victimology puts to the fore the processes that create the victims we 'see' as well as the ones that we do not 'see' (power relations that can both create victims and protect perpetrators) whilst simultaneously recognising that the victim is a human agent who can be active as well as passive (and is someone who can make choices, though not necessarily in every set of circumstances) with their suffering mediated by power and choice. Consequently, critical victimology asks questions about the term 'victim' itself and the circumstances in which it is applied. It focusses attention on the underlying structural processes that lead to the manifestation and/or experience of victimisation and acknowledges the patterning of victimisation that so much of the work associated with positivist victimology has produced, but argues that understanding those patterns needs to appreciate the role of vested interests in the state in (re)producing them. Within this framework, who becomes a victim and who might embrace a victim identity (Rock, 2002) or indeed who might resist such an identity (Walklate, 2011) is neither simple nor straightforward and cannot be read from the patterns of criminal victimisation per se.

Critical victimology has not been without its critics (see for example Spalek, 2006: 45). Nonetheless, Chouliaris (2011: 38) reminds us:

> Critical victimology ... engages in a twofold task: to cast light on the institutions and structural relations that favour specific images of victimisation at the expense of others (contextualization); and to draw attention to situations that, despite producing serious victimization, are not designated as such.

Thus, critical victimology strives to conceive of the victim as a product of the interaction between the cultural and ideological in particular socio-economic circumstances. The agenda implied by a critical victimology takes the power of the state seriously as a self-interested arbiter of the victims (and suffering) that we see and do not see, but whose interests may vary across time and space. Consequently, it places some significance on the power of the victim label, in and of itself, as a unifying device (and frequently used as a uniform concept) for ideological purposes that has inclusive and exclusive properties. So, at an individual level who counts, and whose voice counts as a victim, can change in the light of these properties. Embedded in this position, as in the observations of Chouliaris (2011), are critical questions that relate to Christie's (1986) delineation of the ideal victim. However, before we go on to consider this construct, critical victimology, in the version under discussion here, also stems from a feminist-informed position, so at this juncture it will be useful to say something about the relationship between feminism and victimology.

Feminism and victimology

The tensions, both ideological and conceptual, that have informed the relationship between victimology and feminism have been well documented (see for example Rock, 1986; Rock, 2007; Walklate, 2007). Contemporarily, whilst some of those tensions have been, if not resolved then accommodated, it is important to note that feminist-informed work throws into clear relief the world view of (positivist) victimology in particular. In taking for granted that the world of the white heterosexual male is the norm against which all other forms of knowledge about victimisation are measured, positivist victimology offers a very limited space for victimology and feminism to talk to each other. However, as this chapter has demonstrated so far, there are other visions of victimology, and feminism has had an impact on those different visions. Its emphasis on the power relations of patriarchy clearly speak to the foregrounding of power found within radical victimology. Indeed, critical victimology as understood here was, and clearly is, informed by a feminist agenda, particularly with its emphasis on understanding the relationship between structure and context in producing the victims we see and do not see. Moreover, even within the positivistic orientation embedded in the criminal victimisation survey, it is evident that this method has been used with ever greater success in measuring the nature and extent of the kind of (criminal) victimisation that preoccupies feminist voices: rape, sexual assault, domestic violence. Yet, as Walklate (2014) has suggested, this method still struggles with what to count, how to count, who to count, and what to do with the data once it has been counted, in relation to this kind of violence. As a consequence, feminist-informed work asks profound questions for all social-science endeavours, particularly in relation to victimisation.

If feminism is taken to be a way of thinking that asks fundamental questions about who can know things and how things can be known (qua Harding, 1991), it is possible to frame a victimology that moves beyond the bifurcation between measuring regularities/patterns of criminal victimisation (positivism) and centring power relations (radicalism). Embracing these questions, critical victimology offers an opportunity to appreciate the role of a self-interested state in producing the 'facts' of criminal victimisation at different historical moments, alongside appreciating the toll that individuals can experience from 'crime' in the circumstances in which they find themselves. This does not mean that there are not regular patterns to criminal victimisation but it does mean that we might explain these patterns not by reference to that which differentiates victims from non-victims but by understanding the ways in which the routine practices of everyday life produce and reproduce victimisation. Indeed it is within those routine practices that the power of the state is also produced and reproduced. Thus, 'who acquires the label victim and why' are key questions to ask. It is at this juncture that it will be of value to consider the power of what Christie (1986) called the 'ideal victim'.

The 'ideal victim'

Put simply Christie's (1986) articulation of the 'ideal victim' and the characteristics underpinning it, typically captures the 'little old lady' as victim or 'Little Red Riding Hood' of Grimm's fairy tale: a young, innocent female, out doing good deeds, who is attacked by an unknown stranger. It is of no great surprise that this also resonates with the common-sense stereotype of the 'legitimate' rape victim. This is a stereotype that still carries significant weight across different cultures and jurisdictions that harks back to the early victimological under-standings of culpability and vulnerability discussed above. What Christie (1986) was endeavouring to capture was an appreciation of a process, one that is underpinned by assumptions (around vulnerability, choice and power) in which some people acquire the 'victim' label very readily and easily, and others never acquire it at all. Put simply: to acquire victim status, an individual's victimisation must be acknowledged by others. Acquiring the label 'victim' is a process. Interestingly, van Wijk (2013) has tested the utility of this concept in the context of international crimes. In applying Christie's (1986) characterisation in that setting, he argues that a similar process of acknowledgement is necessary before a response to victims of such crimes is generated. Thus he posits that in order for a victim status of international crimes to be assigned successfully certain conditions need to be met: the conflict must not be complex, it must be unique, short and well timed. Contemporarily, the role and use of the media is particularly pertinent to understanding the conditions of successful acquisition of victim status for these kinds of crime. In putting to the fore the importance of this kind of process van Wijk's (2013) analysis hints at what Furedi (1997) called a culture of victimhood, and we shall turn to an understanding of the emergent shape and form of a cultural victimology later in this chapter.

Importantly, the thoughts of Christie (1986) and latterly van Wijk (2013) lay bare the role that notions of 'innocence', 'legitimacy', and 'deserving' play in the process of acknowledging and assigning the victim label to either an indivi-dual experience or a collective one. Each of these concepts is a dimension of culpability and suffering that we have used in the discussion so far to make sense of the different emphases within the victimological perspectives we have been concerned with. Placing the notions of innocence, legitimacy and deserving centre stage led Carrabine et al. (2004) to identify what they termed a 'hierarchy of victimisation'. At the bottom of this hierarchy would be the homeless, the street prostitute, the drug addict – indeed all those categories of people for whom it is presumed that they expose themselves to victimisation. Thus any claim to the label and status of 'victim' becomes very difficult for these kinds of individuals/groups since arguably what happens to them is a result of the choices they have made. They are not innocent, legitimate or deserving. At the top of this hierarchy would be the elderly person robbed in their own home, the child abused by their parents, and perhaps increasingly an elderly person abused by their children. In other words, these individuals/groups have been subjected to processes not of their choosing. They are innocent, legitimate and deserving. It is important to note that this hierarchy in itself reflects other presumptions, particularly about vulnerability. For example, the elderly and/or children are presumed to be vulnerable (physically weak/fragile and relatively powerless) as a result of their age: that is, innately vulnerable. It is worth noting at this point that this assumption of innate vulnerability is connected to assumptions about the body that Spencer (2014) has usefully illustrated for critical victimology. However, it is also a unidimensional understanding of vulnerability (see Walklate, 2011) that constrains visions of victimhood as a result (which we return to in Chapter 2).

Nonetheless, this hierarchy of victimisation can be applied in different contexts (as illustrated by the work of van Wijk, 2013) and can be used to facilitate an understanding of the ways in which its shape and form changes over time. Some groups and/or individuals acquire victim status and others lose it. McGarry and Walklate (2011), for example, make the case for soldiers – a group for whom the victim label was previously considered anathema – being recognised as victims in the UK as a result of the illegal engagement in conflict in Iraq and Afghanistan from 2003–14. In addition, Aradau (2004) deploys the idea of a 'politics of pity' to make sense of the ways in which trafficked women came to be constructed as victims rather than women seeking work, in order for their abuse to be recognised in terms of policy. In other words, women featured higher up on this hierarchy as they were reconstructed as a group who were innocent, legitimate and deserving. On the other hand, there is evidence to suggest that the political complexities lying behind the mass victimisations in Darfur clearly inhibited international recognition of those experiences as genocide (Hagan and Rymond-Richmond, 2009). In all of these examples, being acknowledged as a victim is a complex process. None of this process implies that such acknowledgement necessarily entails acceptance of the victim label on behalf of an individual or a group (Walklate, 2011) or indeed a victim identity (Rock, 2002), but what all the examples indicate is a role for the 'cultural'. As Mythen (2007: 466) has observed:

> Acquiring the status of victim involves being party to a range of interactions and processes, including, identification, labelling and recognition.

Enter the potential for a cultural victimology.

Cultural victimology

Mirroring developments in the criminological turn to the 'cultural', there has been a recent move towards cultural victimology (Mythen, 2007). This is 'a victimology attuned to human agency, symbolic display, and shared emotion' (Ferrell et al., 2008: 190). Elements of this cultural turn can be found in Furedi's (1997) rather sardonic observations about the emergence of a compensation culture in which we are all victims now (though it should be noted that Quinney, 1972, highlighted similar concerns). The increasing importance of the cultural is also alluded to in Valier's (2004) observations of a return to the Gothic: making public the suffering of the victim. Indeed the rising focus on such cultural preoccupations cannot be divorced from the increasingly visual nature of social life which constantly and consistently places us beside the victim, encouraging us to feel what they feel. Thus Berlant (2004: 5) comments,

> members of mass society witness suffering not just concretely in local spaces but in the elsewhere brought to home and made intimate by sensationalist media, where documentary realness about the pain of strangers is increasingly at the center of both fictional and nonfictional events.

So this turn to the cultural has (at least) two aspects. First, individual and/or collective experiences of victimisation and its aftermath and how those experiences are shared with family or friends, or symbolised more publicly (like, for example, in the roadside shrine or in the 'on the scene' reportage and/or other public media). Second, the ways in which grief, loss and trauma are mapped through the criminal-justice process (see *inter alia* Ferrell et al., 2008; Mythen, 2007). We offer extended thoughts on this in Chapter 8, but for now suffice it to say that we recognise criminal victimisation provokes a range of emotional responses that take their toll on individuals and is not new (see Chapter 2 for a fuller discussion of this). Neither is it novel to observe that emotions pervade the workings of the criminal-justice process (see for example Karstedt, 2002; Green, 2008; Freiberg and Carson, 2009). Arguably what has been a more recent development is the public nature and public voice given to those emotional responses, the public dissemination of them, and the intermeshing of these processes with criminal-justice policy. Thus McEvoy and Jamieson (2007: 425) have commented that 'Suffering becomes reshaped, commodified, and packaged for its public and didactic salience'. One analysis of this intermeshing has been termed 'courting compassion' by Walklate (2012).

Cultural victimology is very much a newcomer to the field of victimological studies, though there have been some tentative incursions into developing an agenda for this kind of work (see for example Walklate et al., 2011; Howie, 2012; Walklate et al., 2014). This agenda carries implications for how we do victimological work (as we go on to discuss in Chapter 8 in relation to the victimologist as witness) and what kind of concepts might inform that work. Carrabine (2012: 467), for example, has observed that 'human suffering should not be reduced to a set of aesthetic concerns, but is fundamentally bound up with the politics of testimony and memory'. If we add 'trauma' to testimony, memory and witnessing, arguably cultural victimology has the capacity to offer something both creative and critical to the study of victims. Cultural victimology foregrounds suffering, our exposure to it, how it is presented to us, and what sense we make of it. It has less to say about choice, either individual or collective (though much media coverage can and does deny the opportunity for choice-making decisions, as Tulloch's [2006] analysis of his experiences as a 'victim' of the bombings in London on 7 July 2005 illustrate in Chapter 4). It does, however, afford the opportunity to think about politics and power relations. At every juncture in the public nature of suffering some voices are heard and others are silenced (as intimated in Wijk's 2013 discussion of the ideal victim of international crimes). Importantly, silencing can frame events in particular ways to the exclusion of others (see Matthieson, 2004). Indeed, as Quinney (1972: 322) commented some time ago, 'To exclude the Vietnamese civilian suffering from criminal war operations is to accept national military policies'. The absences can therefore be powerful. If we were to add to this appreciation of the role of the state an understanding of what Jessop (2010) has called 'complexity reduction', it is possible to connect the cultural with the critical. In some respects, cultural victimology adds an important dimension to critical victimology in so far as it has the potential to extend the latter's desire to situate victimhood within a wider political economy of the state in the context of the cultural. More specifically, the role of the media in all its forms in offering understandings of social reality contributes profoundly to a cultural political economy. From a point of view, mediatised representations of the victims that we see and those that we do not see act as conduits for the interests that serve those of the powerful whilst simultaneously being multilayered.

To summarize: these four theoretical perspectives within victimology offer different understandings of the relationship between choice, power and power relations, and suffering. Implicit in this coverage of them is the recognition that each of them do not have an equal presence in the discipline. Neither do each of them have the same power and influence in the domain of policy. By far the most powerful of these positions has been positivist victimology. This has been exemplified in the ever-increasing presence of the criminal victimisation survey as a source of data about all kinds of victimisations and the use of that data source for informing policy. As that data source has grown, so understandings of victimhood, as reflected in policy, have developed. It is also the case that there are different and more voices now competing for the theoretical space within victimology, and this too has had a recursive relationship with victim policy. So it is to a brief overview of the changing nature of the policy map that we shall now turn, before introducing our first case study as a way of situating these theoretical ideas.

The changing policy map

Arguably, over the last fifty years or so, there have been two phases in the development of policy understandings of victimhood. The first phase takes us from the late 1960s until the early 1990s. The second phase takes us from the mid-1990s to the present. We will briefly address each of these in turn.

Phase one: 1960s–1990s

The introduction of the criminal victimisation survey method, in the late 1960s in the United States and in the early 1980s in the UK, contributed not only to the emergence of victimology as a discipline but also to the subsequent dominance of positivist victimology. The growth and development of this kind of victim-informed survey work, alongside the growth and development of victim-centred support groups, increased awareness of, and focused attention on, the kind of impact that what might be called conventional crime (e.g. burglary, theft, street violence) had on people's everyday lives. It also provided, and still does provide, a considerable database that points to the evidence that, depending upon what kind of crime is being considered, an individual's chance of criminal victimisation can be maximised or minimised by factors such as age, ethnicity, sex and social class. In addition, this kind of data consistently confirms that it is the poorest members of society who bear most of the burden of crime, especially in terms of impact (see for example the work of Dixon et al., 2006 and Chapter 2), thus lending support to the agenda for a radical victimology proposed by Kauzlarich et al. (2001) discussed earlier. However, it should be noted, as Hope (2007) has argued, that there is much left to be desired from this data source in terms of *explaining* the patterning of criminal victimisation. Nonetheless, its use, and the evidence it provides, has been very influential in informing policy initiatives (Van Dijk, 2010) and reorienting the work of criminal-justice practitioners (Garland, 2001; Spalek, 2006; Walklate, 2007).

Alongside the emergent influence of positivist victimology outlined above, the 1960s and 1970s were also marked by the emergence of 'second wave' feminism. These campaigning voices, sparking the development of organisations like Rape Crisis and the Women's Refuge Movement, exposed not only the nature and extent of violence against women (and children) but also the gaps in criminal justice and other responses to these issues. Following on from the seminal survey work of Diana Russell (1990) on the nature and extent of rape, the feminist-informed embrace of the criminal victimisation survey had led to a much improved and informed understanding of the nature and extent of violence against women (see for example Walby and Myhill, 2001) that has had a significant impact on the policy response to these issues on national, regional and international policy agendas.

From this first phase of policy interest it is possible to see that this map of victimhood comprised all those categories of individuals who might be considered to be more or less vulnerable, and thereby more or less deserving of victim status. Thus it is easy to see how the elderly, female victim of crime, the child who has been abused by their parents, or the woman who has been subjected to systematic abuse might feature most readily higher up on the 'hierarchy of victimisation' (qua Carrabine et al., 2004). However, as the recent revelations concerning allegations of historical sexual abuse made against some British celebrities have illustrated, even when the claimants to victim status might be considered ideal (i.e. young and vulnerable), there are all kinds of questions to be asked about who, what, and under what conditions, victimisation is made visible or rendered invisible, and by whom. We return to address this in our case study below.

Phase two: mid-1990s to the present

In the second phase of this policy map, largely as a consequence of the influence of the feminist movement and the increasing awareness of other forms of identity politics, academic research and policy responses became much more sensitive to questions of ethnicity and sexual diversity. Indeed, some of the findings of the criminal victimisation survey data (by now a good deal of repeat data was available), along with its refinement as a tool of measurement, added weight to the need for such sensitivity. This work foregrounded the importance of the impact of power relations experienced as a constant feature of the everyday life for people from ethnic minority groups in particular. For example, the seminal work of Hesse et al. (1992) brought to the fore the problems of racial harassment and the recognition of racially motivated crime in the UK. Feminist work was one impetus for the increasing recognition of not only the diversity of the nature and extent of criminal victimisation amongst women but also amongst men. It centred on men and masculinity as a problem that seamlessly led into an appreciation of other dimensions to victimisation and sexual diversity. This work made important interventions in recognising that men could be victims too (see Hobdell and Stanko, 1993; Goodey, 1997) and even more significantly that this experience applied not only, or even exclusively, to homosexual men.

This brief overview of these developments certainly points to quite a complex and extensive picture of the kind of victim who was the focus of the policy map by the start of the twenty-first century. It was during this time that commentators like Furedi (1997: 97) were also making observations about a 'culture of victim-hood' in which '[a]dvocates of victimhood integrate the themes central to the culture of abuse and imply that once a person has become a victim, he or she will always be a victim'. This is a position echoed by Alison Young (1996), who observed that victimhood had become, if not equated with, then certainly elided with citizenship. Thus, the term 'victim' became a unifier for policy initiatives (not only in the UK but elsewhere, as will be intimated in later chapters of this book) that simultaneously 'celebrates' some victim experiences and erases others. Of course what is being observed here is a cultural shift in the (privileged) attention being given to suffering per se, rather than any *evidenced* claim about the nature and impact of the harm done (by crime). One moment pertinent in these developments was the events in New York on 9/11. Jenks (2003) has called these events transgressive since they challenge our collective and individual understanding of what it is that can be taken for granted in our everyday lives, particularly in relation to what is understood as crime and the nature of criminal victimisation. They have certainly fuelled the assumption that 'we are all victims now' and, as suggested in the Introduction, require a creative and theoretically informed approach in order to grasp their complexity.

So, over the last fifty years the shifting policy map has gone from recognising the (powerful) impact that criminal victimisation can have on individuals, to claims of victim status based on experiences relating to collective identity (racial harassment, for example, which Spalek, 2006, refers to as 'spirit injury'), to a cultural context in which some would say 'we are all victims now'. Within these changing contours it is also possible to discern some consistencies in who is and who is not readily acknowledged as a victim. One way of beginning to explore this is by illustration. The following case study provides some insights into how we might begin to think more clearly about the constitution of who comprises the 'we' of 'we are all victims now' and the extent to which the perspectives on victimhood we have discussed in this chapter aid in this process.

Case study: a tale of two Savil(l)es

Our case study comes in two parts: the events of 30 January 1972 in Derry, Northern Ireland (commonly referred to as 'Bloody Sunday'), and the allegations of abuse perpetrated by UK celebrity Jimmy Savile, which came to light in 2012, a year after his death. They have been chosen for a number of reasons. First of all, whilst some of you reading this book may not be familiar with the precise details and circumstances of each of these events, you will be familiar with similar events that pertain to your own social context. The first set of events here concerns the consequences of questionable violent behaviour on the part of soldiers deployed under difficult national circumstances. Such behaviour is not unique to those soldiers deployed in Northern Ireland in 1972. From the events of Oradaur-sur-Glane in 1944, to My Lai in 1968, to the Mukaradeeb Massacre in 2004 (see Wall and Linnemann, 2014), and many circumstances in between, examples can be found in all societies where similar things have happened. The second set of events draws attention to the consequences of questionable behaviour on the part of an individual whose public image was one of celebrity hero rather than celebrity villain. Again the fall from grace that this example taps into is not unique. The fact that both of these events reflect recurrent if not common experiences is one justification for our choice of them. The second reason we have chosen them is that they provide a useful device for illustrating both the changing contours of victimhood discussed above, alongside the ongoing obstacles to the recognition of victimhood. In particular, they each offer different narratives around choice, power relations and suffering, the key concepts that we have used to present the victimological perspectives under discussion here. In addition they each afford some insight about questions of gender raised by a feminist-informed approach. First we shall say something about each of these events in turn.

The Saville Inquiry, 2010

On 30 January 1972, British soldiers shot and killed thirteen civilians and injured fifteen others (one of whom later died) in Derry, Northern Ireland. All parties seem to agree that the civilians were engaged in a peaceful demonstration in a context charged with tension. In 1972 Northern Ireland was a desperately divided place, with Catholics wanting to leave the United Kingdom and join Eire and Protestants wanting to remain part of the United Kingdom. This divide had led to many violent clashes between the Royal Ulster Constabulary and the paramilitary organisations that existed on both sides. In 1969, after particularly violent events, the British Army was deployed in Northern Ireland to restore law and order. It was in this capacity that the Army was present on what has come to be called 'Bloody Sunday'. Our concern with this event is not to test the veracity of the various interpretations of what happened on that day – though, tellingly, the Saville Inquiry (2010) does comment that there was a 'loss of fire discipline' amongst some of the soldiers deployed – but to bring to these events a victimological imagination: who was/is the victim here? Why? How do we begin to make sense of the ongoing drive to call the soldiers deemed responsible for what happened to justice?

In some respects the answers to these questions are straightforward: unarmed people engaged in asserting their peaceful right to demonstrate died or were hurt. They are clearly victims, as were their families. This happened as a result of heightened tensions, poor communications and loss of fire discipline amongst the particular group of soldiers concerned. To call those responsible to justice, however long after the event, has a rationale to it. For the families concerned, the pain of their suffering has never gone away. This was a series of events that might be classically framed within the positivist concepts of victim proneness and victim precipitation. However, this only offers part of the story. Conway (2009: 407) quotes from the plaque on the Bloody Sunday memorial, part of which is represented below:

> The passage of time has not dimmed the memories or the trauma of those who marched on Bloody Sunday for civil rights and an end to internment. For those who lost loved ones, the hurt is particularly ingrained ... A debt of justice and truth is still owed to the victims.

From this we get a sense of not just an individual wound with individual victims and perpetrators but a collective wound. This is a desire for collective recognition and the admission of collective responsibility.

Here it is possible to discern the strong sense of politics, power and the role of the state of radical victimology. Whatever the legitimacy or otherwise of this view it captures a different sense of victim and perpetrator, one that McEvoy and McConnachie (2013: 503) hint at,

> that in some instances the establishment and reproduction of blame for past hurts may actually obfuscate culpability for either historical or contemporary wrongs, which were actually inflicted by victimised communities.

Here they are discussing the problems of making sense of innocence and victim-hood in transitional societies that can have 'the effect of shining a bright light on the villains while the audience, or indeed those who choose not to watch, can remain safe in the darkness' (McEvoy and McConnachie, 2013: 503). For the purposes of our analysis, these observations serve to remind us that victimhood is contested and a product of processes that can produce and reproduce particular social relations, encouraging the assignation of blame and victimhood in particular ways (qua critical victimology). To date, the hurt caused by Bloody Sunday remains. There appear to be moves to bring prosecutions against individual soldiers who were involved that day, but that action, in and of itself, speaks volumes about what and who is still excluded in terms of victimhood.

The Savile Inquiry, 2013

Our second example is in some respects more recent in the public imagination, though also taps into victim experiences of the past. As has been intimated above, Jimmy Savile was a well-known and popular celebrity noted for his charity work. On 3 October 2012 a television programme presented the stories of five women, all of whom claimed to have been sexually assaulted by him: two whilst they were attending an approved school, three on the premises of the BBC. A public outcry ensued – which Greer and McLaughlin (2012), have labelled 'trial by media' – prompting an investigation of these complaints. This took a number of forms. An inquiry was put in place to understand why the complaints that had been made against Savile whilst he was alive were not proceeded with and a larger inquiry, Operation Yewtree was put in place to consider the wider ramifications of the further complaints that were coming to light after the television programme. In just focusing on the complaints against Savile, Gray and Wall (2013) report that around 450 individuals had alleged sexual abuse complaints against him, 73 per cent were from people under 18 at the time of the incident, 82 per cent were female, with the peak time in which these complaints occurred being 1966–76. Those who reported Savile had their accounts 'discounted', leaving Savile 'hiding in plain sight' (Leavitt, 2013: 6). The disclosures against Savile have resulted in a series of complaints against other celebrities being reported to Operation Yewtree – complaints that have met with varied 'success' in the criminal courts.

Often referred to by the media as historic abuse, these experiences were clearly not historic for the victims, as the Leavitt Report (2013) recognised. Indeed as is often the case with sexual and/or physical abuse, such experiences only come to light when either the perpetrator dies, or when the victim feels confident enough that their voice is going to be heard. In making sense of why these events have come to light now, much has been made of the cultural context at the time they occurred. Indeed it would be misplaced to lose sight of the role of changing tolerances to sexual behaviours. However, in many of the complaints, the victims were underage at the time of the incident and, arguably when faced with a male celebrity, were much less likely to be making a choice. Indeed some were either physically or mentally less capable. They were vulnerable and resonate with Christie's (1986) concept of ideal victims. However, power makes its presence felt here not just interpersonally but also institutionally, from the hospitals to the BBC in which some of this abuse was said to occur, to the poor response by the police when complaints were made to them at the time of their occurrence.

Here again we can see the differential value of the victimological perspectives discussed above. Positivist concepts of victim precipitation and the capacity for victim blaming would fail to capture the institutional 'blind eye' turned to some of these practices (Leavitt, 2013), feminist-informed work would reveal much about the gendered nature of these complaints, and radical victimology could tell us something about the institutional neglect by the police, and others, of these victims at the time. Moreover, a culturally informed critical victimology would reveal much to us about the context of the media response and the presumptions made about human capabilities to cope with stressful events in their lives in the wake of that response (see for example Furedi, 2013).

To summarize, these two incidents have served to illustrate the different ways in which victimological perspectives can shed light on, or fail to shed light on, dimensions of criminal victimisation. Each in its different way also illuminates developments within victimology and the differential attention that has been paid to victims' voices as those concerns have developed. In drawing out those victims' voices our attention is also drawn to how and under what circumstances those voices might be heard, and for what purpose. Throughout this book we have drawn on this feature of victimological concern, testimony (listening to victims' voices), and we develop it as an important resource for empirical data as well as a means for making sense of how such listening might afford the capacity for some healing for the victim. This first case study also raises some interesting possibilities of victimological concern in terms of justice and/or criminal-justice policy; the opportunity for healing/therapy, a possible outcome in the aftermath of the case of Jimmy Savile; or an opportunity for reconciliation in the aftermath of Bloody Sunday. Each of these themes is developed in Chapters 6 and 7 respectively. The two elements of this first case study also, in their different ways, draw attention to the power of the media and media coverage of events in encouraging us all to feel the suffering of others. As Pollard (2011) has observed in relation to the constant media (re)presentation of the events of 9/11, the indirect victimhood experienced by exposure to such images (images that neither space nor time can dilute) is a key ingredient in the contemporary cultural realm that may fuel people's anxieties. It certainly provides fuel for a cultural victimology. Finally, this first case study puts to the fore that not only are individuals troubled by criminal victimisation, as positivist victimology effectively documents for us, but so too are collectivities, as implied by radical victimology. How it might be possible to make sense of that trouble for each of these constituencies is the focal concern of Chapters 2 and 3.

Conclusion

Goodey (2005) observed that most people's experience of crime is 'home grown', that is committed by someone you know. That someone might be a neighbour, your partner, your employer or someone you met on the Internet. Home grown or not, this chapter has illustrated the different ways in which becoming a victim (of crime) can be understood within the context of victimology. In presenting these different ways of thinking, this chapter has illustrated the extent to which victimological thought has paralleled criminological thought and the extent to which that understanding has documented the competing voices that claim to speak for the victim. The chapter has also offered some comment on the links between those competing voices and the changing nature of policy under-standings of who the victim (of crime) may or may not be. Embedded in all of this, in both the academic and policy concerns with the victim of crime, is at least one problem.

Policies are intended to benefit all of us. Victimology as a modern discipline, and a meeting place for campaigners, policymakers and academics, is driven to inform policy at this level. This means that neither the academic perspectives nor the policies themselves readily 'see' the individual. Yet, as is observable in an almost routine fashion, in the contemporary political world it is the individual voices – with experience of a partner murdered or a child lost to rape and murder – who are called upon to inform policy. In a sense this captures part of the present cultural moment: a moment that privileges such individual experiences as a device to engage us all in their emotional distress. Such processes have two effects. They deny the patterning of criminal victimisation that has structural features at the local, national and global level (like, for example, violence against women) and they give voice to what in the past might have been a private matter, the distress caused by stressful life events: increasingly popularised as 'traumatic' (Laqueur, 2010). The invocation of trauma in relation to the impact of crime is the focus of Chapter 2.

Further reading

For a fuller explication of some of the theoretical perspectives discussed in this chapter see Walklate (2007), *Imagining the Victim of Crime*. If you are interested in an analysis of the '9/11 moment' and its potential links with cultural victimology take a look at Howie (2012), *Witness to Terror*. For a very popular and easily accessible introduction to victimology, now in its eight edition, see Karmen (1990), *Crime Victims: An Introduction to Victimology*.

References

Antilla, I. (1974) 'Victimology – a new territory in criminology', in N. Christie (ed.) *Scandinavian Studies in Criminology, Vol. 5*, London: Martin Robertson. pp. 3–7.

Aradau, C. (2004) 'The perverse politics of four-letter words: risk and pity in the securitisation of human trafficking', *Millennium: Journal of International Studies*, 33(2): 251–77.

Berlant, L. (2004) 'Compassion and withholding', in L. Berlant (ed.) *Compassion: The Culture and Politics of an Emotion*. London: Routledge.

Box, S. (1983) *Power, Crime and Mystification*. London: Tavistock.

Carrabine, E. (2012) 'Just images: aesthetics, ethics and visual criminology', *British Journal of Criminology*, 52(3): 463–89.

Carrabine, E., Iganski, P., Lee, M., Plummer, K., and South, N. (2004) *Criminology: A Sociological Introduction*. London: Routledge.

Chouliaris, Λ. (2011) 'The victimological concern as the driving force in the quest for justice for state-sponsored crimes' in R. Lestschert, R. Haveman, A.-M. de Brouwer and A. Pemberton (eds) *Victimological Approaches to International Crimes: Africa*. Cambridge: Intersentia. pp. 35–63.

Christie, N. (1986) 'The ideal victim' in E. A. Fattah (ed.) *From Crime Policy to Victim Policy*. London: Tavistock.

Conway, P. (2009) 'Rethinking difficult pasts: Bloody Sunday (1972) as a case study', *Cultural Sociology*, 3(3): 397–413.

Dignan, J. (2005) *Understanding Victims and Restorative Justice*. Maidenhead, Berkshire: Open University Press.

Dixon, M., Reed, H., Rogers, B., and Stone, L. (2006) *CrimeShare: The Unequal Impact of Crime*. London: IPPR.

Elias, R. (1986) *The Politics of Victimisation*. Oxford: Oxford University Press.

Fattah, E. (ed.) (1992) *Critical Victimology*. London: Macmillan.

Ferrell, J., Hayward, K., and Young, J. (2008) *Cultural Criminology: An Invitation*. London: SAGE.

Freiberg, A. and Carson, K. (2009) 'Evidence, emotion and criminal justice: the limits to evidence-based policy', *New South Wales Bureau of Crime Statistics and Research 40th Anniversary Symposium*, 18–19 February.

Furedi, F. (1997/2002) *Culture of Fear: Risk Taking and the Morality of Low Expectation*. London: Cassell.

——(2013) *Moral Crusades in an Age of Mistrust*. London: Palgrave-Pivot.

Garland, D. (2001) *The Culture of Control*. Oxford: Polity.

Geis, G. (1973) 'Victimisation patterns in white collar crime', in I. Drapkin and E. Viano (eds) *Victimology: A New Focus, Vol. 5*. Lexington, MA: D. C. Heath and Co. pp 86–106.

Giddens, A. (1984) *The Constitution of Society*. Oxford: Polity.

Goodey, J. (2005) *Victims and Victimology*. London: Longmans.

——(1997) 'Boys don't cry: masculinities, fear of crime and fearlessness', *British Journal of Criminology*, 37(3): 401–18.

Gray, D. and Wall, P. (2013) 'Giving victims a voice. Joint report on the sexual allegations made against Jimmy Savile'. London: MPS/NSPCC.

Green, D. (2008) 'Suitable vehicles: framing blame and justice when children kill', *Crime, Media, Culture*, 4: 197–220.

Greer, C. and McLaughlin, E. (2012) 'Media justice: Madeleine McCann, intermediatization and "trial by media" in the British press', *Theoretical Criminology*, 16(4): 395–416.

Hagan, J. and Rymond-Richmond, W. (2009) *Darfur and the Crime of Genocide*. Cambridge: Cambridge University Press.

Harding, S. (1991) *Whose Science? Whose Knowledge?* Buckingham: Open University Press.

Hesse, B., Rai, D. K., Bennett, C., and McGilchrist, P. (1992) *Beneath the Surface: Racial Harassment*. Aldershot: Avebury.

Hindelang, M. J., Gottfredson, M. R., and Garofalo, J. (1978) *Victims of Personal Crime: An Empirical Foundation for a Theory of Personal Victimisation*. Cambridge, MA: Ballinger.

Hobdell, E. and Stanko, E. A. (1993) 'Assaults on men: masculinity and male victimisation', *British Journal of Criminology*, 33(3): 400–415.

Holstein, J. A. and Miller, G. (1990) 'Rethinking victimisation: an interactional approach to victimology', *Symbolic Interaction*, 13: 103–22.

Hope, T. (2007) 'Theory and method: the social epidemiology of crime victims', in S. Walklate (ed.) *Handbook of Victims and Victimology*. Devon: Willan. pp. 62–90.

Howie, L. (2012) *Witnesses to Terror*. London: Macmillan-Palgrave.

Jenks, C. (2003) *Transgression*. London: Routledge.

Jessop, B. (2010) 'Cultural political economy and critical policy studies', *Critical Policy Studies*, 3(3–4): 336–56.

Karmen, A. (1990) *Crime Victims: An Introduction to Victimology*. Belmont, CA: Wadsworth.

Karstedt, S. (2002) 'Emotions and criminal justice', *Theoretical Criminology*, 6(3): 299–318.

Kauzlarich, D., Matthews, R. A., and Miller, W. J. (2001) 'Toward a victimology of state crime', *Critical Criminology*, 10: 173–94.

Laqueur, T. (2010) 'We are all victims now', *London Review of Books*, 32(13): 19–23.

Leavitt, Q. C. A. (2013) 'In the matter of the late Jimmy Savile. Report to the Director of Public Prosecutions'. London: Crown Prosecution Service.

Lestschert, R., Haveman, R., de Brouwer, A-M and Pemberton, A. (eds) (2011) *Victimological Approaches to International Crimes: Africa*. Cambridge: Intersentia.

Matthieson, T. (2004) *Silently Silenced*. London: Waterside Press.

Mawby, R. and Walklate, S. (1994) *Critical Victimology*. London: Sage.

McEvoy, J. and Jamieson, R. (2007) 'Conflict, suffering and the promise of human rights', in D. Downes, C. Chinkin, and C. Gearty (eds) *Crime, Social Control and Human Rights: Essays in Honour of Stan Cohen*. Cullompton, Devon: Willan. pp. 422–41.

McEvoy, K. and McConnachie, E. (2013) 'Victims and transitional justice: voice, agency, blame', *Social and Legal Studies*, 22(4): 489–513.

McGarry, R. and Walklate, S. (2011) 'The soldier as victim: peering through the looking glass', *British Journal of Criminology*, 46(6): 900–917.

Miers, D. (1978) *Responses to Victimisation*. Abingdon: Professional Books.

——(1989) 'Positivist victimology: a critique part 1', *International Review of Victimology*, 1(1): 1–29.

——(1990) 'Positive victimology: a critique part 2', *International Review of Victimology*, 1(3): 219–30.

——(2007) 'Looking beyond Great Britain: the development of criminal injuries', in S. Walklate (ed.) *The Handbook of Victims and Victimology*. Cullompton, Devon: Willan. pp. 337–62.

Mythen, G. (2007) 'Cultural victimology: are we all victims now?', in S. Walklate (ed.) *Handbook of Victims and Victimology*. Cullompton, Devon: Willan. pp. 464–83.

Pollard, J. (2011) 'Seen, seared and sealed: trauma and the visual presentation of September 11', *Health, Risk and Society*, 13(1): 81–101.

Quinney, R. (1972) 'Who is the victim?', *Criminology*, November: 309–29.

Rafter, N. and Walklate, S. (2012) 'Genocide and the dynamics of victimisation: some observations on Armenia', *European Journal of Criminology*, 9(5): 514–26.

Rock, P. (1986) *A View from the Shadows*. Oxford: Oxford University Press.

——(2002) 'On becoming a victim', in C. Hoyle and R. Young (eds) *New Visions of Crime Victims*. Oxford: Hart. pp. 1–22.

——(2007) 'Theoretical perspectives on victimisation', in S. Walklate (ed.) *Handbook of Victims and Victimology*. Cullompton, Devon: Willan. pp. 37–61.

Rothe, D. and Kauzlarich, D. (eds) (2014) *Towards a Victimology of State Crime*. London: Routledge.

Russell, D. (1990) *Rape in Marriage*. New York: Collier.

Soanes, C. and Stevenson, A. (2005). *Oxford Dictionary of English* (2nd edition, revised). Oxford: Oxford University Press. pp. 1963–64.

Spalek, B. (2006) *Crime Victims: Theory, Policy and Practice*. London: Palgrave.

Spencer, D. (2014) 'Corporeal realism and victimology', *International Review of Victimology*, advance access, doi: 10.1177/0269758014547992.

Spencer, D. and Walklate, S. (eds) (forthcoming) *Critical Victimology: Developments and Interventions*. Cambridge, MA: Lexington Books.

Strobl, R. (2010) 'Becoming a victim', in S. G. Shoham, P. Knepper, and M. Kett (eds) *International Handbook of Victimology*. Boca Raton, FL: CRC Press. pp. 1–26.

Tulloch, J. (2006) *One Day in July*. London: Little Brown.

Valier, C. (2004) *Crime and Punishment in Contemporary Culture*. London: Routledge.

Van Dijk, J. (2010) 'The International Crime Victims Survey', in M. Herzog-Evans (ed.) *Transnational Criminology Manual, Vol. 2*. Nijmegen, Netherlands: Wolf Legal Publishers. pp. 631–50.

Van Wijk, P. (2013) 'Who is the "little old lady" of international crimes? Nils Christie's concept of the ideal victim re-interpreted', *International Review of Victimology*, 19(2): 159–79.

Walby, S. and Myhill, A. (2001) 'New survey methodologies in researching violence against women', *British Journal of Criminology*, 41(3): 502–22.

Walklate, S. (1989) *Victimology: The Victim and the Criminal Justice Process*. London: Harvester Wheatsheaf.

——(1990) 'Researching victims of crime: critical victimology', *Social Justice*, 17(3): 25–42.

——(2003) 'Can there be a feminist criminology?', in P. Davies, P. Francis, and V. Jupp. (eds) *Victimisation: Theory, Research and Policy* (2nd edition). Basingstoke: Palgrave. pp. 29–45.

——(2007) *Imagining the Victim of Crime*. Maidenhead, Berkshire: Open University Press.

——(2011) 'Reframing Criminal Victimisation: Finding a Place for Vulnerability and Resilience', *Theoretical Criminology*, 15(2): 175–92.

——(2012) 'Courting compassion; victims policy and New Labour', *Howard Journal of Criminal Justice*, 51(2): 109–21.

——(2014) 'Sexual violence against women: still a controversial issue for victimology?', *Victimology: An International Review*, 20(1): 71–84.

Walklate, S., Mythen, G., and McGarry, R. (2011) 'Witnessing Wootton Bassett: an exploration in cultural victimology', *Crime, Media, Culture*, 7(2): 149–66.

——(2014) 'Trauma, visual victimology and the poetics of justice', in M. Haviid-Jacobsen (ed.) *The Poetics of Crime*. Farnham: Ashgate. pp. 263–84.

Wall, Y. and Linneman, T. (2014) 'Accumulating atrocities: capital, state killing and the cultural life of the dead', in D. Rothe and D. Kauzlarich (eds) *Towards a Victimology of State Crime*. London: Routledge. pp. 33–45.

Whyte, D. (2007) 'Victims of corporate crime', in S. Walklate (ed.) *Handbook of Victims and Victimology*. Cullompton, Devon: Willan. pp. 446–63.

Young, A. (1996) *Imagining Crime*. London: SAGE.

Part I

Trauma

Chapter 2

Traumatised individuals?

Introduction

Chapter 1 offered an overview of different theoretical perspectives on victimisation. Each of those perspectives understood who could be a victim, and what the genesis of their victimisation might be, by offering a differential emphasis on the relationship between power relations, choice and suffering. This chapter will now consider the last of these in greater detail: suffering.

It should be noted at the outset that the concept of suffering is subject to contestation (see *inter alia* Bourdieu et al., 1999; Wilkinson, 2005). This contestation is aptly illustrated in Fassin's (2012: 27) distinction between the 'naturalist' approach to suffering and the 'ironic'. The former takes the extent of suffering as a given condition of the twentieth century and the latter gives prominence to complaining as routine (qua Furedi, 2002). Pointing to problems with each of these approaches (the former assumes that suffering did not occur to the same extent in previous periods in history, and the latter neglects the extent to which suffering is something on which we can all agree), Fassin suggests a third approach that he terms 'critical'. In this approach the question becomes: 'How has this [suffering] come to seem self-evident to us? ... What are the consequences of this representation of the world through pain?' (Fassin, 2012: 29). Our appreciation of the questions raised by Fassin is, in the context of the concerns of this book, intimately connected with the ways in which awareness of the impact of criminal victimisation has been generated by the different victimological perspectives discussed in Chapter 1, along with the way in which the voices of victims have been foregrounded in the search for policy (Chapters 5, 6 and 7). Here, as in the next chapter, we are concerned to trace the narratives that link the conceptual apparatus presented in Chapter 1 with the policy claims addressed in the remainder of this book. In this chapter the focus of attention is on 'suffering' as understood through an appreciation of the impact that criminal victimisation can have on individuals and the tools available to us to make sense of that impact.

Understanding who is impacted by victimisation and under what conditions is neither a simple nor a straightforward process and can be rendered more complex depending upon an individual's structural location and what kinds of resources they have access to in helping them manage these kinds of events. In recognition of this complexity, this chapter considers the impact of victimisation on individuals; the chapter that follows considers the impact of victimisation on collectivities. Of course, in many ways these two dimensions to suffering are interconnected. They are separated here for ease of presentation only.

Since the development of the criminal victimisation survey in the late 1960s, one major way in which the impact of crime has been understood has been through the concept of fear. That survey method and its associated findings has fuelled major research interests in, and questions about, the relationship between people's fear of crime, actual experience of crime, risk from crime and the conundrums that findings in relation to these questions have produced. Here is not the place to review the debates and findings that this work has generated. Suffice it to say that much of this work indicates that people can and do worry about crime, and the extent to which those worries impact upon how they conduct their everyday lives is gendered, classed, ethnicised, racialised, aged and mediated by their sexuality. In others words, there are some patterns to this impact but those patterns do not necessarily predict *individual* behaviours or responses (though there is some evidence to suggest that, once victimised, prior fear of further victimisation can add to the impact that a particular victimisation has – see *inter alia* Kunst and Zwirs, 2014; Hollway and Jefferson, 2000). Indeed, at the individual level, responses to victimisation may well be connected to wider concerns, worries or fears, that is, other things going on in the lives of the individual or their wider community at any particular point in time, as they may be connected with concerns about crime. So whilst the impact of being a victim (of crime) matters to people, the shape and form that might take is perhaps unpredictable at the individual level.

This is not intended to imply that being a victim does not matter. Put simply, being victimised disrupts an individual's sense of well-being as expressed in what they can take for granted on a routine daily basis. This is particularly the case when something happens to them through no fault of their own. These are things that happen to people for which they do not feel responsible, like, for example, being harmed as a result of a terrorist attack, and can take the greatest toll in terms of impact. However, such implied causal links are by no means certain. Human beings are also equipped with the capacity for resilience, and whilst the interconnections between the impact of crime and such capacities is complex (Walklate, 2011; Siapno, 2009) and raise challenging questions for the role of intervention (Christie, 2008), contextualising understandings of the impact of crime in this way affords an important backcloth against which to understand the issues that follow.

In considering the impact of (criminal) victimisation on individuals, it is possible to discern two narratives. The first narrative has emerged, to a great extent, out of the work generated from positivist victimology, the findings associated with the criminal victimisation survey and the focus of attention that has resulted from that work on the efficacy of criminal justice policies and responses from the victim's point of view. For the purposes of this chapter, this has been called the 'victim narrative'. The second narrative emanates from a different, though related, set of concerns within psychology and psychiatry. This narrative centres on an understanding of the traumatic consequences that suffering misfortune can have on individuals. Fassin and Rechtman (2009) have called this 'psychiatric victimology'. For the purposes of this chapter we have called this the 'trauma narrative'. In what follows, each of these narratives will be discussed in turn through the slippage in terminology from one to the other, especially in their respective use of the term 'trauma'. These ideas are explicated in our second case study, which explores the personal testimonies of Jill Saward's *Rape: My Story* and Doug Beattie's *An Ordinary Soldier*. These testimonies differently problematise individual victimisation as a gendered experience through which it is possible to read both a trauma and a victim narrative in perhaps unexpected ways. Thus, throughout, as the question mark at the end of the title to this chapter implies, the presumptions lying behind both narratives will be subjected to critical scrutiny.

The victim narrative

Criminal victimisation can impact upon people in a number of different ways, and at different points in time, in the aftermath of an event. In order to differentiate these different kinds of impact they have been given different labels within the victim literature: primary victimisation, secondary victimisation and indirect victimisation. It will be useful to say a little about each of these in turn.

Primary victimisation

Primary victimisation refers to the direct impact that crime has on a victim. This can range from the financial loss associated with goods stolen, to time taken off work to sort out the aftermath of a burglary, to physical injury as a result of an assault, to the post-traumatic stress syndrome reported by some victims of rape (this latter kind of impact and the level of severity that it implies afford a useful connection with the trauma narrative discussed in more detail below). Drawing on a wide range of studies, the direct effects of victimisation are listed by Hall and Shapland (2007: 3–4) as follows: shock and a loss of trust/faith in society; guilt, often associated with feelings of anger and/or fear; physical injury, minor to severe; financial losses; fear; anger; depression; and changes to lifestyle induced by perceptions of the likelihood of future victimisation. These kinds of wide-ranging consequences to criminal victimisation can vary in their severity according to the particular circumstances of the individual. Maguire and Bennett (1982) reported some time ago that this kind of impact, whilst difficult to predict, is likely to have a greater effect on individuals who are also going through some other stressful event in their lives like a divorce or bereavement. Of course, much of the above draws on findings of studies that have taken a rather conventional and limited understanding of what might be included as criminal victimisation, though Spalek and King's (2007) study of the impact of the collapse of Farepak on its victims (an experience of corporate victimisation that the victims were aware of) resonates with all of those features of primary victimisation listed by Hall and Shapland (2007). (We will go on to consider a more dramatic appreciation of the impact of corporate victimisation in Chapter 5.)

When writ large, of course, for example through an appreciation of the impact of the continued use of white asbestos in poorer countries (Tombs and Whyte, 2006), the direct impact of crime, whilst hugely variable on an individual level, can also be structured by global socio-economic variables (see Whyte, 2007). Such victimisation can also be multifaceted (Rothe and Kauzlarich, 2014) in ways that match well with Hall and Shapland's (2007) list. If we were to widen our lens of criminal victimisation further, to genocide, war crimes and what are sometimes referred to as atrocity crimes, as more recent work within victimology has done (and as we go on to do in our next chapter), then the notion of primary victimisation and its impact perhaps requires less articulation than it once might have done. To talk of civilian casualties in war-torn countries as 'collateral damage' arguably neutralises both the impact of such acts and the power relations that underpin them. Yet some research maintains a value in the distinction between primary and secondary victimisation. Erez and Meroz-Aharoni (2011) have made an interesting intervention using this distinction to make sense of the comparative impact of protracted conflict on victims in Jerusalem and Kigali. Indeed there is some evidence to suggest that there is a continued value in this distinction for documenting the nature and extent of primary victimisation in order to secure wider international recognition and response. This has been demonstrated in the case of genocide in Darfur by the work of Hagan and Rymond-Richmond (2009) and is alluded to by van Wijk (2013) (observations discussed in Chapter 1).

To summarize, the direct impact of criminal victimisation can be hugely variable at an individual level. How individuals respond to this kind of experience will be a reflection of their own coping mechanisms, the nature of their persona, their personal relationships and, for some, the kind of support that they receive. All of which clearly have some associated structural/global dimensions. However, what might be an exceptional experience for an individual is more often than not an ordinary, mundane and routine experience for the criminal justice system. Thus, the exceptional experience for the individual can be made better or worse by how they are treated by the criminal justice system. This is what the victim narrative refers to as secondary victimisation.

Secondary victimisation

Victim Support (2002) defines secondary victimisation as,

> when a victim of crime feels they have been subjected to inadequate, insensitive or inappropriate treatment, attitudes, behaviour, responses

and/or practices by criminal justice and social agencies that compound their original *trauma*.

(quoted by Gekoski et al., 2013: 308, *our emphasis*)

Indeed research has indicated that individuals who are involved in the criminal justice process, as either victims or witnesses, frequently feel let down by that process, through actions such as not being kept informed of what was happening in their case, being treated unsympathetically by the professionals working in the criminal justice process and not being believed when they give their evidence. Thus it is in the space between how victims/complainants/ witnesses might like to be treated, and some of their reported experiences in how they are actually treated, that practices that may further harm them can occur. These kinds of issues have largely been evidenced in relation to allegations of rape. However, the experience of feeling challenged, undermined and accused of not 'telling the truth' is not solely confined to the rape complainant. People as complainants/witnesses across a whole range of different crime categories, and sometimes even professional witnesses, can feel intimidated by the legal process in general and the interrogation aspect of the process in particular.

However, the experience of secondary victimisation is not the sole preserve of victims/witnesses. The families of those who have been murdered (Rock, 1998; Gekoski et al., 2013), families of serious offenders (Condry, 2007), and those who have been subjected to wrongful convictions and their families (Jenkins, 2013), have all been shown to be subjected to secondary victimisation. In relation to family members of murderers, Howarth and Rock (2000: 70) observe:

> Unlike many other traumatised people they ... cannot distance themselves from the other and align themselves morally in a newly polarised world. On the contrary they are stuck between the offender whom they may not have renounced and his victim for whom they may well feel compassion.

So this secondary victimisation can be viewed as a re-victimisation (Dunn, 2007), not only for victims of sexual assault (Clay-Warner and Walklate, 2015) but for a range of victim groups for whom engagement with the criminal justice process is not only a unique experience but also a challenging one. The genesis of this challenge derives from the fact that each of the participants in the criminal justice process starts from a different position in terms of what their role is and the expectations that are associated with that role (Mawby, 2007). Nonetheless, as we shall see in Chapters 6 and 7, the dissatisfactions that have been documented as a result of this kind of secondary victimisation have made their presence felt in the policy arena. In addition, it is interesting to note that this focus on secondary victimisation has become an increasing concern for understanding how professionals who respond to differing kinds of difficult circumstances manage in the aftermath of those events (see for example Dekker, 2013; Ullstrom et al., 2014). Of course, not all of these experiences are necessarily connected to criminal victimisation, but they are illustrative of a wider emergent concern with suffering as a result of criminal victimisation particularly, and exposure to stressful events more generally.

Indirect victimisation

If there can be secondary victims, the victim narrative also points to the phenomenon of indirect victimisation. Spalek (2006) argues that thinking more deeply about the diversity of the crime experience can result in a more finely tuned understanding of what this refers to. She introduces the notion of 'spirit injury' and suggests that,

> embedded within the notion is an assertion of the interconnected self, so that common and recurrent experiences of racist and sexist abuse amounts to a brutalisation of an individual's self-identity and their dignity.
>
> (Spalek, 2006: 88)

She goes on to suggest that thinking in this way allows an understanding of not only the impact that victimisation has on the individual but also on the wider audience who might be indirectly victimised as a result of their shared 'subject position'. The idea of a shared indirect victimisation as a result of crime has some resonance with not only appreciating the importance of cultural and ethnic difference (which Spalek's concept is designed to include) but also taps into other shared experiences of crime. The potential for particularly 'notorious' crimes to impact on the community in which they occurred and wider community relationships, whilst relatively underexplored, can be nonetheless real. For example, it is without doubt that the wider impact of the child murders committed by Ian Brady and Myra Hindley in the UK in the 1960s, and the burial of their victims on Saddleworth Moor in Greater Manchester, captures some of the potential for indirect victimisation on that local community. However, contemporarily the notion of indirect victimisation has been extended to include a wider audience whose 'subject position' may be constituted purely as a result of their collective exposure to a particular event or set of circumstances. Thus, as Eagle and Kaminer (2014: 5) observe, 'individuals become traumatized by virtue of discrimination, oppression, civil war and genocide', leading some to argue that such experiences can be intergenerational. Of note here are the links made between individual experiences, collective experiences, and the use of the concept of trauma, the latter of which is addressed below. In the context of our understanding of 'indirect victimisation', these observations also afford an appreciation of some movement in the victim narrative away from being informed by positivist victimology to being informed by 'cultural' influences.

Chapter 1 noted that a cultural victimology is 'a victimology attuned to human agency, symbolic display, and shared emotion' (Ferrell et al., 2008: 190). This turn to the cultural and the wider public expression of the emotional reflects a constituent element of making public the suffering of the victim (Valier, 2004). As was suggested in Chapter 1, and will go on to be explicated further in Chapter 8, the rising focus on such cultural preoccupations is intimately connected with the increasingly visual nature of social life. This visual culture constantly and consistently places us beside the victim, encouraging us to feel what they feel. This form of indirect victimisation melds the individual with the interpersonal and the collective. Thus Berlant (2004: 5) comments (and was quoted in Chapter 1),

> members of mass society witness suffering not just concretely in local spaces but in the elsewhere brought to home and made intimate by sensationalist media, where documentary realness about the pain of strangers is increasingly at the center of both fictional and nonfictional events.

In the intermeshing of a multilayered contemporary social 'reality', indirect victimisation takes a different tone. As an example, in the aftermath of the terrorist attacks on 9/11, a range of politicians, media professionals, policymakers, opinion pollsters and cultural commentators proclaimed that the world would never be the same again. Indeed McMillan (2004: 383) went on to suggest that this '9/11 moment' resulted in the 'reappraisal [of each American] as inherently dangerous, an invitation for victimisation'. This vision of harm done to the American body (Cole, 2007) reverberated around the world and its media outlets, the consequences of which have been simultaneously widespread and mundane in our collective experience of the uncertainty of the twenty-first century (Howie, 2012). So, as we noted in our introduction, the legacy of 9/11 extends way beyond those that died and their families, and arguably its repeated visualisation haunts witnesses/indirect victims of those events who are less frequently heard – yet, simultaneously, it has had real consequences for them. This is only one example in which these interconnections might be observed. Similar connections can be made in the context of the impact of Hurricane Katrina (Walker, 2010) and the 2004 bombings in Madrid (Burkitt, 2005), amongst many others.

Such 'indirect victimisation' is but one way in which criminal victimisation and its impact can be understood as multifaceted and multilayered, especially in the contemporary visual, multi-mediated world. Thus impact on individuals can be intrinsically tied into, and connected with, impact sustained by the wider community and society at large, more increasingly with global consequences. In this milieu it is perhaps easy to lose sight of the individual victim. As such, we now turn our attention to our second case study and discuss the personal testimonies of two individual victims of very different types of victimisation.

Case study: gendered victimisation? *Rape: My Story* and *An Ordinary Solider*

By way of reviewing how impact can be understood, and in order to facilitate the further development of some underlying issues with which this chapter is concerned, we shall first consider how the experiences of Jill Saward can cast some light on these bigger questions. This is then compared with the personal testimony of Doug Beattie.

Jill Saward (with Wendy Green; 1990): Rape: My Story

Jill Saward was one of the victims in a case that has come to be referred to as the 'Ealing Vicarage Rape Case'. Her story is interesting, not only because she was the first to reject her right to anonymity in such cases and write about her experiences, but also because this case carried major implications for criminal justice sentencing policy.

In the afternoon of 6 March 1986, three men rang the doorbell of the vicarage where Jill lived. Her father answered the door and was confronted by these men, holding weapons, asking for access to the safe. Jill and her then boyfriend were also in the house. Jill's father and boyfriend were badly beaten, both receiving fractured skulls. Jill was taken to another room, vaginally and anally raped by one of the men, who also violated her with the handle of a knife. She was also raped by a second man. Jill, a practising Christian, was a virgin at the time. In her book she documents these experiences, the impact that they had on her, how she was treated in the criminal justice process and how she felt about the outcome. In her words, 'The rape has changed my whole outlook on life. Suddenly something happened that affected everything I did' (Saward, 1990: 143). It is evident that fears for her health (sexually transmitted diseases and the possibility of pregnancy), her experience of flashbacks and suicide attempts constitute primary victimisation of the first order. It should be noted that she has much praise for the police officers who supported her before the case came to court (the reader might like to reflect upon the extent to which the concept of 'ideal victim', discussed in Chapter 1, might underpin these experiences). However, when the case came to court 11 months later, in sentencing the defendants, the judge is reported as saying that, 'Because I have been told the trauma suffered by the victim was not so great ... I shall take a lenient course with you' (reported by Bottoms, 2010: 22), resulting in wide publicity and comment. Bottoms offers a usefully detailed analysis of the relationship between the inference made by the judge in this case concerning the impact of this particular crime, and the sentencing outcome. This need not concern us at this juncture. From Jill's viewpoint, this inference, whilst recognising that she did have a supportive family and a way of viewing the world nestled within her religious beliefs, meaning that she conducted herself with dignity during the court proceedings, belied her actual lived experiences as a result of what had happened to her. The inference was a false one from her point of view (and indeed many others). The question remains: what can be learned from this story?

First of all, Jill's story adds a good deal of legitimacy to the need for understanding primary victimisation and the role of the criminal justice system in exacerbating or alleviating that for the individuals concerned. In addition, the role of the media in this case also merits a mention. Whilst Jill chose to relinquish her right to anonymity, media reporting at the time left little doubt in the minds of the local community as to who had been subjected to the attack in the Ealing vicarage. In relation to the criminal justice system per se, Jill's experiences were uneven. The police in this case are commented on positively. The court experience was not so good. Thus, her story clearly documents the scope for secondary victimisation. The potential for this was self-evidently present and the ensuing policy preoccupations designed to bridge the gap between victims' experiences and criminal-justice practice can be seen to be justifiable (see also Chapters 6 and 7). However, it should also be noted that Jill's story is a particularly dramatic and impactful one. On the one hand, it adds some weight to the power of the concept of the 'ideal victim' and its ambivalent consequences for practice, as alluded to in Chapter 1. On the other hand, it also adds some weight to the power of feminist voices in terms of the impact of sexual violence and the role of the criminal justice system in responding to such violences. But a cautionary question also becomes pertinent: whilst a case like this one might justifiably be used to inform 'best practice' for all like cases, does a case like this capture the experiences of all victims, even rape victims?

Feminism, victims, and rape trauma syndrome

While the general tensions between victimology and feminism have been identified in Chapter 1, it is important to remember that the feminist voice was, and is, primarily preoccupied with the impact that sexual violence has, in all its forms, on women. In the context of rape, the research done by Burgess and Holmstrom (1974) in evidencing a 'rape trauma syndrome' was hugely important in challenging the notion that 'no harm was done' by such violence (qua Jill Saward's experiences). This gave significant impetus to the campaigning voices of the feminist movement in this arena in foregrounding the pain of this kind of criminal victimisation. Much research on sexual violence, in what Rose (1998) refers to as the 'psy' disciplines, has followed in the track of this work and now it is very unlikely that professionals would downplay the impact of rape on the victim. However, appreciation of that impact frequently only comes into play once such victims have been believed. As Jordan's (2004) work has illustrated, barriers to belief persist, particularly amongst criminal-justice professionals, as do beliefs distinguishing real rapes from other rape experiences (Estrich, 1987; Brown and Horvath, 2009). Moreover, the struggle to recognise that men too can be raped, and traumatised by that experience, remains

(Clark, 2014). However, the concern here is not so much with who is recognised as what kind of 'victim' but with the conceptual tools available to make sense of those experiences and the neatness of fit of those concepts with the experiences of individuals.

The evidence that documents the negative impact of rape on both men and women is in many respects beyond dispute. Where dispute has emerged, it has focused on the nature of that impact, and the use of the concept of 'trauma' in making sense of it. Summerfield (1999: 1453) pointedly suggests: 'It is simplistic to regard victims as mere passive receptacles of negative psychological effects which can be judged "present" or "absent"'. There is an irony underpinning this observation. It is ironic to recognise that rape can have a profound impact on individuals, yet simultaneously the process of recognising that impact and defining it as 'traumatic' can result in other kinds of damage. Gavey and Schmidt (2011: 439) express the problem as:

> a universalising presumption of 'no harm done' to an equally universalising presumption of 'severe harm done' ... irrespective of the woman's own views about its place in her life.

Even more worrying might be the tendency to declare the woman to be in denial should she counter the 'psy' discourse for whatever reason. Moreover, the invisibility of male rape in the debates around rape and its impact, whilst changing, has also been historically profound (see *inter alia* Coxell et al., 1999; Lees, 1997) despite the recognition that such violence can be experienced equally as a life-threatening event (Groth and Burgess, 1980), even if it is difficult for men and women to talk about it (Anderson and Doherty, 2008). Arguably, what lies behind these processes has been the power of positivist victimology and the implicit use of the term victim as a uniform and unifying concept for the purposes of policy and practice. However, of interest for our discussion are not only the dangers alluded to above, but also the use and transference of this trauma discourse to other categories of victimisation. Summerfield (1999: 1449) comments:

> One of the features of twentieth-century Western culture – particularly in the last 50 years – has been the way medicine and psychology have displaced religion as the source of explanations for the vicissitudes of life, and of the vocabulary of distress.

The slippage in terminology between primary, secondary and indirect victimisation on the one hand and trauma on the other is one illustration of the 'vocabulary of distress' that Summerfield refers to. For the purposes of mapping the differing narratives of suffering under discussion here, an interesting moment lies in the recognition of post-traumatic stress disorder. Our second case study, and what it reveals in comparison to the first one, provides one vehicle for understanding this moment.

Doug Beattie (2008): An Ordinary Soldier

This personal testimony is the account of one British soldier, Doug Beattie, who received the Military Cross for his role in the capture and defence of Garsmir, Afghanistan, in September 2006. Beattie offers an appreciation from the viewpoint of a soldier about the war in Afghanistan in particular and the difficulties of soldiering more generally. It is a highly detailed and emotionally challenging account that cannot be covered in all its complexity here. There are, however, a number of themes within it that offer some cause for reflection in the context of the issues under discussion in this chapter.

This book is first and foremost a biography. Beattie reveals much about his life and his route to becoming a soldier. He also tells us that the book was written as one way to come to terms with what he had seen and done, and to tell his family about those things. Early on in the book Beattie tells us about the aftermath of witnessing a suicide bomber attack:

> The effects of the detonation assaulted all my senses … here laid out in front of me, all the possible horrors of war had come together in one nightmarish scene.
>
> (Beattie, 2008: 4)

And later, learning that another attack might be imminent and that only he and one colleague were left to deal with it, he says,

> I was terrified. My stomach churned and my heart raced … This was now a game of chance with the odds stacked against me.
>
> (Beattie, 2008: 6)

He and his colleague came through this particular event, and it is in its aftermath that he learns he has been awarded the Military Cross for earlier combat activity. In learning of this he details his feelings of pride, embarrassment and guilt. It provokes deep reflection of his deservingness, and self-doubt over why he survived when so many of his colleagues did not. Much later in the book, he comments that on returning to the UK, feelings of guilt and worthlessness overcame him, and despite knowing where he could go for help, he did not choose to do that (Beattie, 2008: 294). He goes on to describe both the struggle he had coming to terms with the death of an Afghan colleague whom he respected and the barriers to talking to his wife about his experiences.

This brief overview hopefully gives the flavour of what is a compelling read, but what are we to take from this account? As the title of the book implies, in so many ways this is indeed an ordinary story. However, under this ordinariness lies a challenge. Beattie's account transgresses the assumption of the soldier as a non-victim as much as it simultaneously endorses the brute force and violence necessary for the task. Moreover, it provides some insight into the kind of suffering intimately connected with soldiering and the ways in which the implied assumptions of masculinity, and what it is to be a man, can act as barriers to managing those experiences. To paraphrase Wilkinson (2005: 162), through Beattie's story we are afforded an opportunity to envisage a more complete account of what suffering can do to people, and that includes men.

Gendered victimisation?

The two parts of the case study outlined above in many ways offer a gendered view of the impact of distressing and stressful events on individuals. Put simply, they remind us of what we all 'know': women are vulnerable, men are not. They also capture gendered understandings of criminal victimisation. Again, put simply, we know that women are victims (particularly of violence) and men are perpetrators (of violence). Yet, as both personal testimonies in our case study illustrate, the coping strategies of both of these individuals in the face of life-threatening events are very different but equally remarkable. This does not mean that these events did not take their toll. They did. Moreover, these individual testimonies also lead us to consider who, and what, has been included and excluded from the victim narrative discussed above and the trauma narrative to be discussed below. As has been argued elsewhere (Newburn and Stanko, 1994; Walklate, 2007), men have more often than not been the victimological other. They are outside of the victim narrative gaze. So much so that being a man and being a victim becomes a contradiction in terms. However, when it comes to the harms experienced by men as soldiers (as in the case of Beattie), the presumption of their 'latent invisibility' (Walklate, 2007; McGarry and Walklate, 2011) as both men and victims is challenged. This challenge is not new and historically coincided with the emergence of the second narrative we are concerned with here: the trauma narrative.

The trauma narrative

To date, and as illustrated above, we have witnessed what might be referred to as 'trauma creep' into the world of victimology and criminal victimisation. The word 'trauma' itself, of course, carries a range of meanings, having its origins as a medical term referring to wounds sustained by the body. However, trauma has also come to be used as a metaphor for almost anything unpleasant, and contemporarily refers more to psychological distress than it does to physical unpleasantness (see Hacking, 1995). Indeed Eagle and Kaminer (2014: 3) have commented that contemporarily it is a concept that has come to have dual usage: as delineating a traumatic event and traumatic impact. Such a conflation of usage, alongside a shift in emphasis from the physical to the psychological, is important to understand in appreciating the growth and development of 'trauma creep'.

Trauma, as a psychic concept, has its origins in the work of Charcot in the 1860s. He was primarily interested in the psychological impact of railway accidents and other workplace incidents (Fassin and Rechtman, 2009; Hacking, 1995). For Charcot, trauma was triggered by an external event in which the role of the psychiatrist determined the veracity of the event. That veracity justified, or failed to justify, any claim for workplace compensation. A decade or so later, Freudian analysis, through seduction theory and later fantasy theory, took the understanding of trauma to a different level. Freud understood trauma to be the result of an internal psychic problem from which psycho-pathological problems developed. These two different ways of thinking about trauma – the first as an external event with internal consequences (fear, anxiety and so on), and the second as an internal psychic problem from which deeper problems might emerge (anxiety states, psychopathological disorders and so on) – were evidenced in the different ways in which they were applied to people so afflicted. Fassin and Rechtman (2009) report, for example, that both these approaches to trauma could be found in the practices of the medical military profession during the First World War. For such medical professionals, driven as they were to search out 'malingerers', their solution (particularly in France) to claims of trauma was to put them to a physical test by the use of electric shock treatment. This was intended to elicit a confession from malingerers that they were not really ill at all and wanted to return to the front. It would weed out the real sufferers from those who were not. Most returned to the front. Such practices added a moral dimension to the concept of trauma, to add to its already existing medical and psychical understandings. Put simply, 'normal' people (men) did not shirk from their moral duty to fight for their King and Country, and following on from this trauma – now constituted as a moral, medical and psychological problem – became the province of particular pro-fessional expertise: psychiatric victimology (see Fassin and Rechtman 2009, particularly Chapter 5). This understanding of trauma and the role of profes-sionals in determining its presence was given added impetus in the late 1960s and early 1970s. Chamberlin (2012: 362) states of the Diagnostic and Statistical Manual of Mental Disorders (DSM-III), which brought the category of PTSD into psychological and popular discourse following the war in Vietnam:

> The type of traumatic events that were now understood as potentially leading to PTSD included … military combat, violent personal assault, being kidnapped or taken hostage, terrorist attack, torture, incarceration as a prisoner of war … natural or manmade disasters, severe automobile accidents, or being diagnosed with a life-threatening illness.

Published in 1980, DSM-III marked the culmination of work with individuals in distress that meant that the veracity of the victim was no longer in question. This work also included women who had been raped (Burgess and Holmstrom, 1974). Coinciding with the concerns of the (American) feminist movement alongside the (American) peace movement (Herman, 1992), 'A new era of thinking about trauma had begun' (Fassin and Rechtman, 2009: 77). PTSD now became the preserve of professional judgement rather than individual claims making, and whilst reservations were expressed about the inclusion of PTSD and its associated symptoms in DSM-III (potentially identifying 20 to 30 per cent of the American population with this condition), from this point, 'suffering is no longer something that should be hidden from others or concealed from oneself: it is something that can be legitimately described in others and oneself' (Fassin, 2012: 41–42).

As such, a number of processes lay behind, and contributed to, the recognition of PTSD: the growth of the women's movement from the 1960s onwards bringing to the fore, in particular, the nature and extent of sexual abuse of women and children; the legacy of the Vietnam War and the impact of that conflict on those who participated in it; and, as noted by Alexander (2012), the trial of Adolf Eichmann. (This latter event is of particular interest here given that the early victimologists, particularly Mendelsohn, were concerned that the focus of this new 'discipline' of victimology should be wide ranging and include the atrocities of war and genocide – see Rafter and Walklate, 2012.) Taken together, these three processes not only contributed to a change in understanding of individual trauma and its manifestation as reflected in DSM-III, they also contributed to what came to be labelled as 'cultural' trauma (Alexander 2012). However, in terms of our understanding of 'traumatised individuals', a further exploration of this particular moment will be of value.

Wither the victim narrative

The 'My Lai Massacre' (1968) committed by American soldiers on Vietnamese people, sent shockwaves around the United States. Up until that point in time many people in the United States believed that they were involved in a 'just' war in Vietnam. The reporting of My Lai and the investigation that it generated prompted serious questions about that involvement and how it was that conceivably ordinary men could commit such atrocities. Were these men monsters or did the exceptional circumstances render them capable of such horrific acts? These kinds of questions were not very dissimilar from those posed by the increasing awareness and recognition of the Holocaust prompted by the trial of Adolf Eichmann. Alexander (2012) reminds us that the Holocaust was not always referred to as such. Indeed in the 1930s, during the Second World War, and even on the discovery of the concentration camps, doubt and disbelief were expressed about what had been found. In the decade or so immediately after the war came to a close, the dominant political desire was to rebuild after victory rather than dwell on the horrors of the past. That was until the trial of Adolf Eichmann. Captured by the Israelis, Eichman was tried in Jerusalem, in part to ensure that the victims were not forgotten. Karstedt (2010) has commented on the telling absence of victims' voices (of the Holocaust) in the post-war years, and the trial of Eichmann confronted the German and other publics in this respect. Arendt's (1965) analysis, postulating that Eichmann represented the 'banality of evil', sent reverberations around the intellectual world, particularly in the United States, and simultaneously informed responses to the My Lai Massacre. That massacre left big question marks around the US involvement in Vietnam, and raised the question, as Alexander (2012: 72) postulates, of the possibility of other democratic nations to engage in mass atrocity in war.

We return to this final point in Chapter 3, but taken together in historical context the convergence of these different events and social movements gave space to listening to victims' voices. Those voices ranged far and wide – from the Holocaust, to rape crisis centres, to the claims made by veterans from the Vietnam War and their victims, and the incipient rise of victim support organisations more generally from the late 1960s to the early 1970s. The impact that that these voices had was profound. Taken alongside the increasing awareness of the impact of rather more mundane events of ordinary crimes on people's everyday lives being generated by criminal victimisation surveys, and the growth of victim-oriented support groups outwith the feminist movement, the slippage in thinking about the impact of criminal victimisation as no longer constituting 'primary victimisation' but 'trauma' is perhaps easy to appreciate. Importantly, these wider social processes marked the beginnings of recognizing PTSD (trauma) not only as a psychic problem for individuals but also as a problem for collectivities. Moon (2009) observes, for example, that the emergence of what has been referred to as the 'new wars' in the 1990s (wars that minimised the harm done to military personnel but resulted in a greater number of casualties amongst civilian populations) added weight to the view that such war-torn societies constituted traumatised collectivities in need of therapeutic intervention. This issue is also addressed by Fassin (2012) and is something that we shall return to in the next chapter.

To summarize, the emergence of this trauma narrative lends some weight to the analysis offered by Alexander (2012). Whilst his work is primarily concerned with understanding how the Holocaust achieved the status of a master narrative when equally atrocious events did not acquire this status, Alexander (2012) provides a framework in which to make sense of the apparent convergence between the victim narrative and the trauma narrative as presented here. He suggests four elements need to be present for a master narrative around trauma to emerge: the kind of pain incurred, who the victim is, the capacity to relate the victim's trauma to a wider audience, and the attribution of responsibility for that pain (Alexander, 2012). Arguably these four elements have been increasingly present for the victim of crime from the mid-1970s through to the early 1980s to the present day, and increasing evidence of the pain of criminal victimisation emerged. This included the proliferation of the criminal victimisation survey; the evidence generated by those surveys of a relatively powerless victim (gendered, aged, classed and racialised); the proliferation of victim-centred organisations making claims on behalf of victims' voices (see for example Rock, 2004); and in the light of these kinds of (and other) findings, the attribution of responsibility to criminal-justice practitioners in particular and the system of justice more generally for the further pain endured. Thus primary, secondary and indirect victimisation slip neatly into, and become conflated with, trauma.

To review and reiterate, the victim narrative, dominated by what has been referred to as a 'conservative victimology' (Karmen, 1990), clearly reflects certain assumptions about the impact of crime and who is likely to be vulnerable to that impact. Originally informed by concepts emanating primarily from positivist victimology, like victim precipitation, lifestyle and the ideal victim, that easily leant themselves to understandings of a deserving and undeserving victim, it is easy to see how a hierarchy of victimisation (Carrabine et al., 2004) is operable. Those considered most vulnerable (the elderly, the young, the frail and so on) could readily be situated at the top of this hierarchy, and as a result it would be assumed that the impact of victimisation would take their greatest toll on these groups of individuals. The trauma narrative challenged this. In the trauma narrative even those least likely to be considered vulnerable (soldiers, for example) could find themselves suffering as a result of their exposure to the violences of war. Moreover, women subject to sexual (and other) violences were no longer to be blamed for what happened to them. In the intermeshing of victimhood and trauma implied by thinking about the impact of crime in this way, we can observe, qua Fassin (2012), the transition from suffering as naturalistic (given by the data of criminal victimisation surveys) to suffering as ironic (routine and a possibility for all of us): hence we are all victims now (Furedi, 2002). In presenting these narratives and their points of interconnection we are by implication adding some weight to the position of critical victimology. Whilst the increasing influence of a mediated world might suggest that we are all increasingly vulnerable to indirect victimisation, as the constantly available and unchanging images of the collapse of the Twin Towers of 9/11, or images of different violence(s) disseminated on YouTube, might imply (see Pollard, 2011), it is also the case that individuals recover from bad experiences and have the capacity to deal with horrendous circumstances in a myriad of different ways. How and under what conditions this happens is a moot point. As Rock (2002) observed some time ago, little is known about who embraces a 'victim identity' and why.

Conclusion: towards a cultural economy of trauma?

The impact of criminal victimisation can be multifaceted and multilayered. It can range from feelings of fear and insecurity through to much more profound psychological damage. It can take its toll on individuals both economically and it terms of their health. As such it is possible to calculate the wider economic costs that the impact of crime can have on society as a whole (see for example Dixon et al., 2006). Yet despite all that is known about the impact of crime on individuals, whether that has been generated as part of the victim narrative or the trauma narrative, who is likely to experience what kind of impact and how they might deal with it is still difficult to predict. Thus it can be argued that neither the victims' narrative nor the trauma narrative captures the *lived experiences* of individuals. The first fails in part because it is generated by data that aggregates individuals into groups and the latter does not necessarily reveal anything about the former. The second fails because of the same problem in reverse. Its claims are generated by data rooted in an in-depth appreciation of individual experience that is used to make claims about the impact of events on groups. In addition, in the convergence that has occurred between the victim narrative and the trauma narrative that this chapter has endeavoured to document, it is possible to observe other shortcomings.

The historical moment that brought together a range of voices rooted in different social movements, but nonetheless contributed to the recognitions of post-traumatic stress disorder in DSM-III, has also resulted in the conflation of suffering with trauma. Arguably, suffering is something that is felt. Trauma is something that happens that results in suffering. In addition, as Eagle and Kaminer (2014) observed, there is confusion as to whether or not trauma is to be understood as an event or as the impact of an event. Such conflations and confusions notwithstanding, the claims to trauma and the import of their presence, either in popular terms (qua Laqueur, 2010) or as a master narrative (qua Alexander, 2012), cannot be denied. In political and policy space, whilst neither the victim narrative nor the trauma narrative necessarily provide the *evidential* basis for action, each arena proceeds as though the opposite were the case. In terms of responding to individuals this is problematic (as the discussion above of the potential impact of rape trauma syndrome implies) because, in order to be considered worthy of policy or practice intervention, an individual's response to their experiences has to be pathologised. This is rather contrary to evidence that suggests that being distressed as a result of a life-threatening experience is normal (see Eagle and Kaminer, 2014). Only when such responses are rendered abnormal is it possible to put in place a response to render them once again normal. Thus in the convergence of the victim and trauma narratives the normal is pathologised in order for intervention to normalise that which has been deemed to be pathological. It is against this backcloth that some 'victim' voices are listened to, and indeed become the voice and conduit for policy changes, and others are not.

Arguably, underpinning all of these processes it is possible to observe ways in which 'Suffering becomes reshaped, commodified, and packaged for its public and didactic salience' (McEvoy and Jamieson, 2007: 425), best evidenced in the growing influence of victim voices in policy formation. This commodification puts to the fore individual suffering rather than collective suffering, as aptly observed by Fassin and Rechtman (2009: 281):

> Both before and after the tsunami survivors in Aceh were already victims of political domination, military repression, and economic marginalisation … Trauma is not only silent on these realities, it actually obscures them.

Of course, as we shall see in Chapters 6 and 7, this does not mean that both narratives have not been used in support of policy interventions. Indeed it can be argued that the current preoccupation in the UK and beyond in devising policy responses to take account of victims has occurred directly as a result of this convergence. Moreover, on the international stage it is similarly possible to observe the underlying presence of such political-economic processes that foreground some aspects of victimhood and erase others (see Chapter 7). Interestingly, one way in which we have been able to gain some insight into the efficacy of each of these narratives has been by drawing on 'data' not routinely included within the academic or policy sphere of victimology: autobiographical accounts. Each account within the case study used in this chapter casts different light on the problems and possibilities inherent in the narratives under discussion here, including the challenges that they pose for people's own coping mechanisms. The potential of this kind of material for victimology is discussed more fully in Chapter 4. However, before we can complete our appreciation of what kind of impact crime has under what conditions, we shall explore how these issues have been considered for collectivities.

Further reading

Readers might like to consider taking a look at either of the accounts referred to in this chapter in the case study – Saward (1990), *Rape: My Story* or Beattie (2008), *An Ordinary Soldier* – and read them in full in the light of the issues discussed here, or indeed any other biographical account of an individual's experience of being a victim. Those interested in the emergence of the trauma narrative will find Fassin and Rechtman's (2009) *Empire of Trauma* an invaluable read. Any victimological textbook will provide an overview of the impact of crime, but a particularly interesting contribution is made by Green (2007), 'Crime, victimisation and vulnerability', in Walklate's *Handbook of Victims and Victimology*.

Bibliography

Alexander, J. (2012) *Trauma: A Social Theory*. Cambridge: Polity.

Anderson, I. and Doherty, K. (2008) *Accounting for Rape*. London: Routledge.

Arendt, H. (1965) *Eichmann in Jerusalem*. Harmonsworth: Penguin.

Beattie, D. (2008) *An Ordinary Soldier*. London: Simon and Schuster.

Berlant, L. (2004) 'Compassion and withholding', in L. Berlant (ed.) *Compassion: The Culture and Politics of an Emotion*. London: Routledge. pp. 1–14.

Bottoms, A. (2010) 'The "duty to understand": what consequences for victim participation', in A. Bottoms and J. V. Roberts (eds) *Hearing the Victim: Adversarial Justice, Crime Victims and the State*. Cullompton, Devon: Willan Publishing. pp. 17–39.

Bourdieu, P. (1999) *The Weight of the World: Social Suffering in Contemporary Society*. Cambridge: Polity.

Brown, J. and Horvath, M. (2009) 'Do you believe her? Is it real rape?', in M. Horvath and J. Brown (eds) *Rape: Challenging Contemporary Thinking*. London: Routledge-Willan. pp. 325–42.

Burgess, A. W., and Holmstrom, L. L. (1974) 'Rape trauma syndrome', *American Journal of Psychiatry*, 131: 981–86.

Burkitt, I. (2005) 'Powerful emotions: power, government and opposition in the war on terror', *Sociology*, 39: 679–95.

Carrabine, E., Inganski, P., Lee, M., Plummer, K., and South, N. (2004) *Criminology: A Sociological Introduction*. London: Routledge.

Chamberlin, S. E. (2012) 'Emasculated by trauma: a social history of post-traumatic stress disorder, stigma, and masculinity', *Journal of American Culture*, 35(4): 358–65.

Christie, N. (2008) 'Fertile ground for victim-movements', *Keynote Speech at the Third Nordic Conference of Victimology and Victim Support, Conference Report*. Helsinki, March.

Clark, J. (2014) 'A crime of identity; rape and its neglected victims', *Journal of Human Rights*, 13(2): 146–69.

Clay-Warner, J. and Walklate, S. (2015, forthcoming) 'Victimisation and Revictimisation', in B. Francis and T. Sanders (eds) *The Oxford Handbook of Sex Offenders and Sex Offences*. Oxford: Oxford University Press.

Cole, A. (2007) *The Cult of True Victimhood*. Stanford, CA.: Stanford University Press.

Condry, R. (2007) *Families Shamed*. Cullompton, Devon: Willan.

Coxell, A., King, M., Mezey, G., and Gordon, D. (1999) 'Lifetime, prevalence, characteristics and associated problems of non-consensual sex in men: cross sectional survey', *British Medical Journal*, 318: 846–50.

Dekker, S. (2013) *Second Victim*. New York: CRC Press.

Dixon, M., Reed, H., Rogers, B. and Stone, L. (2006) *Crime Share. The Unequal Impact of Crime*. London: IPPR.

Dunn, P. (2007) 'Matching service delivery to need', in S. Walklate (ed.) *Handbook of Victims and Victimology*. Cullompton, Devon: Willan. pp. 255–81.

Eagle, G. T., and Kaminer, D. (2014) 'Traumatic stress: established knowledge, current debates and new horizons', *South African Journal of Psychology*. doi: 10.1177/0081246314547124.

Erez, E. and Meroz-Aharoni, T. (2011) 'Primary and secondary victims and victimisation during protracted conflict. National trauma through a literary lens in Jerusalem and Kigali', in R. Letschert, R. Haveman, A.-M. de Brouwer and A. Pemberton (eds) *Victimological Approaches to International Crimes: Africa*. Cambridge: Intersentia.

Estrich, S. (1987) *Real Rape*. Harvard: Harvard University Press.

Fassin, D. (2012) *Humanitarian Reason*. Berkeley and Los Angeles: University of California Press.

Fassin, D., and Rechtman, R., (2009) *Empire of Trauma*. Princeton: Princeton University Press.

Ferrell, J., Hayward, K., and Young, J. (2008) *Cultural Criminology: An Invitation*. London: SAGE.

Furedi, F. (2002) *Culture of Fear: Risk Taking and the Morality of Low Expectation*. London: Cassell.

Gavey, N., and Schmidt, J. (2011) '"Trauma of rape" discourse: a double-edged template for everyday understandings of the impact of rape', *Violence against Women*. Published online 5 April 2011. doi: 10.1177/1077801211404194.

Gekoski, A., Adler, J. R., and Gray, J. M. (2013) 'Interviewing women bereaved by homicide: Reports of secondary victimisation by the criminal justice system', *International Review of Victimology*, 19(3): 307–29.

Green, S. (2007) 'Crime, victimisation and vulnerability', in S. Walklate (ed.) *Handbook of Victims and Victimology*. Devon: Willan. pp. 91–118.

Groth, A. N. and Burgess, A. W. (1980) 'Male rape – offenders and victims', *American Journal of Psychiatry*, 137(7): 806–10.

Hacking, I. (1995) *Rewriting the Soul*. Princeton: Princeton University Press.

Hagan, J. and Rymond-Richmond, W. (2009) *Darfur and the Crime of Genocide*. Cambridge: Cambridge University Press.

Hall, M. and Shapland, J. (2007) 'What do we know about the effects of crime on victims?', *International Review of Victimology*, 14: 175–217.

Herman, J. (1992) *Trauma and Recovery: From Domestic Abuse to Political Terror*. London: Pandora.

Hollway, W. and Jefferson, T. (2000) 'The role of anxiety in the fear of crime', in T. Hope and R. Sparks (eds) *Crime, Risk and Insecurity*. London: Routledge. pp. 31–49.

Howarth, G. and Rock, P. (2000) 'Aftermath and the construction of victimisation: "the other victim of crime"', *Howard Journal of Criminal Justice*, 39: 58–78.

Howie, L. (2012) *Witnesses to Terror*. London: Palgrave Macmillan.

Jenkins, S. (2013) 'Secondary victims and the trauma of wrongful conviction: families and children's perspectives on imprisonment, release, and adjustment', *Australian and New Zealand Journal of Criminology*. 46(1): 119–37.

Jordan, J. (2004) *The Word of a Woman: Police, Rape and Belief*. New York: Palgrave Macmillan.

Karmen, A. (1990) *Crime Victims: An Introduction to Victimology*. Belmont, CA: Wadsworth.

Karstedt, S. (2010) 'From absence to presence, from silence to voice: victims in international and transitional justice since the Nuremburg trials', *International Review of Victimology*, 17: 9–30.

Kunst, M. J. and Zwirs, B. W. (2014) 'Post-traumatic stress disorder symptom severity and fear of personal crime: exploring their interrelationship as a function of risk estimation', *Psychology, Crime and Law*, 20(9): 921–32.

Laqueur, T. (2010) *We Are All Victims Now*. London Review of Books 32(13), 8th July pp. 19–32.

Lees, S. (1997) *Ruling Passions*. Buckingham: Open University Press.

Maguire, M. with Bennett, T. (1982) *Burglary in a Dwelling*. London: Heinemann.

Mawby, R. (2007) 'Public sector services and the victim of crime', in S. Walklate (ed.) *Handbook of Victims and Victimology*. Cullompton, Devon: Willan. pp. 209–39.

McEvoy, K. and Jamieson, R. (2007) 'Conflict, suffering and the promise of human rights' in D. Downes, C. Chinkin, and C. Gearty (eds) *Crime, Conflict and Human Rights: Essays in honour of Stan Cohen*. Cullompton, Devon: Willan. pp. 422–41.

McGarry, R. and Walklate, S. (2011) 'The soldier as victim: peering through the looking glass', *British Journal of Criminology*, 46(6): 900–917.

McMillan, N. (2004) 'Beyond representation: cultural understandings of the September 11 attacks', *Australian and New Zealand Journal of Criminology*, 37(1): 380–400.

Moon, C. (2009) 'Healing past violence: traumatic assumptions and therapeutic interventions in war and reconciliation', *Journal of Human Rights*, 8: 71–91.

Newburn, T. and Stanko, E. A. (eds) (1994) *Just Boys Doing Business*. London: Routledge.

Pollard, J. (2011) 'Seen, seared and sealed: trauma and the visual presentation of September 11', *Health, Risk and Society*, 13(1): 81–101.

Rafter, N. and Walklate, S. (2012) 'Genocide and the dynamics of victimisation: some observations on Armenia', *European Journal of Criminology*, 9(3): 514–26.

Rock, P. (1998) *After Homicide*. Oxford: Clarendon Press.

——(2002) 'On becoming a victim', in C. Hoyle and R. Young (eds) *New Visions of Crime Victims*. Oxford: Hart. pp. 1–22.

——(2004) *Constructing Victims' Rights: The Home Office, New Labour and Victims*. Oxford: Oxford University Press.

Rose, N. (1998) *Inventing ourselves: psychology, power and personhood*. Cambridge: Cambridge University Press.

Rothe, D. and Kauzlarich, D. (eds) (2014) *Towards a Victimology of State Crime*. London: Routledge.

Saward, J. with Green, W. (1990) *Rape: My Story*. London: Bloomsbury.

Siapno, J. A. (2009) 'Living through terror: everyday resilience in East Timor and Aceh', *Social Identities,* 15(1): 43–64.

Spalek, B. (2006) *Crime Victims: Theory, Policy and Practice*. London: Palgrave.

Spalek, B. and King, S. (2007) 'Farepak victims speak out'. London: Centre for Crime and Justice Studies.

Summerfield, D. (1999) 'A critique of seven assumptions behind psychological trauma programmes in war-affected areas', *Social Science and Medicine,* 48: 1449–62.

Tombs, S. and Whyte, D. (2006) 'Risk and work', in G. Mythen and S. Walklate (eds) *Beyond the Risk Society: Critical Reflections on Risk and Human Security*. Maidenhead, Berkshire: Open University Press. pp. 169–93.

Ullstrom, S., Sachs, M. A., Hansson, J., Øvretveit, J., and Brommels, M. (2014) 'Suffering in silence: a qualitative study of second victims of adverse events', *BMJ Quality and Safety,* 23: 325–31.

Valier, C. (2004) *Crime and Punishment in Contemporary Culture*. London: Routledge.

Van Wijk, P. (2013) 'Who is the "little old lady" of international crimes? Nils Christie's concept of the ideal victim re-interpreted', *International Review of Victimology,* 19(2): 159–79.

Walker, J. (2010) 'Moving testimonies and the geography of suffering: perils and fantasies of belonging after Katrina', *Continuum: Journal of Media and Cultural Studies,* 24(1): 47–64.

Walklate, S. (2007) 'Men, victims and crime', in P. Davies, P. Francis, and C. Greer (eds) *Victims, Crime and Society*. London: SAGE. pp. 142–64.

——(2011) 'Reframing criminal victimisation: finding a place for vulnerability and resilience', *Theoretical Criminology,* 15(20): 179–94.

Whyte, D. (2007) 'Victims of corporate crime', in S. Walklate (ed.) *Handbook of Victims and Victimology*. Cullompton, Devon: Willan. pp. 446–63.

Wilkinson, I. (2005) *Suffering: A Sociological Introduction*. Cambridge: Polity.

Young, A. (2007) 'Images in the aftermath of trauma: responding to September 11th', *Crime, Media, Culture,* 3(1): 30–48.

Chapter 3

Traumatised collectivities?

The previous chapter introduced two narratives used to make sense of the impact crime can have on individuals. In this chapter, drawing on the legacy of radical victimology discussed in Chapter 1, we consider the efficacy of these narratives for making sense of traumatised collectivities. As was indicated in Chapter 1, there have been moves within radical victimology towards a more thoroughgoing analysis of state crime victimisation which draws power relations into the centre of victimological concerns (see Kauzlarich et al., 2001; Rothe and Kauzlarich, 2014). In adding to those concerns, this chapter connects the traumatised individual to the traumatised collectivity by drawing out the layered experience of mass victimisation which, in many ways, begins with the story of individuals. This appreciation is developed throughout the chapter in the context of war.

Jamieson (1998: 480) observes,

> war offers a dramatic example of mass violence and victimisation in extremis … these issues of violence and violations of human rights are accomplished inter alia through state action.

And although war and its impact have gained increasing interest within crimi-nological and victimological literature, as Jamieson also comments, much remains to be said. The mass victimisation caused as a result of war has far-reaching consequences transcending the individual acts of violence that constitute it. For C. Wright Mills (1959: 9–10, *our emphasis*),

> the structural issues of war have to do with its causes … with its effects upon economic and political, family and religious institutions, with the *unorganized irresponsibility* of a world of nation-states.

Here this is taken to mean that the conditions created before, during and after war impact upon the structural conditions of social life and cause a wider range of victimisation than currently recognised by some versions of victimology, particularly positivist victimology. For example, quantifying death and violence in terms of a 'victim narrative' is done at the expense of understanding the broader violences and victimisation caused by war (qua Woolford, 2006). So, building on some aspects of Chapter 2, the victim narrative and the trauma narrative are deployed to engage with the victimisation of war as it might be connected with the 'terrorism of everyday life' (Furedi, 2005). It is important to note that 'war' is multifaceted. Indeed Alvarez (2010) reminds us that acts of genocide frequently take place during acts of war, so, mindful of this, the current chapter addresses a broad range of victimisations experienced by 'traumatised collectivities'.

This introduces our third case study. Following Friedrichs (2000), we make connections between acts of individual murder and the collective experience of genocide during war. The death of Stephen Lawrence in 1993, understood as a product of 'hate crime', is used as a platform to explore the deaths associated with the 2003 war in Iraq. In so doing both victimising events are considered to be characterised by essentialism, domination by 'hate groups,' and the systematic 'othering' of those victimised, and both events are explored through the narratives introduced in Chapter 2.

Case study: Stephen Lawrence and the invasion of Iraq

This case study is presented in two parts and focuses on two separate high-profile acts of violence ten years apart; the first against a murdered individual, the second against a collectivity.

Murder of Stephen Lawrence, 1993

On 22 April 1993 Stephen Lawrence, a young black teenager, was murdered in an unprovoked racist attack by white youths in London. In the aftermath of his murder, Stephen was found to have received poor attention and first aid by the London Metropolitan Police, who had treated his victim status with scepticism, presuming that both he and his accompanying friend, Dwayne Brooks, were somehow complicit in their own victimisation. The apparent ineptitude of the police became one of the many unfortunate legacies of Stephen's death. Following complaints to the police from the Lawrence family that not enough was being done to investigate Stephen's death, between May and June 1993 three men were arrested (Neil Acourt, Gary Dobson and Luke Knight), two of whom (Acourt and Knight) were formally charged with Stephen's murder. These charges were subsequently dropped by the Crown Prosecution Service in July 1993 due to a lack of evidence, prompting a private prosecution against the three men by the Lawrence family. This prosecution ran from September 1994 to April 1996 and resulted in an acquittal. In February 1997, having persistently campaigned against the injustice of Stephen's death, a public inquest reached a verdict of unlawful death in an attack motivated by racism. What followed was a judicial inquiry into Stephen's death, beginning in July 1997. The resulting *Macpherson Report* (1999) had a remit to re-examine the failed police inquiry into Stephen's death, learn lessons about the investigation of racially motivated crimes, and to look at the wider issues of public trust and confidence between the police and ethnic minority communities in the UK (see Macpherson, 1999). The *Macpherson Report* is now well known for becoming an influential and damning investigation of the police as an institution and added some weight to the earlier *Scarman Report* (1981), which had implicated the police in racist practices with racist officers. The *Macpherson Report* found that, in addition to professional incompetence, the failure to convict Stephen's killers was a direct result of what the report termed 'institutionalised racism'. In brief, Stephen's death fractured the UK's domestic sense of justice and pushed legal and operational concepts of hate crime to the top of the political agenda.

Invasion of Iraq, 2003

Some 10 years later, in March 2003, US and Coalition forces invaded Iraq, employing a campaign of military airstrikes referred to as 'shock and awe'. The invasion of Iraq in 2003 was, however, prefixed by instances of mass victimisation to collectivities, events that cumulatively facilitated and were indeed used to 'legitimise' the invasion of Iraq in 2003.

Under the dictatorship of Saddam Hussein, the head of state for Iraq and leader of the Baath Party, his regime had been responsible for the mass victimisation of a diverse Iraqi population. Seeking to lessen the Iranian influence in Iraq, Saddam had pursued the religious persecution of the predominant population of Shiite Muslims in Iraq. Under this persecution Shiite militants had attempted to assassinate Saddam without success in the town of Dujail. Saddam responded by ordering the slaughter of approximately 150 people in that town in 1982, including children. Saddam had also sought to persecute the traditional population of Kurdish Iraqis, who suffered at the hands of the al-Anfal Campaign (1986–89), resulting in the mass extermination of approximately 180,000 Kurds in the north of Iraq. He also persecuted the Shiite Marsh Arabs in southern Iraq, reducing their numbers through starvation and persecution from 250,000 to approximately 30,000. Then in 1990 Saddam's Baath Party invaded Kuwait, considered part of Iraq's sovereignty. This move was met with international condemnation, causing the United Nations Security Council to respond with a set of Resolutions made under Chapter VII of the UN Charter to defend Kuwait against Iraq. For simplicity these are listed below:

Resolution 660: condemnation of Iraq's invasion of Kuwait; demanded Iraq to withdraw from Kuwait immediately due to the invasion constituting a breach of international peace and security.
Resolution 678: sanctioned UN members to cooperate with Kuwait and uphold Resolution 660 by all necessary means, giving the authority which resulted in the first Gulf War.

Resolution 687: following the ceasefire of this conflict in 1991 this Resolution instructed Iraq to disarm its Weapons of Mass Destruction (WMD: nuclear, biological and chemical weapons) and agree to UN weapons inspections.

Following international action led by the US and UK (the Gulf War to liberate Kuwait), Iraq was subsequently subjected to UN sanctions, imposing an economic and military blockade on the country under UN Resolution 661 in 1990 (introduced for refusing to adhere to UN Resolution 660). These sanctions drove the Iraqi state and its people into a humanitarian crisis, causing widespread victimisation as an indirect result of the war.

Ten years on from the 1991 Gulf War, terrorist attacks in the US on 11 September 2001 (9/11) witnessed four domestic American aircraft[1] deliberately crashed into three separate locations of US economic, military and political significance by members of Al Qaeda (see Benjamin and Simon, 2002). The first struck the economic target of the Twin Towers of the World Trade Center[2] claiming 2,996 lives in its collapse; the second hit the military target of the Pentagon[3] killing 189 people; the third political target (reportedly the White House) was never reached – the aircraft[4] crashed in a remote field, killing all 45 of its passengers. The US responded by invading Afghanistan just 26 days later on 7 October 2001, engaging Coalition forces in a war lasting over 13 years, with an estimated 11,614 civilians killed since 2007 (United Nations Assistance Mission in Afghanistan, 2007; 2008; 2014). However, attention was also redirected towards Iraq as being complicit in the attacks, returning the US and its allies to previous UN policy, implemented during the Gulf War, in order to fashion a corresponding military attack in the Middle East:

An attempt was made to use Article 51 (right for a nation to defend itself) as justification to invade Iraq by the US as self defence for 9/11. This was not granted by the UN.

Resolution 1441: passed in 2002 acknowledging that Iraq had failed to abide by regulations under Resolution 687 to disarm its WMD. Iraq was given a final opportunity to disarm, give way to UN weapons inspections and allow humanitarian aid to access those who needed it within Iraq.

Following Resolution 1441 the UN Monitoring, Verification and Inspection Commission stated Iraq had actively begun movements towards fulfilling its obligations under Resolution 687 during 2003.

Nevertheless, Resolution 1441 became the lynchpin to rationalize the invasion of Iraq without the consent of the UN Security Council (see Kramer and Michalowski, 2005; 2006 for a detailed discussion). Reviving Resolution 678 (the justification to enact hostilities against Iraq in 1990) without justification, and relying on falsely evidencing the non-compliance of Resolution 687 (the request for Iraq to disarm WMD), was used as justification to employ military force under Resolution 1441. Under this skewed rationale, US and Coalition forces invaded Iraq in 2003. Lasting just three weeks, from 20 March to 9 April, the shock and awe campaign killed more than 6,700 civilians (Iraq Body Count, 2013). The yearly totals of civilians killed from violence in Iraq have consistently remained high since the initial invasion in 2003, averaging over 12,000 deaths per year. Saddam was later captured by US forces, tried and sentenced to death by a local – not international – court for war crimes committed in Dujail in 1982. To date, over 10 years on since the shock and awe campaign initiated the war in 2003, over 149,000 civilians are reported to have been killed as a direct result of violence in Iraq (Iraq Body Count, 2014). As we go on to discuss, the country has been left in disarray ever since.

Connecting individual and collective victimisation

This case study connects 'street' crime with victimisation by the state in ways encouraged by both Friedrichs (2000) and Young (2007). For the purposes of this chapter it will be useful to explicate some of the basic connections between each element of this study before going on to consider its relevance for our appreciation of the impact of 'crime' and its relevance for victimology.

Both parts of this case study address different scales of victimisation. Stephen Lawrence was an individual direct victim, murdered in cold blood in an overtly racist attack. In Iraq the deaths of over 149,000 direct victims of war violence far outweighs the scale of any street crime likely to be experienced in a domestic context (though note the case study in Chapter 7 as a potential exception to this). However, as Howarth and Rock (2000) have demonstrated, murder creates a wider impact of victimisation other than the direct victim. This wider impact includes those who witness and experience acts of violence indirectly, suffering the consequences of harm directly inflicted upon others. For Strobl (2004), both direct and indirect victims experience different classifications of victimisation. Direct victims can fall foul of victimisation that is 'personal' (caused by the offence, with the intent to cause harm to the victim) or 'vicarious' (caused by the offence but not motivated to cause harm to the victim); indirect victims suffer differently through instances of victimisation that are either 'mediated' (neither caused by the offence nor motivated to cause harm to the victim) or 'collective' (not caused by the offence but motivated to cause harm to the victim). However, there is perhaps another difference between these two cases of victimisation too. The murder of Stephen Lawrence was felt intimately in the UK, and its consequences hit at the heart of the criminal justice process. The same cannot be said for the deaths of 149,000 Iraqi civilians, distanced from the West by space, culture and politics, though hugely impactive, of course, within the local, regional context. This in itself reveals much about Western priorities.

Both elements of our case study can also be read in terms of victim culpability (Mendelsohn, 1974; see also Chapter 1). The ill-founded perception of the London Metropolitan Police in the immediate aftermath of Stephen

Lawrence's murder – that both he and Dwayne Brooks had been actively involved in the perpetration of their own victimisation – was based upon suspicions related to their ethnicity. In the eyes of the police they were 'culpable'. Appositely in the months following 9/11 and in the build up to the war in Iraq, Saddam Hussein's perceived lack of compliance under Resolution 1441 afforded the opportunity for US and UK governments to make a case that his dictatorship and the Baath Party posed a direct and imminent threat to the West. On the basis that he was harboring 'Weapons of Mass Destruction', which he is now commonly understood not to have possessed, the US and UK governments presented the invasion in the context of 'victim blaming' (Amir, 1967; see also Chapter 1). Saddam presented a threat to the West through non-compliance of Resolution 1441 and therefore 'deserved' the violent military response that his relationship with the West provoked. Some of these points are returned to in more detail below; for now they alert us to a question raised in Chapter 1 that usefully sets out the next line of inquiry: to what extent do victims of such violence possess characteristics that made them more prone to victimisation?

Making sense of trauma and victimisation: from the individual to the collective

With all that we now know about these two cases it may be more appropriate to consider the victimisation exacted in terms of 'victim proneness' (von Hentig, 1940). Stephen Lawrence was a young male victimised by a group of older men intent on causing him harm – not for a threat that he posed but for the difference the colour of his skin presented. The nation of Iraq was similarly vulnerable to the might of Western military power following its persecution under UN sanctions following the Gulf War. The subsequent justifications for the invasion in 2003 were based upon a mix of humanitarian intervention for the Iraqi people and a need to disarm Saddam of WMD (see Robinson et al., 2010). This mix of vulnerability and threat created a 'rejected victim' status (Strobl, 2004) of the East by the West. Thus, this geopolitics of war made possible the victim status of the already 'traumatised' collectivity of the people in Iraq (through economic sanctions and internal persecution) subservient to the perceived importance of the violation of international norms committed by Saddam. As a result, 'the need to react to the norm violation [by the East] … led to arbitrary justice and other forms of norm violations [by the West]' (Strobl, 2004: 296, *our inserts*).

Much has already been written about such norm violations by a number of critical criminologists in the decade following the 2003 invasion. Green and Ward (2004) analyse the complicity between Saddam's crimes against humanity in Iraq and the West's involvement in supporting his regime pre 1990, and subsequent persecution of the Iraqi state by the UN and US thereafter. Kramer and Michalowski (2005; 2006) document the illegality of the invasion of Iraq in 2003 by US and Coalition forces based upon their manipulation of the aforementioned UN Resolutions, using 9/11 as a catalyst for an illegal war. Whilst Whyte (2007) provides an insight into the 'economic domination' of Iraq during its subsequent occupation by the West following the 2003 invasion, perpetuating state-corporate criminality and rife profiteering from Iraq's natural resources. However, whilst we agree with the critical outlook of such analyses, there are other ways in which these events can be understood that draw attention to victimisation in terms of what Rafter and Walklate (2012) have termed 'victimality'. This they define in the following way:

> Just as 'criminality' means a capacity for criminal behaviour, so 'victimality' means a capacity for victimisation; and, just as the former fluctuates over time, so does the latter ... Note that in neither case does 'victimality' connote blameworthiness. Rather, victimality refers to the potential of an individual for victimisation, not a fault.
>
> (Rafter and Walklate, 2012: 517)

Victimality is imagined as a way to redefine victim precipitation. In other words, a victim may already possess different degrees of 'victimality', meaning that they are vulnerable to victimisation time and time again (Rafter and Walklate, 2012). How does this concept help connect traumatised individuals with traumatised collectivities?

Traumatised individuals: hate crime

Stephen Lawrence's death and the subsequent Macpherson Inquiry contributed to the introduction of the *Crime and Disorder Act* (1998). Under Section 28 of this Act, offenders considered (by the victim) to have expressed hostility towards the victim before, during or following the commission of a criminal act were to be reported as perpetrators of 'hate crimes'. McLaughlin (2013: 211) defines a hate crime as constituting

> a criminal act which is motivated by hatred, bias or prejudice against a person or property based on the actual or perceived race, ethnicity, gender, religion, disability or sexual orientation of the victim.

Advocating hate crime legislation as a positive social process of re-moralization (see also Mason, 2013) establishing values of tolerance and multiculturalism, McLaughlin (2002) set his position in contrast with such commentators as Jacobs and Potter (1998) who, he argues, downplay its severity and perceive the concept as a divisive instrument appropriated by state, media and vulnerable groups seeking protection within the law. Nestled between these opposing debates, Hall (2013) outlines the many problematic definitional aspects of hate crime, suggesting that in addition to needing to be understood legally and operationally (by the police) it also needs to be understood conceptually.

For Mason (2014), the application of the concept of hate crime within existing laws, in those countries who recognise it, has been ascribed a set of general characteristics. First, crimes need to be understood as being *motivated* by prejudice towards a victim's identity. Second, individuals or groups need to be *selected* for victimisation either because of their personal characteristics or belonging to a social group; or offenders have to demonstrate prejudice towards victims *before, during or after* the commission of a criminal act. Third, hate crime laws are not specifically needed for this category of crime to exist since this understanding aligns it with established crimes that often attract a heavier sentence if found to have been perpetrated due to the above criteria (Mason, 2014). Finally, and most controversially (qua Jacobs and Potter, 1998), the judgement of hate crime within either pre-existing or specifically designed laws is laden with identity politics: some victim characteristics are protected while others are not (Mason, 2014). However, following Perry (2001), Hall (2013) adds that hate crime can also be understood as perpetuating hegemonic power and oppression of already marginalised groups that reaffirm the hierarchies shaping social order. In the context of this debate it is not so much the application of hate crime within legal statutes that we wish to press here. Instead it is the two latter characteristics that are of interest: who is included and/or excluded from categories of hate crime and what hierarchies are reaffirmed by its existence. So whilst there may be a grasp on how hate crime helps make some sense of the experiences of individuals subjected to it, in what ways does this facilitate an understanding of traumatised collectivities and how is this connected to war?

Traumatised collectivities: extending the concept of hate crime

Chakraborti and Garland (2012) suggest that conceptual understandings of hate crime should go further, to include the 'ordinariness' and intricate experiences and motivations between offenders and victims (see also Garland, 2011 and Spalek, 2006 on 'spirit injury'). A more ambitious reading of hate crime victimisation allows an appreciation of

> the more individualized acts of hate borne from boredom, jealousy or unfamiliarity with 'difference'; our awareness of those groups of victims whose experiences have been marginalised because they typically lack access to resources or political representation or because they are seen as less worthy than other more 'legitimate' victim groups.
>
> (Chakraborti and Garland, 2012: 510)

There is room for the concept of hate crime to be pressed further to include an even wider range of mass victimisation frequently marginalised from hate crime (and victimological) discourses: the victims of war. Following the logic of Garland (2011) and Chakraborti and Garland (2012) in part, Perry's (2001) conceptual model also has some value when discussing traumatised collectivities. This model permits conceiving of acts of violence that are not only motivated by prejudice but also perpetuate the 'otherness' of those victimised, further oppress already marginalised individuals or groups, and reaffirm established hierarchical dualities of normal/difference, wanted/unwanted, superiority/inferiority, good/evil (Perry, 2001). Taking this step requires some further rethinking of what is meant by hate crime and its relationship with 'victimality' (Rafter and Walklate, 2012).

Reconceptualizing hate crime

Simply stating that war is an act of hate crime because it is committed by powerful states on weaker opponents is too broad and problematic to afford analytical meaning. As McLaughlin (2013: 211, *our emphasis*) continues, 'hate crime encompasses racist crime, sex crime, homophobia, anti-Semitism, sectarianism, and links across to ethnic cleansing and *genocide*'. By introducing genocide McLaughlin opens a narrative within which to discuss a much broader continuum of victimisation that can be experienced across a wide variety of prejudice-based violence. Indeed Young (2007) makes a case for understanding acts of violent terrorism experienced in the domestic context as having fundamental connections with acts of violence perpetrated during war. Key to this analysis is the identification of a paradox that exists in the 'banality' of violence in both domains. This leads Young (2007: 163 *our insert*) to ask the question: 'How do normal people do these [violent] things?' So asking a similar question in a different way we pose: How is such violence made possible, and what are its consequences for victims?

The answer to the first part of this question is essentialism, a term that is also useful in connecting hate crime and genocide. As Young (1999: 117) explains, 'Essentialism greatly facilitates the process of social exclusion. It furnishes the targets, it provides the stereotypes, it allows the marshalling of aggression'. For Stephen Lawrence, essentialism was evidenced in him being targeted based on the colour of his skin by perpetrators expressing overt racism. His victimisation typifies 'essentializing dualisms' (Perry, 2001: 143) between perceptions of superiority/inferiority of race by his murderers. For Young (1999), the parallels between hate crime and war similarly become apparent through acts of violence based on essentialism; the justification of which requires the identification of perceived hostile groups (Perry, 2001) and the creation of a 'good enemy' deserving of the violent conduct they receive (Young, 1999: 116). Wider essentialism of this kind identifies an opposing nation's moral differences as dangerous and a threat to the West, thus generating aggression towards a divergent group: hostility that legitimises the use of violence as an appropriate means of action (Young, 1999; see also Mooney and Young, 2005). This point is returned to below.

Those who are therefore 'marshalling aggression' are those who perpetuate hate crime victimisation. Thus essentialism of entire groups or nations may instead be understood as being carried out by 'hate groups' (Perry, 2001: 137) rather than individual offenders. Such groups range from extreme racist organisations such as the Ku Klux Klan and 'skinheads' to quasi-legitimate political organizations, such as the British National Party (BNP) and UK Independence Party (UKIP), who foster overtones of prejudice within their political rhetoric. However, according to Perry (2001), there are hate groups connected to mainstream politics who do not have implicit or overtly prejudiced or racist connotations but manage to orchestrate hate crime more subtly through supposedly 'legitimate means'. For the radical victimologist such groups may be emblematic of states or governments, a much more diffuse entity to attribute with criminal wrongdoing, particularly as their violences are secreted under legality and notions of 'justness' (Mooney and Young, 2005). This inexorably leads to a deeper consideration of the connections between hate crime, war and acts of genocide.

Traumatised collectivities of war: hate crime and genocide

Mooney and Young (2005) suggest that the ways in which violence is engaged in between states in the East (Orient) and the West (Occident) can be understood as a process of simplification and beautification; both the East and West are fearful of stereotypes of the other, feeding essentialism and a process of 'othering' to legitimise violence. In terms of making connections between hate crime and genocide, the crux of this process is the instrument of essentialism between national, ethnic and religious groups. However, this is not enough to permit violence, it merely facilitates it (Mooney and Young, 2005). It is instead the extent of essentialism which allows the 'other' to be placed on the 'periphery of humanity' that permits violence to take place, and it is the perceived threat of the 'other' which legitimises violence (Mooney and Young, 2005: 119). For Jamieson (1999), it is the process of social exclusion facilitated by essentialism in this way, rather than the violence itself, that is the core characteristic of genocide.

Genocide defined

Coined by Raphael Lemkin in 1944 (Hirsh, 2003), the term genocide refers to the destruction of a nation or the extermination of entire ethnic groups, and was conceptualized to signify the mass murder of the global Jewish population by Nazi Germany during the Holocaust (Hirsh, 2003). It is asserted as the most severe crime to occur during peace or war (McLaughlin, 1996, cited in Croall, 1998: 296) and, as noted above, is conceivable as the most extreme form of hate crime imaginable (McLaughlin, 2003). It is not our intention to labour the intricacies of this concept further. Suffice it to say that as a subject matter it has already received wide and varied attention within criminological and victimological literature (see Alvarez, 1997; Jamieson, 1999; Friedrichs, 2000; Woolford,

2006; Morrison, 2007; Maier-Katkin, Mears and Bernard, 2009; Hagan and Rymond-Richmond, 2009; Cameron, 2012; Hagan et al., 2012; Rafter and Walklate, 2012). Instead the intention here is to provide the legal and conceptual parameters within which to discuss genocide for the purposes of this chapter.

Genocide is a specific international crime (Hirsh, 2003). Within the *United Nations Convention on the Prevention and Punishment of the Crime of Genocide* (1948, cited in Alvarez, 2010: 11–12), genocide constitutes

> acts committed with the intent to destroy, in whole or in part, a national, ethnical, racial or religious group [by] …
>
> > Killing members of the group;
> > Causing serious bodily or mental harm to members of the group;
> > Deliberately inflicting on the group conditions of life calculated to bring about its physical destruction in whole or in part;
> > Imposing measures intended to prevent births within the group; [or]
> > Forcibly transferring children of the group to another group.

However, Alvarez (2010) points out that capturing genocide in one definitional form is problematic, particularly given that it regularly occurs during acts of war and its crimes frequently overlap with war crimes and human rights violations, making it hard to distinguish legally from other misdemeanors. The act of genocide also involves much more than simply using violence to kill large numbers.

> Genocide has been perpetrated not only with gas, guns, machetes, clubs and other similar kinds of weapons, but also through less direct methods that include disease, malnutrition and starvation, forced sterilization and displacement and rape.
>
> (Alvarez, 2010: 7)

Thus it is important to note that any one of these elements can constitute the act of genocide and for those who are killed, they are murdered not for what they have done, but for *who* they are and *what* they may become (Jamieson, 1999). For Jamieson, there is nothing that the direct, primary or indirect victims of genocide could or could not do – be they submissive or militant – that would prevent their attempted eradication. However, genocide is not simply an 'eruption of hatred', it requires a widespread acceptance of legitimacy and acceptance of state policies to carry it out (Alvarez, 2010). It is a planned, rational and bureaucratic act of direct or indirect violence and social exclusion in extremis, legitimised through an essentialism of difference, positioned as serving and protecting public interests (Jamieson, 1999). Furthermore, different genocides have different motivations (i.e. political rivalry, religious ideology, retribution, colonisation, or the political/economic exploitation of a region) and the act itself evolves over time (Alvarez, 2010). These legal and conceptual notions of genocide provide the analytical context inviting the legacies of war into a trauma narrative of collective victimisation.

Hall (2013) points out that under conventional legal applications of hate crime anyone can claim to be a victim if they believe their victimisation has been motivated by prejudice toward them. Whilst this aims to afford direct victims more agency in how their victimisation has been experienced, it also renders the term fragile, with the risk of it being overused and thus losing its significance (Hall, 2013). Similar arguments have been made regarding the use of the term genocide. It too carries a double-edged meaning. International authorities discussed in Chapter 7, such as the UN Security Council, International Criminal Court (ICC) and members of the Western international community, are said to use the official term 'genocide' as a means of prudently identifying mass victimisation so as not to trivialise the Holocaust (Hirsh, 2003), and avoid reducing perceptions of genocidal acts to instances of brutality rather than mass murder (Furedi, 2005). This usage, it is suggested, protects Western states from engaging in humanitarian assistance and masks their own acts of violence. It is a term scarcely used by member states of the Genocide Convention (1948) (Morrison, 2005) to reduce the pressure for international intervention, as witnessed by the inaction of the US during the 1994 Rwandan genocide (Hirsch, 2003; see also Cameron, 2013). Indeed the US has also been accused of committing acts of mass murder on civilians, such as those occurring during the Vietnam War (see Storr, 1991).

However, despite advocating that the use of the term genocide be employed prudently so as not to trivialise the Holocaust, Woolford (2006) avers we should also not be restricted by the limits placed on its use by its legal definition: to do so sidelines the issue of power and restricts what might be considered harmful to a 'victim narrative'. As an example of this, Jones (2002) highlights the accusations of genocide against the West during the Gulf War. In 1996 former US Attorney General Ramsey Clark accused leaders of the US, UK and UN of genocide at the International Court for Crimes against Humanity Committed by the UN Security Council on Iraq for imposing an economic and military blockade on Iraq under UN Resolution 661 in 1990, introduced for refusing to adhere to UN Resolution 660 (demand for Iraq to withdraw from Kuwait) (see Clark, 1996). Following the Gulf War these sanctions were linked to upholding Resolution 687 (the request for Iraq to disarm WMD) and led the population of Iraq into a widespread humanitarian crisis:

> The direct consequence of such acts and others is direct physical injury to the majority of the population in Iraq, serious permanent injury to a substantial minority of the population and death to more than 1,500,000 people including 750,000 children under five years of age.
>
> (Clark, 1996)

The imposition of economic sanctions under Resolution 661 denied billions of dollars of aid to an Iraqi population suffering the consequences of an estimated 88,000 tons of explosives dropped in 1991, 70 per cent of which landed on civilian Iraqi areas (Kelly, 2003), in addition to increasing child and adult fatalities as a result of UN sanctions and depleted uranium from US missile attacks (Fisk, 2003). In 1996 the oil-for-food programme was introduced in Iraq, regulating the country's oil-selling potential to £6 billion of oil per year to ease UN sanctions and buy humanitarian resources (Fisk, 2003; Teather, 2005). The oil-for-food programme, intended to alleviate the humanitarian damage caused to the population of Iraq by the sanctions (Jones, 2012) is alleged to have been introduced as a means of avoiding further accusations of genocide (Nimri Aziz, 2003). This suggests that the population of Iraq has been a collectivity traumatised by the West since 1990 at the behest of the US, UK and UN, and stands as illustration of the hegemonic dominance referred to in Perry's (2001) understanding of hate crime. Arguably it also has the effect of further removing these events from the victimological gaze.

Was the 2003 Iraq War genocide?

In an analysis of the Rwandan and Bosnian genocides, Jamieson (1999) suggests that, not being recognised by the international community at the outset as acts of genocide, such events become even more prescient for criminological (read victimological) attention as a result. In a similar way, by employing criminological and socio-legal work to demonstrate that the Iraq War was conducted without the authorisation of international humanitarian law, Kramer and Michalowski (2005) aver that it too becomes part of the criminological/victimological gaze. So, following Woolford's (2006) lead, we return to the definition of genocide and attempt to transcend its confines in the critical spirit proposed by Jamieson, Kramer and Michalowski. In so doing, what this has to say of the extent of victimisation caused by war violence is quite profound for the study of victimology.

(i) Destruction of groups partially or completely by killing group members

As Green and Ward (2009) note, following the 2003 invasion, Iraq became the non-state terrorism capital of the world, suffering more deaths from violent attacks than any other country. As stated earlier, in the three weeks – from 20 March to 9 April 2003 – of the shock and awe campaign, more than 6,700 civilians were killed (Iraq Body Count, 2013). The yearly totals of civilians killed from violence in Iraq have consistently remained high since the initial invasion in 2003, averaging over 12,000 deaths per year (Iraq Body Count, 2014). Using the Iraq Body Count we could go on intricately listing the extent of deaths per year, but this is only part of the story. Here we reiterate that to date more than 149,000 civilians have been killed as a result of violence in Iraq (Iraq Body Count, 2014), including a combination of deaths caused during the initial invasion, subsequent occupation of the country by US and Coalition forces and other attendant violence occurring as a result.

(ii) Causing bodily or mental harm

Levy and Sidel (2013) establish that the extent of war-related illnesses and injuries experienced by Iraqi civilians is not known. However, some inferences can be made regarding the extent of physical injuries experienced as a result of the Iraq War since 2003. In the first six months following the invasion Dardagan et al. (2003) reported that for every one death experienced in Iraq, three other injuries were experienced. They estimate that at the start of July 2003 more than 21,000 people had been injured as a result of war violence. Applying this logic (median injury-death ratio of 2.85 × number of deaths) to the number of deaths experienced in Iraq as of 2014, this number rises to over 400,000 physical injuries. According to Faber and Saggurthi (2013), approximately 155,000 of Iraq's population of 31,000,000 require prosthetic or medical devices to assist with their injuries. Moreover, they inform us that of the large numbers of people registered at the Red Cross physical rehabilitation centre in one of Iraq's major cities in the north of the county, more than 6,000 people have suffered amputated limbs, mostly caused as a result of the 2003 war or other attendant violence (Faber and Saggurthi, 2013). In addition, Bolton (2013) reports that a survey by the Iraq Mental Health Survey (see World Health Organisation, 2009; Alhasnawi et al., 2009) indicated anxiety disorder to be the most common group recorded, with depression being the most common disorder amongst the reporting populations. Kurds in the north of the country and populations in southern Iraq are said to have 'substantial symptoms of depression, anxiety, and post-traumatic stress' (Bolton, 2013: 880). Although little research has been conducted on the mental health of Iraq's population (Bolton, 2013), particularly in the aftermath of the war, the extent of psychological problems suffered by military personnel, who participated in this war and were stationed in Iraq for comparatively short periods compared to the population who live there, perhaps indicates the potential for psychological trauma to be widespread. However, not only is the mental health provision in Iraq lacking to support its current need, there remains a cultural stigma attached to poor mental health that presents a number of practical and familial barriers to those suffering poor mental health to seek the treatment that they need (Bolton, 2013).

(iii) Destruction of the condition of life partially or completely

Hagan et al. (2012) have recently noted the economic victimisation of the Iraqi population. Drawing on two large data sets, they indicate the extent of the monetary costs of the invasion and subsequent violence experienced in Iraq. They note that one in five households in Baghdad had experienced some form of 'index violation' (i.e. assault, burglary, looting, theft or confiscation) in the six months following the 2003 invasion, with approximately 250,000 households having at least one member experiencing victimisation of this sort (Hagan et al., 2012). In the five subsequent years following the invasion it is estimated that over a million households across Baghdad had experienced some form of index or 'non-index' violation (i.e. killings, displacement, targeted assassinations, mass lethal attacks, abduction, torture, threats, abuses of various sorts). Other monetary costs incurred in Baghdad alone (i.e. blackmail, kidnapping/ransom payments, medical expenses incurred due to violence, moving costs to escape violence and insecurity, losses of businesses, homes, cars and other large costs) amount to over $90 billion, with the country as a whole suffering an estimated economic cost of $309 billion; at the upper limit this estimate rises to over $1 trillion (Hagan et al., 2012). These costs pertain solely to household victimisation and do not include the economic costs to Iraq as a nation (i.e. infrastructure and other public costs). The extent of the infrastructural damage to the health provision, food and water supply, sewage and sanitation facilities in Iraq following the invasion is indicated by Levy and Sidel (2013) to have worsened the prevalence of injury and ill-health of Iraqi civilians. Instances of index violations noted above have also affected core health services, which were looted and damaged in the years following the invasion, including many health workers and physicians being displaced or leaving Iraq (Levy and Sidel, 2013). Hilfi et al. (2013) also report that healthcare services in Iraq are still struggling to recover following years of sanctions under Resolution 661 and the post-2003 invasion, with Iraq's healthcare system continuing without a coordinated strategy capable of tackling key health problems such a communicable diseases, which were rife during the years following the invasion.

(iv) Prevention of births and transfer of children

Although there is no evidence of this final element, Levy and Sidel (2013) do note that following five years of the war approximately 2,200,000 people fled Iraq as refugees, many leaving for Syria and Jordan; in addition a further 2,700,000 people were internally displaced in Iraq, many of whom faced greater health risks through a lack of food, shelter and vulnerability to insecurity. In a country with half of its population under the age of 18 (Webster, 2013) it is a fair estimation that many pregnant women and children would have been exposed to these conditions during the invasion and in the years thereafter. Moreover, according to Webster (2013: 892), the rate of children dying before the age of one in Iraq is 32 for every 1,000 children born alive, with 84 women in every 100,000 dying in childbirth. 'Iraq is among the group of 68 countries that account for 97 per cent of all maternal and child deaths globally', with 90 per cent of its young (under 18) population 'deprived of essentials such as healthcare, nutrition, water and sanitation, protection and shelter'.

Victimality, power and the problem of intent

The range and extent of deaths caused by the shock and awe campaign, and subsequent destruction caused by the military occupation of Iraq, provides evidence of a dramatic power differential during the 2003 Iraq War. The scale of the impact of this and the trauma generated (in every sense of the term) sits comfortably within the designated definition of genocide. Moreover, the extent of harm experienced over such a long period by the people of Iraq firmly demonstrates their victimality: openness to repeated state victimisation (Rafter and Walklate, 2012).

However, when questioning the 'legitimacy' of such power, the allegations raised against the US, UK and UN in 1996 offer further clarity. Jones (2012), drawing on Gordon (2010), suggests that for the allegation of genocide to be legally viable, *mens rea* must be present: an intent to conduct criminal violence at war with the purpose of achieving the range of mass victimisation articulated in the definition of genocide. For Jones (2012: 141), 'if understandings of genocidal intent could be expanded to place greater emphasis on *general* rather than *specific* intent, the term would be apt'. As such, despite creating the legacy of traumatised collectivities in Iraq, the 2003 war is not *legally* considered to be an act of genocide. However, if not an act of genocide, in what ways do these events speak to a victimological agenda? Jones (2002: 135) continues, although non-state entities or campaign groups 'lack an ability to enforce their verdicts … they can do much to bring crimes to light that liberal states have a vested interest in suppressing'. If an appreciation of the political economy of trauma, as suggested in Chapter 2, is added to this observation, the relevance of these events to victimology becomes clear. In order to facilitate this, it will be useful to return to the connections to be made between individual trauma and collective trauma.

The death of Baha Mousa in 2003 evidenced a watershed moment of victimisation during the war in Iraq (Baha Mousa Inquiry, 2011). He was a civilian hotel worker who died whilst in the custody of the British Army during the country's occupation. From the images released of Baha he is seemingly unconscious, his face battered and bruised, having clearly undergone physical trauma and 'personal victimisation' (qua Strobl, 2004). Further disturbing imagery of individual trauma was provided by the US Army soon after (see Hamm, 2007). By now the images of abuse of Iraqi prisoners from Abu Ghraib prison need little introduction:

> You know the ones: the hooded figure standing on a box with wires running from his hands, the pile of men with Lyndie England leering and pointing down at them, the prisoner on the leash held by England.
>
> (Ferrell et al., 2008: 12)

These images of traumatised individuals being victimised amid the mass traumatised collectivity of war coldly reflect the purest form of essentialism against the 'other'. They are starkly emblematic in terms of their prejudice and violence, not that far removed from the murder of Stephen Lawrence. By situating the victim on the 'periphery of humanity', as Mooney and Young (2005: 119) describe, essentialism of this nature becomes the precipice where victimisation takes place, legitimising violence through the perceived threat of the essentialised 'other'. There is nothing indirect about these forms of victimisation, nor any room to hide behind the well-crafted legality within which they have each been addressed subsequently. They are not 'mediated' by accident or without direct damage caused to those who experience them (qua Strobl, 2004). For the direct victims of such violence these acts are deeply personal: full of intent to debase, harm and traumatise. As such, a trauma narrative for victimology holds power relations at its core, when committed against both individuals and collectivities. This victimisation is 'deliberate and knowing, and deeply *indifferent to the human consequences*' (Gordon, 2012: 224, our emphasis).

Conclusion

This chapter has illustrated the ways in which the victimological imagination can be used to address state crime victimisation and genocide. In so doing it has travelled through the victimological terrain, from understanding the impact that crime has on individuals through to an appreciation that such events have on collectivities. The analysis of the case study has utilised a full range of victimological concepts to do this – some drawn from the victim narrative and some from the trauma narrative discussed in Chapter 2. Underpinning this analysis, it is possible to discern the deeper presence of the geopolitics that frame how events like those discussed are understood; implicitly framed here as a political economy of trauma (qua Fassin and Rechtman's, 2009, moral economy of trauma). Moreover, the practices of denial (Cohen 2001) and the processes of othering that have been evidenced in both elements of the case study demonstrate the emotional pull that the ideal victim (discussed in Chapter 1) has in the public and legal domains.

Mason (2014) suggests that to gain compassion and be brought into focus, victims must not only be publicly definable as undeserving of the prejudice they have suffered, but also have their suffering recognised as serious enough to warrant state intervention. This jostling for public recognition as a deserving victim contributes to the hierarchy of victimisation (Carrabine et al., 2004), a process contingent upon being able to claim public sympathy: a key hallmark of the 'ideal victim' (see also Chapter 1). Indeed, as Mason (2014) goes on to suggest, the identities of victim groups, involved in hate crime or other forms of victimisation, play their own role in shaping the moral force of the law. The murder of Stephen Lawrence, and the campaigning voices that have persisted since that event, have ensured that hate crime and the protection of minority ethnic groups from crime motivated by prejudice remains high on political agendas. However, the same cannot necessarily be said for the people of Iraq. The Iraqi people have been placed at too far a distance from the centre of public compassion in the UK for them to achieve a lofty position within any victim hierarchy. The obscuring of the Iraqi population in the ways we have outlined here illuminates the ways in which they have been denied 'ideal victim' status, despite the humanitarian compassion and work of the agencies and NGOs that might suggest otherwise. Even their presence is arguably tainted by presumptions of trauma as taking priority over presumptions of political economy (see for example Fassin, 2012). Moreover, this chapter has also illustrated how, and under what circumstances, the victim narrative and the trauma narrative discussed in Chapter 2 can work in making sense of the impact of crime, not only for individuals but also for collectivities.

Further reading

We would recommend reading Stan Cohen's (2001) *States of Denial* as an excellent sociological account of the range of broad issues relating to state violence and victimisation discussed in the latter part of this chapter. For further information relating to the extent of victimisation and death suffered by the Iraqi people, we suggest readers review the 2013 Special Issue of *The Lancet* dedicated to Iraq, in addition to the Iraq Body Count website (www.iraq bodycount.org).

Notes

1 American Airlines Flight 11, United Airlines Flight 175, American Airlines Flight 77, and United Airlines Flight 93 (Benjamin and Simon, 2002: 33–37).
2 American Airlines Flight 11 struck the north tower at 8.46 a.m. United Airlines Flight 175 struck the south tower at 9.02 a.m. (Benjamin and Simon, 2002: 33)
3 American Airlines Flight 77 struck the west side of the Pentagon at 9.40 a.m. (Benjamin and Simon, 2002: 34).
4 United Airlines Flight 93 (Benjamin and Simon, 2002: 35).

References

Alhasnawi, S., Sadik, S., Rasheed, M., Baban, A., Al-Alak, M. M., Othman, A. Y., Othman, Y., Ismet, N., Shawani, O., Murthy, S. AlJadiry, M., Chatterji, S., Al-Gasseer, N., Streel, E., Naidoo, N., Ali, M. M., Gruber, M. J., Petukhova, M., Sampson, N. A. and Kessler, R. C. (2009) 'The prevalence and correlates of DSM-IV disorders in the Iraq Mental Health Survey (IMHS)', *World Psychiatry*, 8: 97–109.
Alvarez, A. (1997) 'Adjusting to genocide: the techniques of neutralization and the Holocaust', *Social Science History*, 21(2): 139–78.
——(2010) *Genocidal Crimes*. Oxon: Routledge.
Amir, M. (1967) 'Victim precipitated forcible rape', *The Journal of Criminal Law, Criminology, and Political Science*, 58(4): 493–502.
Arnove, A. (ed.) (2003) *Iraq Under Siege: the Deadly Impact of Sanctions and War*. London: Pluto Press.
Baha Mousa Inquiry. (2011) 'Independent report: the Baha Mousa public inquiry report'. Available at https://www.gov.uk/government/publications/the-baha-mousa-public-inquiry-report.
BBC News (2003, May 2) 'Bush speech: full text'. Available at http://news.bbc.co.uk/1/hi/world/americas/2994345.stm.

Benjamin, D. and Simon, S. (2002) *The Age of Sacred Terror*. New York: Random House.

Bennetto, J. and Kirby, T. (2005, December 8) 'War criminals', *The Independent*: 1–2.

Bolton, P. (2013) 'Mental health in Iraq: issues and challenges', *The Lancet*, 381: 879–81.

Cameron, H. (2013) *Britain's Hidden Role in the Rwandan Genocide: The Cat's Paw*. Oxon: Routledge.

Carrabine, E., Iganski, P., Lee, M., Plummer, K., and South, N. (2004) *Criminology: A Sociological Introduction*. London: Routledge.

Chakraborti, N. and Garland, J. (2012) 'Reconceptualising hate crime victimisation through the lens of Vulnerability and 'difference', *Theoretical Criminology*, 16(4): 499–514.

Clark, R. (1996) 'Ramsey Clark: charges against US, British and UN leaders', *International Action Centre Anti-Sanctions Project*. Available at http://www.iacenter.org/warcrime/charges.htm.

Cohen, S. (2001) *States of Denial: Knowing about Atrocities and Suffering*. Cambridge: Polity Press.

Croall, H. (1998) *Crime and Society in Britain*. Essex: Longman.

Dardagan, H., Sloboda, J., and Williams, K. (2003) *Adding Indifference to Injury*, Iraq Body Count. Available at http://www.iraqbodycount.org/analysis/beyond/indifference-to-injury.

Edkins, J. (2003) 'The rush to memory and the rhetoric of war', *Journal of Political and Military Sociology*, 31(2): 231–50.

Faber, J. and Saggurthi, P. (2013) 'Physical rehabilitation services in Iraq', *The Lancet*, 381: 881–83.

Fassin, D. (2012) *Humanitarian Reason*. Berkeley: University of California Press.

Fassin, D. and Rechtman, R., (2009) *The Empire of Trauma*. Princeton, NJ: Princeton University Press.

Ferrell, J., Hayward, K., and Young, J. (2008) *Cultural Criminology: An Invitation*. London: Sage.

Fisk, R. (2003) 'The hidden war', in A. Arnove (ed.) *Iraq Under Siege: the Deadly Impact of Sanctions and War*. London: Pluto Press. pp. 121–32.

Friedrichs, D. O. (2000) 'The crime of the century? The case for the Holocaust', *Crime, Law and Social Change*, 34: 21–41.

Furedi, F. (2005) *The Politics of Fear: Beyond Left and Right*. London: Bloomsbury Continuum.

Garland, J. (2011) 'Difficulties in defining hate crime victimisation', *International Review of Victimology*, 18(10): 25–37.

Gordon, J. (2012) *Invisible War: The United States and Iraq Sanctions*. Cambridge, MA: Harvard University Press.

Green, P. and Ward, T. (2004) *State Crime: Governments, Violence and Corruption*. London: Pluto Press.

——(2009) 'The transformation of violence in Iraq', *British Journal of Criminology*, 49(5): 609–27.

Hagan, J. (2009) 'Prosecuting ethnic cleansing and mass atrocity in the former Yugoslavia and Darfur', *Journal of Scandinavian Studies in Criminology and Crime Prevention*, 10: 26–47.

Hagan, J. and Rymond-Richmond, W. (2009) *Darfur and the Crime of Genocide*. Cambridge: Cambridge University Press.

Hagan, J., Kaiser, J., Rothenberg, D., Hanson, A., and Parker, P. (2012) 'Atrocity victimisation and the costs of economic conflict crimes in the battle for Baghdad and Iraq', *European Journal of Criminology*, 9(5): 481–98.

Hakki, M. M. (2006) 'War crimes and the war in Iraq: can George W. Bush and Tony Blair be held legally responsible?', *The International Journal of Human Rights*, 10(1): 3–17.

Hall, N. (2013) *Hate Crime* (2nd edition). Oxon: Routledge.

Hamm, M. S. (2007) '"High crimes and misdemeanors": George W. Bush and the sins of Abu Ghraib', *Crime, Media, Culture*, 3(3): 259–84.

Hilfi, T. K. A., Lafta, R., and Burnham, G. (2013) 'Health services in Iraq', *The Lancet*, 381: 939–48.

Hillyard, P. (1993) *Suspect Community: People's Experiences of the Prevention of Terrorism Acts in Britain*. London: Pluto Press.

Hirsh, D. (2003) *Law against Genocide: Cosmopolitan Trials*. London: Glasshouse Press.

Howarth, G. and Rock, P. (2000) 'Aftermath and the construction of victimisation: "the other victims of crime"', *The Howard Journal*, 39(1): 58–78.

Iraq Body Count (2013, March 19) 'The War in Iraq: 10 years and counting'. Available at https://www.iraqbodycount.org/analysis/numbers/ten-years.

——(2014) 'Documented civilian deaths from violence'. Available at https://www.iraq bodycount.org/database.

Jacobs, J. and Potter, K. (1998) *Hate Crimes: Criminal Law and Identity Politics*. New York: Oxford University Press.

Jamieson, R. (1998) 'Towards a criminology of war in Europe', in V. Ruggiero, N. South, and I. Taylor (eds) *The New European Criminology: Crime and Social Order in Europe*. Oxon: Routledge. pp. 480–506.

——(1999) 'Genocide and the social production of immorality', *Theoretical Criminology*, 3(2): 131–46.

Jones, A. (2002) 'The politics of genocide', *International Studies Review*, 4(1): 129–42.

——(2012) 'Genocide and structural violence', in A. Jones (ed.) *New Directions in Genocide Research*. Oxon: Routledge. pp. 132–48.

Kauzlarich, D., Matthews, R. A. and Miller, W. J. (2001) 'Towards a victimology of state crime', *Critical Criminology*, 10: 173–94.

Kellner, D. (2003) *From 9/11 to Terror War: The Dangers of the Bush Legacy*. Oxford: Rowman & Littlefield.

Kelly, K. (2003) 'Raising voices: the children of Iraq, 1990–99', in A. Arnove (ed.) *Iraq Under Siege: The Deadly Impact of Sanctions and War*. London: Pluto Press. pp. 145–60.

Kramer, R. C. and Michalowski, R. J. (2005) 'War, aggression and state crime: a criminological analysis of the invasion and occupation of Iraq', *British Journal of Criminology*, 45(4): 446–69.

——(2006) The invasion of Iraq, in. R. J. Michalowski and R. C. Kramer (eds) *Wrongdoing at the Intersection of Business and Government*. New Brunswick: Rutgers University Press. pp. 199–214.

Levy, B. S. and Sidel, V. W. (2013) 'Adverse health consequences of the Iraq War', in *The Lancet*, 381: 949–58.

MacAskill, E. (2005, October 7) 'George Bush: "God told me to end the tyranny in Iraq"', *The Guardian*: 1 & 16.

Macpherson, W. G. (1999) 'The Stephen Lawrence Inquiry'. London: HMSO.

McLaughlin, E. (2002) 'Rocks and hard places: the politics of hate crime', *Theoretical Criminology*, 6(4): 493–98.

——(2013) 'Hate Crime', in E. McLaughlin and J. Muncie (eds) *The SAGE Dictionary of Criminology*. London: SAGE. pp. 211.

Maier-Katkin, D., Mears, D. P. and Bernard, T. J. (2009) 'Towards a criminology of crimes against humanity', *Theoretical Criminology*, 13(2): 227–55.

Mason, G. (2014) 'The symbolic purpose of hate crime: ideal victims and emotion', *Theoretical Criminology*, 18(1): 75–92.

Mendelsohn, B. (1974) 'Victimology and the technical and social sciences: a call for the establishment of victimology clinics', in I. Drapkin and E. Viano (eds) *Victimology: A New Focus*. Lexington, MA: D. C. Heath.

Mills, C. W. (1959) *The Sociological Imagination*. Oxford: Oxford University Press.

Mooney, J. and Young, J. (2005) 'Imagining terrorism: terrorism and anti-terrorism terrorism, two ways of doing evil', *Social Justice*, 32(1): 113–25.

Morrison, W. (2005) 'What is crime? Contrasting definitions and perspectives', in C. Hale, K. Hayward, A. Wahidin, and E. Wincup (eds) *Criminology*. Oxford: Oxford University Press. pp. 3–21.

——(2007) *Criminology, Civilization and the New World Order*. Oxon: Routledge.

Nimri Aziz, B. (2003) 'Targets – not victims', in A. Arnove (ed.) *Iraq Under Siege: The Deadly Impact of Sanctions and War*. London: Pluto Press. pp. 161–70.

Nobel Foundation. (2005, December 8) 'Pinter v the US', *The Guardian: G2*: 9–13.

Perry, B. (2001) *In the Name of Hate*. New York: Taylor and Francis.

Rafter, N. and Walklate, S. (2012) 'Genocide and the dynamics of victimisation: Some observations on Armenia', *European Journal of Criminology*, 9(5): 514–26.

Robinson, P., Goddard, P., Parry, K., Murray, C., and Taylor, P. M. (2010) *Pockets of Resistance: British News Media, War and Theory in the 2003 Invasion of Iraq*. Manchester: Manchester University Press.

Rothe, D. L. and Kauzlarich, D. (eds) (2014) *Towards a Victimology of State Crime*. Oxon: Routledge.

Scarman, L. G. (1981) *The Brixton Disorders, 10–12 April 1981: Report of an Inquiry by the Right Honourable the Lord Scarman, OBE*. London: Her Majesty's Stationary Office.

Spalek, B. (2006) *Crime Victims: Theory, Policy and Practice*. Basingstoke: Palgrave Macmillan.

Storr, A. (1991) *Human Destructiveness: The Roots of Genocide and Human Cruelty*. Oxon: Routledge.

Strobl, R. (2004) 'Constructing the victim: theoretical reflections and empirical examples', *International Review of Victimology*, 11(2/3): 295–311.

Sykes, G. M. and Matza, D. (1957) 'Techniques of neutralization: a theory of delinquency', *American Sociological Review*, 22(6): 664–70.

Teather, D. (2005, October 28) 'Abuse claims against 2,400 firms', *The Guardian*: 11.

United Nations Assistance Mission in Afghanistan. (2007) 'Civilian Casualties During 2007'. Available at http://www.unama.unmissions.org/Portals/UNAMA/human%20rights/PoC -Civilian-Casualties-report-2007.pdf.

——(2008) 'Afghanistan: annual report on protection of civilians in armed conflict, 2008'. Available at http://www.unama.unmissions.org/Portals/UNAMA/human%20rights/ UNAMA_09february-Annual%20Report_PoC%202008_FINAL_11Feb09.pdf.

——(2014) 'Civilians casualties rise by 24 per cent in first half of 2014. Ground engagements and crossfire now killing and injuring more Afghan civilians than IEDs'. Available at http:// www.unama.unmissions.org/LinkClick.aspx?fileticket=OhsZ29Dgeyw%3d&tabid=12254& mid=15756&language=en-US.

von Hentig, H. (1940) 'Remarks on the interaction of the perpetrator and victim', *Journal of Law and Criminology (1931–1951)*, 31(3): 303–9.

Walklate, S., McGarry, R., and Mythen, G. (2014) 'Trauma, visual victimology and the poetics of justice', in H. V. Jacobsen (ed.) *The Poetics of Crime: Understanding and Researching Crime and Deviance through Creative Sources*. Farnham: Ashgate. pp. 263–83.

Webster, P. C. (2013). 'Roots of Iraq's maternal and child health crisis run deep', in *The Lancet*, 381: 891–94.

Whyte, D. (2007) 'Crimes of the neo-liberal state in occupied Iraq', *British Journal of Criminology*, 47(2): 177–95.

Woolford, A. (2006) 'Making genocide unthinkable: three guidelines for a critical criminology of Genocide', *Critical Criminology*, 14: 87–106.

World Health Organisation (2009) 'Iraq Mental Health Survey – 2006/7 Report'. Available at http://applications.emro.who.int/dsaf/EMRPUB_2009_EN_1367.pdf

Young, J. (1999) *The Exclusive Society*. London: SAGE.

——(2003) 'Merton with energy, Katz with structure: the sociology of vindictiveness and the criminology of transgression', *Theoretical Criminology*, 7(3): 389–414.

——(2007) *The Vertigo of Late Modernity*. London: SAGE.

——(2011) *The Criminological Imagination*. London: Polity Press.

Part II

Testimony

Chapter 4

Testimony as data?

Introduction

Having considered the various ways in which crime can impact upon victims, in this chapter and the next we consider how we might listen to victims' voices as a means of making sense of their experiences: testimony. This chapter considers the individual victim and asks: how do we listen to their voice and what kind of 'data' might that constitute for victimological work? The first case study used in Chapter 1 alluded to some of these issues. This chapter adds some weight to that discussion by considering the role of personal testimony as a methodological device within victimology. Personal testimonies raise conceptual and methodological challenges in offering insights into the experiences of harm and victimisation. It is worth briefly indicating what these challenges look like before going on to consider the wider value of personal testimonies for victimological research.

Mendelsohn (1974) advocated that victimological research explore all types of victimisation. At the same time, in his earlier work (1963), he suggested that victimology only maintained its validity as an academic area of study when placed alongside criminology. This reasoning placed firm parameters on the victimological imagination and posed a conceptual dilemma twinning the broad study of victims with a discipline preoccupied with crime and criminality – a discipline that Barton et al. (2007: 2) argue 'remains largely a self-referential, self-perpetuating practice that lacks the ability to look outside itself'. Thus viewing the study of victims through the prism of criminology significantly narrows who is conceived of as a victim and under what circumstances; it becomes bounded by a 'crime narrative' comprising the law and the functional imagination of the criminal justice system (Separovic, 1973). The result of this has been that victimology has succumbed to the same constraints as mainstream criminology, having difficulty, as Newburn and Stanko (1994) suggest, in operating outside of the polarised legal constructions of the victim and the criminal. In this way, criminology and victimology have, in many aspects of their development, been inward-looking disciplines with a narrow focus on victims of 'conventional crimes' (i.e. acquisitive crime, theft, assault), leaving many peripheral victims, outwith legal definitions of criminal activity, unimagined (i.e. state violence, natural disasters, miscarriages of justice).

The clearest evidence of these conceptual challenges is reflected in the preferred methodological approaches to studying victims, in what has been described as 'empirical victimology': the study of people and their experiences of *crime* victimisation (Hope, 2007). As noted in earlier chapters, for several decades large-scale studies of the causes and experiences of crime victimisation have relied upon the use of government-supported surveys, such as the British Crime Survey of England and Wales (see Hough and Mayhew, 1983), national criminal victimisation surveys from the Bureau of Justice Statistics (2013) in the US, and the International Criminal Victimisation Survey. For Hope (2007), despite the associated issues of selectivity, bias and methodological ambiguity, victimological research has been tied to these particular (statistical) methods. However, these sources of data abstract the lived experiences of victimisation from their 'embeddedness' in everyday life. Attempts to overcome this, and to more reliably observe the causes of crime victimisation, take the form of longitudinal surveys, with alternative methods such as the use of biography, being dubbed a 'teleological fallacy' (Hope, 2007: 64) because of their lack of comparability and questionable veracity. However, claims to understanding the experience of victimisation, as documented in quantitative surveys and police recorded statistics, are problematic for more reasons than solely the methodological. Whilst these data sources go some way to uncover the 'dark figure' of crime and illustrate the problems associated with the 'grey figure' of police reporting, in abstracting victimisation from its embedded everyday lived experience they also inhibit more progressive victimological research and do little more than turn our heads to view those harms that continue to go on 'behind our backs' (see Walklate, 1989). Victimisation *is* frequently embedded within the structural conditions of the lives people lead; it can be random (as we will go on to evidence in the following case study), but it is regularly mundane and routine, and a wide variety of victimisation (i.e. child abuse, corporate and state crime) frequently continues to go unrecognised (Walklate, 1989; see also the case study in Chapter 1).

Victimologists need to find ways that do not abstract the experience of victimisation, but turn and face it head on and indulge in the lived reality of people's experiences at their source. Whilst the victim of crime conventionally understood within criminology is of key concern within this book, it is precisely the embeddedness of these experiences, and those that go on unrecognised, unseen or hidden in plain sight, that equally require the creative attention of victimologists. As Separovic (1973) urges, despite the origins of victimology being sutured to criminology, this should not restrict the scope of our interests from extending to other criminal and non-criminal related areas of concern. Despite an institutional fixation with victimisation surveys, victimology has become more progressive and is not constrained to the use of quantitative methods. Although seemingly fatalistic to do in isolation of the broader church of 'scientific knowledge' (qua Sebba and Berenblum, 2014) a brief review of the *International Journal of Victimology* gives some indication as to the progressive nature of victimological research with the adoption of a range of qualitative (see Yurman, 2008), quantitative (see Wikstrom and Dolmén, 2001) and mixed methods (see Newburn and Rock, 2006) approaches used to investigate a variety of victims' experiences, including those of hate crime, war tribunals, violence against women, and secondary victimisation, to name but a few (see respectively Funnell, 2014; Horn et al., 2009; Ba-Obaid and Bijleveld, 2002; Gekoski et al., 2013). As such, Walklate (2008: 334) surmises,

> It would seem, therefore, that differentiated imaginings of the crime victim are possible and indeed, are being tried. However, despite these imaginings there are structural, cultural and political limitations to their realization.

So further innovation is possible, and arguably desirable, in getting closer to the lived emotional experiences of victimisation that transgress traditional and unimaginative frameworks of studying victims of crime (see for example Moore and Shepherd, 2007).

This chapter creates some space within which we can begin to expand our methodological and victimological imaginations. We aim to introduce a creative approach to studying the experiences of victimisation through the use of written personal testimony. First this is set in context by outlining the concept of 'auto/biography' as our particular methodological frame of reference. Observing the intermittent presence of biographical research within the discipline of criminology allows us to infer that its subject matter has disproportionally concerned itself with criminal lives over attention to the lived experiences of victimisation. The absence of auto/biography within victimological literature becomes the point of departure to explore the use of personal testimony as 'data' within victim research through the application of *testimonio*. To demonstrate the use of this method of exploring the lived experiences of victimisation a sympathetic reading of its form and content is provided before drawing upon its existing application within written autobiographies. This framework is used to present our fourth case study, *One Day in July,* the autobiographical memoir of John Tulloch, a victim of the terrorist attacks in London on 7 July 2005. Our reading of this case study demonstrates the value of exploring individual victims' experiences as a way of both situating the experience of victimisation in the temporal and spatial contexts in which they occur, and facilitating ways of thinking about the accounts people provide as a critical and perhaps cultural victimology. In conclusion, we suggest some further innovative uses of *testimonio* that would permit an engagement with legal materials and ethnographic methods.

A narrative, life story or biographical approach?

The suggestions above imply that the victimological desire to *generalise* the experiences of victimisation as a consequence of its relationship with criminology results in its inability to deal with victims on an individual basis and a disciplinary forgetfulness that victims too are people with thoughts, feelings and emotions (Walklate, 2008). Accessing the lived experience of victimisation in ways that do not abstract its meaning from the context in which it occurs implies that we need to consider those individual experiences as a primary source of victimological inquiry. Situated in direct contrast to 'empirical victimology', the appeal is to let victims speak for themselves and for us – as social scientists – to trust in their words, indulge their experiences, and to comprehend the social world on their terms. Becker (1992) highlights that empirical phenomenological research takes account of people's lived experiences, ranging from the mundane features of everyday life to extreme and rare experiences not found in day-to-day living (Denscombe, 2003). Although studies looking to explore the phenomenological experience of victimisation are said to be rarely found within victimological studies (Hope, 2007), Becker (1992: 45–47) suggests that empirical phenomenological research is an appropriate means of studying the lived experience of criminal victimisation by seeing the world through the eyes of the victim. Recent research on the secondary victimisation associated with homicide has demonstrated the worth of obtaining the direct experience of victims 'to accept, respect and document their stories of … victimisation as their reality' (Gekoski et al., 2013: 309). Clearly there are benefits in undertaking semi-structured interviews within victimological research (see for example McGarry and Walklate, 2011; Van Camp and Wemmers, 2013). However, here the interest is with personal testimony as a source of data.

Chase (2005) suggests that the terms used within qualitative research to describe the methods and materials under study have flexible meaning. With reference to personal testimony there is a varied terminology used to demonstrate the methodological nuances around which first-hand experiences can be interpreted. For example, Polkinghorne (1995) outlines the aims of 'narrative' research as being to: (i) identify the start and finish of a story; (ii) provide criteria for the selection of events to be included into the story; (iii) order events into a rolling continuum until the coda is reached; and (iv) access and understand the relationship between people's experiences and their choices following certain events. When using 'life story' in empirical research Goodley et al. (2004) instruct that this approach provides an insight into the personal experiences of individuals and their public and collective interpretations of the social worlds in which they live. This is achieved without focussing on a particular theme, asking leading questions or imposing or prioritising the researcher's theoretical interests over events that are significant to those being studied (Goodey, 2000). Similarly, the approach of 'life history' is said by Chase (2005) to have a range of meanings of its own, from specifically describing extensive biographies, to presenting a person's biography in terms of social science research. It is also suggested that the term 'life history' may be used interchangeably with 'life story' to describe: (i) a person's biography from birth to present, (ii) a significant event or turning point, or (iii) a 'compelling topical narration' via 'personal narratives' (Chase, 2005: 652). In addition, Goodey (2000) comments that the use of 'biography' provides the researcher with an opportunity to be guided through specific details of an individual's life, acknowledging significant events along the way. In attempts to consolidate these meanings, Stanley's (1992) concept of 'auto/biography' offers one way of encompassing these particular approaches. Defined as the 'ideological accounts of "lives" which in turn feed back into everyday understandings of how "common lives" and "extraordinary lives" can be recognised' (Stanley, 1992: 3), auto/biography offers a single methodological point of reference to work discussed within this chapter, whilst simultaneously allowing us to be cognizant of the various attendant approaches from which we are also drawing meaning. Consequently, although each approach takes the temporal experiences of an individual as the locus of study, the terms narrative, life story and biography have interchangeable meanings and capture personal testimony in variously nuanced ways. The question remains: how is this conceptual framework applicable to victimological interests?

The biographical turn in criminology

The use of personal testimony as spoken and interpreted accounts of peoples' lives has influential origins within sociological theorising and is at the empirical core of criminological thinking. Indeed C. Wright Mills (1959: 6) reminds us,

> The sociological imagination enables us to grasp history and *biography* and the relations between the two within society. That is its task and its promise.

The essence of the sociological imagination is to facilitate an interpretation of the social world that includes a reflexive understanding of biography in order to help recognise how peoples' lives and the lives of others are located within broader social, historical and cultural contexts (Mills, 1959). Without being situated in this way individual biographies make little sense, and without a reflexive approach to biography a more complete analysis of the social world is impossible (Mills, 1959) (this point is returned to in Chapter 8, when we consider our own biographical role in victimological research).

Although influential, sociological work taking account of biography had been ongoing for some time before Mills made these comments. As a reaction against biological and psychological tendencies to explain criminal behaviour in terms of degeneracy and 'feeblemindedness', attempts to adopt sociological approaches to social problems emerged from the Chicago School of Sociology during the early twentieth century. Here the lived experiences of individual criminals became a prolific source of empirical data to be analysed and theorised. In the Chicago School biographical research was used to research deviant subcultures (i.e. gangs, petty criminals and juveniles) in order to understand how criminals and their environment interact and influence one another. A classic example of this type of research is Clifford Shaw's *The Jack Roller* (1930/ 1966), the culmination of six years of research into the early biography of one adolescent boy ('Stanley') from an unstable background, who subsequently experienced deprivation and homelessness, before ending up in prison and being rehabilitated under the guidance of Shaw. Upon introducing this method, Shaw (1930/1966: 1) states:

> The life-history record is a comparatively new device of sociological research in the field of criminology, although considerable use has been made of such material in other fields. The life record itself is the delin- quent's own account of his experiences, written as an autobiography, as a diary, or presented in the course of a series of interviews. The unique feature of such documents is that they are recorded in the first person, in the boy's own words, and not translated into the language of the person investigating the case.

Sutherland (1937) followed this tradition some time later by researching the biographical accounts of another petty criminal, Chic Cornwell, in *The Pro- fessional Thief*. Reflecting upon these studies as accounts of *criminal men* by *men interested in crime* they too tell a tale of the biography of criminology as a 'malestream' (Walklate, 2007) discipline. As such the female experience of crime went largely unaccounted for within biographical research in criminology until Pat Carlen and colleagues (1985) published *Criminal Women*. As a study of four women who experienced imprisonment and its criminalising label long after their release,

> The autobiographical accounts demonstrate in fine detail how, under certain material and ideological conditions ... law-breaking ... may indeed comprise rational and coherent responses to women's awareness of the social disabilities imposed upon them by discriminatory and exploitative class and gender relations.
>
> (Carlen et al., 1985: 8–9)

This gendered reading of crime is also noteworthy in Goodey's (2000) later use of 'hegemonic masculine biography' as a practical and empirical means of mapping the lived experiences of *criminality* within the life stories of *men* on a 'biographical continuum'.

All of these biographical pieces are noteworthy contributions to the criminological canon. However, the significance of *The Jack Roller* was singled out in a special issue of *Theoretical Criminology*. This issue presents numerous appreciative interpretations of Shaw's (1930/1966) work, but it also suggests that despite biographical research in criminology being intermittent, there is a 'new generation' of criminological work dedicated to using biographical approaches (Gelsthorpe, 2007). These 'newcomers' to the biographical scene in criminology are varied and have adopted narrative (see Maruna, 2001); autobiographical (see Nellis, 2002); ethnographic (see Cromwell, 2010); life course (see Benson, 2013); and autoethnographic (see Wakeman, 2014) approaches. It now perhaps seems imprudent of Goodey (2000) to have suggested that a lack of evidence of biographical research in criminological work implies that such methods are more of an 'idea' rather than a practice. The evidence above squarely challenges this assertion. However, although providing myriad exemplars of the intermittent attention biographical work has gained within criminology, and demonstrating the damaging effects of criminalisation upon offenders, there is no significant presence of the victims of the criminal transgressions within these accounts, and a near complete absence of biographical work within the victimological agenda.

Despite its concentration upon male victimisation, the model of a 'biographical continuum' proposed by Goodey (2000) is flexible enough to satisfy interpretations of different materials in different contexts (i.e. experiences of criminality and victimisation, see McGarry and Keating, 2010). More specifically, entrenched within this methodological approach to biography is the notion of 'epiphany' or significant turning points in a person's life; defined by Denzin (1989: 70) as 'interactional moments and experiences which leave marks on people's lives'. These experiences have been employed by Goodey (2000) to include life events which are (i) major: impacting entirely on a person's life; (ii) cumulative: reactions to experiences which have been ongoing over a period of time; (iii) minor: symbolic of a major incident in a person's life; and (iv) relived: an incident that is prescribed meaning once recounted. This interpretation of epiphany facilitates a shift in attention from the biographical work within criminology to that of victimology. Adapting these characteristics to the lived experiences of victimisation enables past events to be considered in the context of present and future circumstances and to be mapped on a 'biographical continuum' as suggested by Goodey (2000). However, this is methodologically limited as an analytical reading of victims' experiences. As Schüetz (1992) and Goodey (2000) observe, some events considered as epiphany by the researcher may not be so by the participant, meaning that a researcher interpreting a person's lived experience of victimisation via interview (for example) becomes the mouthpiece for the individual and disempowers them. So, how might it be possible to allow victims to speak for themselves?

Turning to testimony

Notwithstanding Goodey's (2000) work as a 'cogent argument' for a return to biography within criminological research (Walklate, 2007: 100), for victimology the use of biography remains conspicuous in its absence. Spalek (2006) has previously advocated the extended use of biographical and narrative methods to help tease out a more emotionally sensitive understanding of the experiences of victimisation. However, this does not mean that biographical approaches to victims can simply be transferred from criminology to victimology.

Quinney (1972) observes that crime generates 'victims' as the result of both an act of direct – legally identifiable – harm, and as a result of a structurally derived status complete with its own code of practices, remuneration schemes and support services. However, whilst this label may be awarded objectively, it is a much more subjective, contestable and problematic process for those who acquire it. Not only can the word 'victim' be interpreted to suggest vulnerability, passivity and defeat to those who have experienced harm, it can also have disempowering connotations for an individual or group (Rock, 2007; see also Chapter 1). This is not to suggest that the label of a 'criminal' does not have similarly stigmatising connotations; the work of Carlen et al. (1985) indicates that it does and is. However, in looking to capture the experiences of victims in ways that build upon, but are distinct from, the criminological uses of biography, the problematic imposition of a given status by the state and others is arguably a critical point of departure. In order to situate the voices of those who have suffered harm, oppression or victimisation into victimological inquiry it is necessary to look for other kinds of sources that can facilitate this, as Sebba and Berenblum (2014) suggest. Sources more closely associated with auto/biography (qua Stanley, 1992).

Testimonio

In Latin American literature the use of what is termed *testimonio* (testimony) implies the telling of truth in legal and religious contexts. Beverley (2004: 3) interprets this in this way: '*dar testimonio* means to testify, to bear truthful witness'. This literary genre does not assume that the sources of testimonio are restricted to these institutional contexts, quite the opposite. Popularised in Latin American literature during the 1960s, this genre came to represent the telling of harmful experiences from people subjugated or marginalised from conventional cultural norms, class positions and identities (Beverley, 2004). Indeed testimonio can take many forms and requires some creative, but sympathetic, methodological innovation to make it suitable for victimology. In order to do so first requires a sensitive reading of this genre's form, purpose and intention.

Testimonios are intended to engage readers by providing what Stanley (1992: 119) describes as the 'slices of lives' of each narrator. In its common form testimonio is understood to be, a novel or novella-length narrative, produced in the form of a printed text, told in the first person by a narrator who is also the real protagonist or witness of the events she or he recounts. Its unit of narration is usually a 'life' or a significant life experience.

(Beverley, 2005: 547)

However, this is not fictional or objective storytelling. Its intentions are to illustrate the lived experiences of harmful events in ways that are purposefully emotive, truthful and critical. To ensure that each testimonio has 'ethical and epistemological' authority over the experiences being described, there are a range of attendant characteristics that afford them authenticity (Beverley, 2004: 3). We shall say a little about each of these in turn, drawing from a popular work, Beverley's (2004) Testimonio, before moving on to elaborate on how this can be employed for victimological analysis.

Relationship between the narrator and the reader

The first concern for testimonio is the relationship being shaped between the narrator and the reader. The narrator must have lived through the experiences they are describing, either directly or indirectly through relationships with family, friends or associates; seeking to engage the reader in events that are 'real' with the intention of developing solidarity between the reader and the narrator.

Relationship between narrator and the wider public

Next a testimonio is not communicating the life of the narrator per se, despite being an individual account. Instead it is concerned with an 'urgency' to recount the lived experiences of harm, oppression or marginalisation (i.e. racism, violence, genocide) as experienced by others. In doing so, the literary presence of the narrator is replaced by their symbolic voice speaking of, and for, marginalised and oppressed groups who have similar experiences. This raises awareness of the plight of others through recounting their individual experiences, without asserting a hegemonic masculine or hierarchical status. The connection to a wider group experience is a fundamental component to the authenticity of testimonio.

Form and shape as a genre

Although the lived experiences found within testimonio are often captured and edited by an interlocutor (such as a writer, journalist or anthropologist) due to the frequent lack of literary skills on behalf of the narrator, testimonio has no literary or academic aspirations, setting itself as distinct from oral history and biography as found within the criminological literature described above. In doing so, the voices within testimonio do not speak of, or for, civil society (as they might when depicted in films, novels or essays); instead the subjugated voices of others are brought *into* the public domain so that they can be heard with their own authority and agency.

Relationship with power

A vital aspect of the use of testimonio is its relationship with power. It intends to assert an individual voice from a position of marginalisation, demanding to be recognised and looking to impose itself upon the institutions of power who have served to subjugate the people it represents. The voices within testimonios emanate from 'outside the limits of the state' and help to 'trace the frontiers' of state institutions and their practices (Beverley, 2004: 19). In fostering readers' solidarity, testimonio seeks to engage the reader with their own sense of social justice by informing the public of causes distant but not unfamiliar to their own lives, tabling issues of poverty, inequality and oppression caused by imbalances of power that need to be challenged.

As a source of scrutiny

Testimonio looks to situate the reader in a similar position to a jury member in a trial, compelled to be told the truth and make subjective assessments on its veracity. In this way its truthfulness (as well as its value as an academic source of data) is open to scrutiny. This aspect of testimonio was made imperative following the accounts of social activist and Nobel Peace Prize winner Rigoberta Menchú (1984) (see Nobelprize.org, 2014). Her acclaimed testimonio *I, Rigoberta Menchú* depicted her and her family's experiences of atrocities committed by the Guatemalan army throughout the civil war during the 1980s. However, the authenticity of her account was subsequently challenged by the anthropologist Stoll (1999) as containing inaccuracies and misrepresenting some aspects of the experiences of others during this period. Thus we may feel compelled to question whether or not we believe what we are being told, or whether or not we are satisfied as readers with the authenticity of the events put before us.

Problems and possibilities

Finally, Reyes and Rodríguez (2012) point out that the telling and documenting of testimonio can be double edged. It is intended for liberation and emancipation but it can equally have the potential to harm. Recounting the lived experiences of harmful events can cause the narrator to revisit their past in ways counter-productive to their own healing. Moreover, speaking out against oppression and marginalisation against state actors can expose narrators with dissenting voices and open them to further marginalisation and oppression (Beverley,

2004). So the process of testimonio has the potential to be experienced as a form of secondary victimisation. However, recent use of testimonio has encouraged its adaptation to be used more broadly and interchangeably with 'testimony', 'narrative' and 'biography' (Reyes and Rodríquez, 2012). This offers some flexibility on its interpretation and connection with auto/biography as defined earlier. Beverley (2004) also indicates a wider interpretation of testimonio to identify the depiction of 'truthful narratives' across a range of different sources of inquiry, including interviews and witness statements, amongst others which are returned to below. So despite having quite specific theoretical under-pinnings, a sympathetic reading of testimonio offers an opportunity for its use as a methodological device of auto/biography.

Using testimonio for victimological research

As Hoffman (2009) notes, testimonio derives from a similar life-story tradition found in criminology, in particular Clifford Shaw's (1930/1966) *The Jack Roller*. However, although both seek to deconstruct the identity politics of a subjugated 'other', it is the characteristics outlined above that set testimonio apart from criminological use of biography. For Hoffman (2009) these differences are particularly notable in the imposition of an academic authority onto the inter-pretation of the experiences being depicted, and the appropriation of the narrator's identity, subsumed by the author's own 'voice'. For example, Menchú's (1984) use of experience and emotion as key features of authority and authenticity in her testimonio situate it in contrast to the preoccupation with dispassionate, objective methods within criminological research (qua Wakeman, 2014). As such, testimonio has the potential to allow victimologists to harness the use of subjective and emotive experiences as a credible source of analysis that can develop the victimological imagination.

From this reading of testimonio it is possible to see that there are connections to be made with the victimological perspectives discussed in Chapter 1. Obser-ving the subjugated positions of 'others' as a means of accessing state processes and structures that perpetuate harm, and its capacity to facilitate campaigns or movements, shares similar characteristics with Elias' (1986) vision of radical victimology (discussed in more detail in chapter 5). A concern with identity politics within testimionio also serves as a platform to launch further inquiry from feminist and critical victimological perspectives by centring on the voices of 'victims', challenging how they have been constructed, and questioning their positions of marginality. It also has the purpose of directing the 'reading public' to harms experienced by the Victimological Other that 'go on behind our backs' (qua Walklate, 2007) so that they can be faced and confronted. However, more than this, testimonio, as a distinct method of observation, has commonalities with Quinney's (1998) depiction of the criminologist as a witness and a 'moral entrepreneur' of violence, suffering and marginalisation experienced in everyday life. Some of these connections with the role of the victimologist as witness have been made elsewhere through the use of photo-graphy (Walklate et al., 2014). This is returned to in more detail in Chapter 8 as a potential component of cultural victimology, but for now we look to develop a different kind of 'witnessing' through the adaptation of testimonio to personal auto/biography.

Testimonio and auto/biography

From the reading of related military memoires of British soldiers who had served in Afghanistan since 2001, Woodward and Jenkings (2012) employed testimonio analytically to foreground the lived experiences of violence within this literature, gain more comprehensive understandings of contemporary war, and offer a renegotiation of the moralities underpinning the perpetration and experience of violence. Although not equating military memoirs with testimonio, Woodward and Jenkings (2012) use the attendant features of testimonio, as previously described, to help elicit some of the salient critical features of each auto/biographical account. It may not be possible to identify all of these characteristics within particular written personal testimonies, but the overarching concern of testimonio is to communicate harmful experiences that have con-nections with a similar wider group experience. The adaptation of testimonio in this way provides a sound model for applying this mode of analysis to other relevant auto/biographical work. Our fourth case study illustrates how the use of testimonio may be applied to an instance of victimisation.

London, 7 July 2005

On the morning of 7 July 2005 (7/7) a small group of male Islamic fundamen-talists detonated four explosions in a coordinated suicide attack on the London transport system. Led by Mohammad Sidique Khan, a 30-year-old primary school learning mentor from Beeston, Leeds, the three other men responsible for these attacks included: Shezad Tanweer, a 22-year-old chip-shop worker from Leeds; Germaine Lindsay, a 19-year-old father, husband and carpet fitter living in Aylesbury; and Hasib Hussain, an 18-year-old former student from Leeds. With the exception of Germaine Lindsey, who was born in Jamaica and converted to Islam later in life, the other three men were British-born Muslims. The locations that these men targeted included three trains on the London Underground: the first situated between Liverpool Street and Aldgate stations (Tanweer), and two others which had each recently departed Edgware Road (Sidique Khan) and King's Cross (Lindsay) stations respectively. Approximately one hour later a fourth explosion occurred on a bus located at Tavistock Square (Hussain). In addition to each of the men taking their own lives during these attacks, the explosions collectively killed 52 civilians and left over 700 injured. In a pre-recorded video message Sidique Khan stated that the attacks were in response to British involvement in the invasion and subsequent war in Iraq in 2003. These events resulted in the identification of short-comings in victim compensation awards for those killed and injured, raised questions regarding the centring of 'victims' at the heart of the criminal justice process (as promised in the New Labour white paper *Justice for All*) and were used to identify instances of secondary victimisation at the hands of deficient criminal justice policy. However, these events also had deleterious effects on the force and expansion of the British security estate: evidenced by the subsequent death of an innocent civilian – Jean Charles de Menezes (see Independent Police Complaints Commission, 2009) – shot and killed by London Metro-politan Police having been mistaken for a suspected suicide bomber; and the introduction of the *Terrorism Act* (2006), extending police powers to hold terrorist suspects for up to 28 days without charge. The case study below focuses on the lived experiences of a victim of these attacks.

Case study: John Tulloch, *One Day in July*

Travelling on the tube leaving Edgware Road that fateful day was John Tulloch, a professor of journalism at Brunel University at the time of the attacks. Tulloch had found himself travelling in the same carriage as Sidique Khan, seated just feet away from him. He survived the explosion but suffered a range of serious injuries. As he emerged from the Underground bloodied, bandaged and chaper-oned by emergency workers, his image was captured by the British press and used by the *Sun* newspaper to campaign for the further proliferation of counter-terrorism measures (i.e. 90-day detention without trial for terrorist suspects). This was done without his consent. As a staunch protestor against the war in Iraq in 2003 and a non-advocate of extending the security estate, his 'ideal victim' status was appropriated and used for purposes that he was opposed to. In response to his experiences during and after 7/7, Tulloch (2006) published a personal testimony entitled *One Day in July*. In what follows there is a brief depiction of his experiences, read as a form of testimonio. Although documenting his individual experiences of 7/7, as an academic writing his own account of these events one might assume that the intentions of Tulloch's (2006) personal testimony might be to appeal to that specialist audience. However, there are explicit messages throughout *One Day in July* directed to a broad readership, speaking of wider harm and victimisation, that implicate the state and transcend notions of ideal victimhood.

Reading *One Day in July* as testimonio

Although Tulloch was reticent at first to tell his story to the public, in part as a result of the constraints put on him by his injuries, this did not last. In the months that followed he began telling of his experiences with 'urgency' to help counter the narrative being shaped around his 'iconic' image (Tulloch, 2008) and what he describes as 'multiple identities' (Tulloch, 2006). As Beverley

(2004: 24) notes, post-9/11 the American public became a 'testimonial people' having faced catastrophe, trauma, death and mourning collectively, giving rise to testimonio that derives from common disaster. Similar to 9/11, 7/7 created victims indiscriminately from across a variety of stratified social groups, uniting a society divided by social class, ethnicity and gender through collective victimisation by a seemingly 'common enemy' (Beverley, 2004). However, such unity also brought to public attention the power relations that divide societies, pointing to the presence of social inequality, relative deprivation and oppression that germinate the roots of fundamentalism (Beverley, 2004). Tulloch's (2006) intentions in this regard are clear. In starting to depict the 'truth' of his experiences in *One Day in July* the deeper complexities of how he perceives what has happened to him and why are unravelled. He voices his concerns about the war in Iraq and threats to British civil liberties, epitomised by the death of Jean Charles de Menezes. He also raises difficult questions about what compelled Sidique Khan and others to commit acts of violence against the British state and offers a thought for how their families must feel following the attacks.

Tulloch is not passive in recounting his experiences. He wants to engage the reader in solidarity for the 'cultural wound' suffered by the UK following the attacks, but not sympathy for his personal injuries. He guides the reader through a critical construal of policy, politics and the divisive power relations of the media in assembling a security agenda based on fear and essentialism (as discussed in Chapter 3), of which he became an unwitting pawn. This is not just personal conjecture. Tulloch is acutely aware that he is not alone in his opinions or experiences and is keen to communicate this to the reader and a wider receptive audience:

> There are many people in Britain who feel the way I do. Some of the other victims of your [Sidique Khan's] attack on 7 July have said so publicly. They are all part of a powerful rhetorical force emerging out of a continued, disempowered silence.
>
> (Tulloch, 2006: 222)

Moreover, in a further call to action in an associated account of *One Day in July*, Tulloch (2008: 34) makes his desire to impose his voice – and the voices of others – known as counter narratives to state action, indicating ways he believes this can be achieved:

> There are many fine media professionals out there, and there is room for much more 'public intellectual' engagement in the media than we might think. For academics, I believe there is no more important activity in the face of the growth of the criminal justice system.

As a victim of a terrorist attack suffering physical and psychological injuries, Tulloch's experiences sit comfortably with direct and primary victimisation and notions of the 'ideal victim' (Christie, 1986). His lifestyle activities had led him into the Tube, but not in the ways that could have predicted his victimisation as positivist victimology would have it. Although victimised by Sidique Khan via an act of terrorism, his story tells of his subjugation at the hands of power relations between the British press and the government, using him as a muse for counterterrorism policy. Instead his story is hinged on a critical and radical victimological reading. No more so is this evident than in an open address to Sidique Khan in the postscript of *One Day in July*, wherein Tulloch (2006: 222) fractures the structurally derived labels afforded to both him and his aggressor by stating,

> I don't accept the label of innocent victim that the media want to give me, any more than I accept the label of mindless psychopath they give you. My British and Australian governments have taken that innocence away, and helped create more terrorists.

There are, of course, various ways in which *One Day in July* does not meet the criteria of testimonio. Tulloch was invited by a publisher to write about his own experiences and as the author of many books before *One Day in July,* this negates a vanquished literary position. As the author he is speaking for himself and reflecting the problematic construction of his identity with those of other oppressed groups that Sidique Khan was claiming to avenge. The projection of his experiences have helped speak for others who hold the same views as him regarding British foreign and domestic policy, and highlighted the oppression of Muslim communities in the UK and the suffering caused to Iraq as a Muslim nation during war (as discussed in Chapter 3). However, try as he might, Tulloch does not and cannot speak on behalf of these populations in either Iraq or the UK as he has not experienced their marginalisation first hand. These constraints notwithstanding, the fundamental characteristic of a testimonio resides at the core of this personal testimony and speaks to a trauma narrative concerned with suffering, choice and power relations. Through narrating his *individual* experiences of a terrorist attack he is perhaps letting us know that we are '*all* victims now' in the aftermath of these events, in one way or another (Mythen, 2007: 464, our emphasis).

Wider uses of testimonio for victimology

A further detailed reading of Tulloch's (2006) work will no doubt afford a more nuanced interpretation of his experiences. However, from the brief interpretation here it is clear that testimonio has contemporary significance and much potential for using personal testimony of this kind as data within victimological research. Finally, in adopting testimonio as a methodological device in this chapter we have sought to develop one possible use for its application in auto/biographical work. There are other ways in which testimonio has been used which affords it more methodological flexibility for victimological research.

Testimonio and legal narrative

In the role of the 'victim of crime' as traditionally understood, their 'voice' is frequently heard within the criminal justice process in the following forms: the giving of factual information in witness statements or recounting personal feelings within the objective constraints of a victim impact statement (discussed further in Chapter 6). Both of these particular mediums are widely used by authorities and generate considerable amounts of 'data' although they are seldom understood in this way. For Trinch (2010: 186),

> within the criminal justice system, the notion that narrative might be used for any purpose other than an accounting of the facts is nearly non-existent.

Witness statements can be read as testimonio to highlight the position of the narrator; role of the interlocutor; purpose of the narrative being given; and the (re)production of power in the telling and recording of the lived experiences of victimisation (Trinch, 2010). In providing a legal testimony, the subjective experience of the narrator must be transformed into a legally acceptable standard to afford it authenticity and legitimacy as the 'truth' (Trinch, 2010). From this point onwards testimonio can challenge a legal narrative account and can demonstrate the further subjugation of the narrator to the behest of legalese, and may help to identify the further risks that this entails for 'witnesses' within the criminal justice process.

Testimonio and ethnographic methods

The three exemplars of testimonio described throughout this chapter have all been restricted to written accounts of personal testimony in various forms: a 'novella-length' story (qua *testimonio*, Beverley, 2004; 2005); auto/biographical accounts; and legal narrative. However, there are other ways in which testimonios that are shorter in length (when in written form) can be used, more aligned to ethnographic methods. Researching the lived experiences of asylum seekers across three continents (North America, Asia and Europe), Witteborn (2012) demonstrated the use of testimonio through several different means of engaging with personal testimony as data:

Public testimonio: conducted by observing public events during which people spoke of their lived experiences of harm and voiced politically active positions.
Face-to-face testimonio: conducted via interviews, asking questions to elicit a life story of the lived experiences of the narrator.

Virtual testimonio: through an engagement with letters and personal testimonies posted on credible online resources by narrators.

Using testimonio eclectically stretches its use in ways that are further appealing to victimological research. This, of course, comes with its own unique limitations that challenge the form and function of this approach (i.e. narrating experiences via facilitated public talks; using interpreters to communicate with narrators; and the efficacy of an online web presence) (Witteborn, 2012). However, listening to and reading lived experience in these imaginative ways allows narrators to speak with reference to their own identities rather than those ascribed to them. They can draw attention to processes of harm and marginalisation to broader public audiences, that 'morally implicate the listener' (Witteborn, 2012: 437), resonant of Quinney's (1998) aspiration for the criminologist as witness.

Reflecting upon these uses of testimonio, it becomes clear that they place demands upon a reader's sense of social justice. It urges us not to merely seek out the inequality of those who have experienced harm, oppression and marginalisation; it also encourages us to ask similar questions of those who perpetrate violence, in order to gain a fuller understanding of the aetiologies of victimisation. MacNair's (2005) work illustrates how psychological trauma can latently become caused through having engaged in violence as an aggressor. Schütz's (1992) research, eliciting the lived experiences of survivors of the Holocaust and Nazi German soldiers, explored similar questions. Tulloch's account of 7/7 encourages a further delineation of these victimological problems, returning to the maxim of Quinney (1972) to simply ask: who are the victims of these events? The civilians killed and injured in these attacks are easily identifiable as deserving and 'ideal' victims, and those responsible as a designated 'enemy' are undeserving and 'rejected' victims (Strobl, 2004). However, what if a perpetrator's background is non-violent and familiar – as was the case with Sidique Khan – but their actions perpetrate mass victimisation? Who is the victim then? As 'witnesses', should we be equally as compelled to understand the experiences of those who cause victimisation and not just those we comfortably understand to be 'victims' as the recipients of harm? Is the victimological imagination stretchy enough to grasp this level of embedded lived experience when we witness the 'spirit injury' (Spalek, 2006) perpetrated by the state on those marginalised by it? These types of questions are intended as analytical rather than sympathetic and certainly challenge how we might work with the concept of the ideal victim (Christie, 1986).

Conclusion

In this chapter we have suggested a way of progressing victimological inquiry using personal testimony as a source of data. We centred on the use of biography as found within criminological research, and the absence of the 'victim' within such work to act as a point of departure to uncover ways in which similar work could be read and foreground the role of the victim rather than the criminal. By looking to the genre of *testimonio* we have offered a sympathetic reading of a critical and emancipatory approach that is contingent upon the unencumbered telling of the lived experiences of harm. Being creative with this approach does require a sensitive reading of its purposes, form and functions, as well as its limitations. What we have demonstrated is that there are indeed ways of engaging with the lived experiences of victimisation that overcome the need to abstract them into quantifiable data or pool them from a representative sample. Instead we urge for the individual experiences of victimisation to be trusted to speak in their own phenomenological terms. We have depicted an exemplar of reading written auto/biographical work as testimonio, with an awareness of its nuances which affords some critical reflexivity in permitting its use confidently and creatively (though see Albert and Couture, 2014 for a particularly unsympathetic adaptation of testimonio). There are other ways in which testimonio can be modified: for example, to interrogate the sanitised legal testimonies of victims within the criminal justice process, or the experiences of a Victimological Other who would otherwise be voiceless. In the chapter that follows, we leave the methodological questions raised by testimonio behind and look to the ways in which victims' voices might be heard through practice.

Further reading

Good material on victimological methods are difficult to find, but we recommend Hope's chapter in Walklate's (2007) *Handbook on Victims and Victimology*, and Walklate's chapter in King and Wincup's (2008) *Doing Research on Crime and Justice*. Other journal articles that hit at the sentiment we are advocating here include Goodey's (2000) article on biography in criminology in *Theoretical Criminology,* and more recently Wakeman's (2014) article on autoethnography in the *British Journal of Criminology*. For further insight into the method of *testimonio* we recommend Beverley's (2004) collection of essays *Testimonio: On the Politics of Truth* as an authoritative and intellectually engaging book on the subject.

References

Albert, M.-N. and Couture, M-M. (2014) 'To explore new avenues: experiential testimonio research', *Management Decision*, 52(4): 794–812.
Ba-Obaid, M. and Bijleveld, C. C. J. H. (2002) 'Violence against women in Yemen: official statistics and an exploratory survey', *International Review of Victimology*, 9: 331–47.
Barton, A., Corteen, K., Scott, D., and Whyte, D. (2007) 'Introduction: developing a Criminological Imagination', in A. Barton, K. Corteen, D. Scott, and D. Whyte (eds) *Expanding the Criminological Imagination: Critical Readings in Criminology*. Cullompton, Devon: Willan. pp. 1–14.

Becker, C. S. (1992) *Living and Relating: An Introduction to Phenomenology*. London: SAGE.

Benson, M. L. (2013) *Crime and the Life Course: An Introduction* (2nd edition). Oxon: Routledge.

Beverley, J. (2004) *Testimonio: On the Politics of Truth*. Minneapolis: University of Minnesota Press.

——(2005) 'Testimonio, subalternity, and narrative authority', in N. K. Denzin and Y. S. Lincoln (eds) *The SAGE Handbook of Qualitative Research* (2nd edition). London: SAGE. pp. 555–65.

Bureau of Justice Statistics. (2013) 'National crime victimization survey (NCVS) API'. Available at http://www.bjs.gov/developer/ncvs/index.cfm.

Carlen, P., Hicks, J., O'Dwyer, J., Christina, D., and Tchaikovsky, C. (1985) *Criminal women: autobiographical accounts*. Cambridge: Polity Press.

Chase, S. E. (2005) 'Narrative inquiry: multiple lenses, approaches, voices' in N. K. Denzin and Y. S. Lincoln (eds) *The SAGE Handbook of Qualitative Research* (3rd edition). London: SAGE. pp. 651–80.

Christie, N. (1986) 'The ideal victim', in E. A. Fattah (ed.) *Crime Policy to Victim Policy*. London: Macmillan. pp. 17–30.

Cromwell, P. (2010) *In Their Own Words: Criminals on Crime* (5th edition). Oxford: Oxford University Press.

Denscombe, M. (2003) *The Good Research Guide: For Small Research Projects* (2nd edition). Maidenhead, Berkshire: Open University Press.

Denzin, N. K. (1989) *Interpretive Biography*. London: SAGE.

Elias, R. (1986) *The Politics of Victimisation: Victims, Victimology and Human Rights*. Oxford: Oxford University Press.

Funnell, C. (2014) 'Racist hate crime and the mortified self: an ethnographic study of the impact of victimisation', *International Review of Victimology*, online first: doi: 10.1177/0269758014551497.

Gekoski, A., Adler, J. R., and Gray, J. M. (2013) 'Interviewing women bereaved by homicide: reports of secondary victimisation by the criminal justice system', *International Review of Victimology*, 19(3): 307–29.

Gelsthorpe, L. (2007) 'The Jack-Roller: telling a story?', *Theoretical Criminology*, 11(4): 515–42.

Goffman, E. (1961) *Asylums*. Harmondsworth: Penguin.

Goodey, J. (2000) 'Biographical lessons for criminology', *Theoretical Criminology*, 4(4): 473–98.

Goodley, D., Lawthom, R., Clough, P., and Moore, M. (2004) *Researching Life Stories: Method, Theory and Analyses in a Biographical Age*. London: Routledge-Falmer.

The Guardian (2014) '7 July London attacks'. Available at http://www.theguardian.com/uk/july7.

Hoffman, B. (2009) 'Conquest traditions, conflict transformation, and the cultural boundaries of criminology: Rigoberta Menchú and criminological science', *Contemporary Justice Review*, 12(2): 171–89.

Hope, T. (2007) 'Theory and method: the social epidemiology of crime victims', in S. Walklate (ed.) *Handbook of Victims and Victimology*. Cullompton, Devon: Willan. pp. 62–90.

Horn, R., Charters, S., and Vahidy, S. (2009) 'The victim-witness rxperience in the special court for Sierra Leone', *International Review of Victimology*, 15: 277–98.

Hough, M. and Mayhew, P. (1983) 'The British crime survey: first report. Home Office Research Studies 76'. London: HMSO.

Independent Police Complaints Commission. (2009) 'The Stockwell investigation: fatal shooting of Jean Charles de Menezes'. Available at http://webarchive.nationalarchives

.gov.uk/20100908152737/http://www.ipcc.gov.uk/index/resources/evidence_reports /investigation_reports/the_stockwell_investigation.htm.

Jupp, V. (1989) *Methods of Criminological Research*. London: Routledge.

MacNair, R. M. (2005) *Perpetration-Induced Traumatic Stress: The Psychological Consequences of Killing*. Santa Barbara, CA: Praeger/Greenwood.

McGarry, R. and Keating, M. (2010) 'Auto/biography, personal testimony and epiphany moments: a case study in research informed teaching', *Enhancing Learning in the Social Sciences (ELiSS) Journal*, 3(1): 1–31.

McGarry, R. and Walklate, S. (2011) 'The soldier as victim: peering through the looking glass', *British Journal of Criminology*, 51(6): 900–917.

Maruna, S. (2001) *Making Good*. Washington, DC: APA Press.

Menchú, R. (1984) *I, Rigoberta Menchú: An Indian Woman in Guatemala*. London: Verso Books.

Mendelsohn, B. (1963) 'The origins of the doctrine of victimology', *Excerpta Criminologica*, 3: 239–45.

——(1974) 'Victimology and the technical and social sciences: a call for the establishment of victimology clinics', in I. Drapkin. and E. Viano (eds) *Victimology: A New Focus*. Lexington, MA: D. C. Heath.

Mills, C. W. (1959) *The Sociological Imagination*. London: Penguin.

Moore, S. C. and Shepherd, J. (2007) 'Gender specific emotional responses to anticipated crime', *International Review of Victimology*, 14: 337–51.

Mythen, G. (2007) 'Cultural victimology: "are we all victims now"?' in S. Walklate (ed.) *Handbook of Victims and Victimology*. Cullompton, Devon: Willan. pp. 464–83.

Nellis, M. (2002) 'Prose and Cons: offender auto/biographies, penal reform and probation training', *The Howard Journal*, 41(5): 434–68.

Newburn, T. and Rock, P. (2006) 'Urban homelessness, crime and victimisation in England', *International Review of Victimology*, 13: 121–56.

Newburn, T. and Stanko, E. A. (1994) 'When men are victims: the failure of victimology', in T. Newburn. and E. A. Stanko (eds) *Just Boys Doing Business: Men, Masculinities and Crime*. London: Routledge. pp. 153–65.

Nobelprize.org (2014) 'Rigoberta Menchú Tum – Biographical'. Available at http://www .nobelprize.org/nobel_prizes/peace/laureates/1992/tum-bio.html.

Polkinghorne, D. E. (1995) 'Narrative configuration in qualitative analysis', in J. A. Hatch and R. Wisniewski (eds) *Life History and Narrative*. London: Taylor & Francis. pp. 5–24.

Quinney, R. (1972) 'Who is the victim?' *Criminology*, 10: 314–23.

——(1998) 'Criminology as moral philosophy, criminologist as witness', *Contemporary Justice Review*, 1: 347–64.

Reyes, K. B. and Rodriguez, J. E. C. (2012) 'Testimonio: origins, terms and resources', *Equity and Excellence in Education*, 45(3): 525–38.

Rock, P. (2007) 'Theoretical perspectives on victimisation', in S. Walklate (ed.) *Handbook of Victims and Victimology*. Cullompton, Devon: Willan. pp. 37–61.

Schütz, F. (1992) 'Pressure and guilt: war experiences of a young German soldier and their biographical implications (part 1)', *International Sociology*, 7(2): 187–208.

Sebba, L. and Berenblum, T. (2014) 'Victimology and the sociology of new disciplines: a research agenda', *International Review of Victimology*, 20(1): 7–30.

Separovic, Z. P. (1973) 'Victimology: a new approach in the social sciences', in I. Drapkin and E. Viano (eds) *Victimology: A New Focus. Volume I, Theoretical Issues in Victimology*. London: Lexington Books.

Shaw, C. R. (1930/1966) *The Jack-Roller: A Delinquent Boy's Own Story*. Chicago: University of Chicago Press.

Spalek, B (2006) *Crime Victims: Theory, Policy and Practice*. Basingstoke: Palgrave Macmillan.

Stanley, L. (1992) *The Auto/biographical I*. Manchester: Manchester University Press.

Stoll, D. (1999) *Rigoberta Menchú and the Story of All Poor Guatemalans*. Boulder, CO: Westview Press.

Strobl, R. (2004) 'Constructing the victim: theoretical reflections and empirical examples', *International Review of Victimology*, 11(2/3): 295–311.

Sutherland, E. H. (1937/1956) *The Professional Thief, by a Professional Thief*. Chicago: University of Chicago Press.

Trinch, S. (2010) 'Risky subjects: narrative, literary testimonio and legal testimony', *Dialectical Anthropology*, 34(2): 179–204.

Tulloch, J. (2006) *One Day in July: Experiencing 7/7*. London: Little, Brown.

——(2008) 'Becoming iconic', *Criminal Justice Matters,* 73(1): 33–34.

Van Camp, T. and Wemmers, J.-A. (2013) 'Victim satisfaction with restorative justice: more than simply procedural justice', *International Review of Victimology*, 19(2): 117–43.

Wakeman, S. (2014) 'Fieldwork, biography and emotion: doing criminological autoethnography', *British Journal of Criminology*, 54(5): 705–21.

Walklate, S. (1989) *Victimology: The Victim and the Criminal Justice Process*. London: Unwin Hyman/Oxon: Routledge.

——(2007) *Imagining the Victim of Crime*. Maidenhead, Berkshire: Open University Press.

——(2008) 'Researching victims', in King, R. D. and Wincup, E. (eds) *Doing Research on Crime and Justice* (2nd edition). Oxford: Oxford University Press. pp. 315–39.

Walklate, S., McGarry, R. and Mythen, G. (2014) 'Trauma, visual victimology, and the poetics of justice', in M. H. Jacobsen (ed.) *The Poetics of Crime: Understanding and Researching Crime and Deviance through Creative Sources*. Surrey: Ashgate. pp. 263–83.

Wikstrom, P.-O. H. and Dolmén, L. (2001) 'Urbanisation, neighbourhood social integration, informal social control, minor social disorder, victimisation and fear of crime', *International Review of Victimology*, 8: 121–40.

Witteborn, S. (2012) 'Testimonio and spaces of risk: a forced migration perspective', *Cultural Studies*, 26(4): 421–41.

Wolfgang, M. E. (1957) 'Victim precipitated criminal homicide', *The Journal of Criminal Law, Criminology, and Police Science*, 48(1): 1–11.

Woodward, R. and Jenkins, K. N. (2012) '"This place isn't worth the left boot of one of our boys": geopolitics, militarism and memoirs of the Afghanistan war', *Political Geography*, 31: 495–508.

Yurman, A. (2008) 'The victimisation motif as a guiding principle of Israeli discourse', *International Review of Victimology*, 15: 59–83.

Chapter 5

Testimony as practice?

Introduction

Chapter 4 has presented the case for the methodological importance to victimology of connecting with the embedded individual experiences of victims as a vantage point to view wider instances of victimisation. As victimologists, it is important to trust victims to speak for themselves and on behalf of others with similar experiences. This chapter concentrates on the ways in which personal testimony can be used as a means of social action, and makes broader critical observations about the consequences of victimisation to collectivities. This chapter is set in the problematic dual positioning of what constitute victim 'needs' and how they may be delivered as victim 'rights'. What victims 'need' and what they should expect as a 'right' has had a long and controversial history within criminal-justice policy and victimology. While we do not wish to embroil ourselves in lengthy debates about this tension within this chapter, it is important to recognise what victim 'needs' are and acknowledge the extent to which they are claimable as 'rights', formalised in legal statute or policy of some sort.

As Walklate (1989) avers, having experienced criminal victimisation, at a minimum, victims are said to have a desire for information about the management of their offender and subsequent criminal prosecution; support with either practical or emotional issues arising from their experience; and compensation to assist with the restitution of their harm. To these requirements Goodey (2005: 121–22; see also Walklate, 2007: 106) later added that victims of crime require: reassurance and counseling; medical assistance; financial and practical assistance to secure property; information about case progress; guidance about what to expect in court; the chance to express how crime has affected them; assistance with filling out forms for state compensation; and information about the release of their offender. Taken together, these broadly constitute the requirements of victims, as conventionally understood, having experienced *criminal* victimisation. Set within this context we look to make some international observations relating to these broadly constituted 'needs'.

Previously, Mawby and Walklate (1994) situated the victim within non-Western societies (in, for example, parts of Asia, Africa and the Antipodes) as experiencing tensions between formal bureaucratic structures of justice in the legacy of postcolonial systems and indigenous informal, community-based resolutions, in which Western style criminal-justice processes are privileged. However, Mawby and Walklate (1994) did not consider the position of the victim in non-Western societies who sit outside of formal or informal justice processes, and the ways in which they respond to instances of victimisation at the hands of more powerful bodies who have the capacity to suppress their experiences. The intention of this chapter is to fill this gap by exploring the extent to which a large group of victims of corporate crime had their needs met (i.e. medical, financial, psychological and emotional assistance) and the role of campaign groups in aiding that process. Thus we consider another source of data for victimologists: the work of campaign groups and campaigning voices, testimony as practice.

In order to do this the chapter is presented in two interconnected parts. It begins by briefly situating our argument in an overview of international and European victim policy and the core concern for their testimony (or 'voice') to be present within the criminal-justice process. This is followed by our fifth case study, the 1984 Bhopal industrial disaster: a well-evidenced case of corporate victimisation, the effects of which are still being felt. This part of the chapter draws on the events of Bhopal to explore a deeper understanding of corporate victimisation. It does so by illustrating the roles of collective alternative victim movements and individual personal testimony as vehicles for critical inquiry into the prevalence and denial of trauma for victims of this event. The chapter concludes with some brief observations on the nature of victims' movements and what, as victimologists, we might learn from a critical engagement with them.

Victim assistance and the changing landscape of victim policy

Identifying what victims' 'needs' are and devising ways to cater for them as claimable 'rights' is a highly politicised process (see *inter alia* Mawby and Walklate, 1994). What constitutes victim 'needs' sits against the historical backdrop of the victim movement in the West, spanning post-war welfarism during the 1950s, the feminist movement during the 1960s–1970s, and the construction of the victim as a 'consumer' of criminal justice from the 1980s onwards (see Chapter 2 and Mawby and Walklate, 1994 for a detailed overview of this period). Picking out two strands within this period, Walklate (1989) noted that whilst the feminist movement for victims of crime has been progressive and influential in speaking out against gendered forms of victimisation disproportionally experienced by women (i.e. sexual assault and domestic violence), and the harms of invisible 'others' within criminal justice (i.e. the elderly, children), during the 1970s and early 1980s it was bounded by its own remit and, as a result, often on the margins of the policy process. At the same time, setting a broader, more politically and sexually neutral agenda was the

victim support movement (Walklate, 1989). This was a voluntary sector movement, initially often operating with the support of the probation service, designed
to provide practical and emotional assistance to victims of crime (i.e. interpersonal
violence, acquisitive crime). Founded in the UK during the 1970s, the voluntary
organisation Victim Support (www.victimsupport.org.uk) came to epitomise this
movement – witnessing 'active' citizens helping themselves and others in the
face of diminishing state welfare (see Reeves and Dunn, 2010 for a detailed
discussion). Victim Support was not only well suited to the political shifts from
welfarism to 'active citizenship' within policymaking under a British Conservative government, but it also constructed an image of a structurally neutral
crime victim (Mawby and Walklate, 1994). Thus Victim Support became an
attractive resource for the UK Home Office and easily gained support and
funding as a result of its alignment with state policy (Walklate, 1989). Victim
Support has now become a major force in policymaking in the UK as the
National Victims Service, with whom the Home Office consult. However,
the victim movement did not just have domestic influence on the formation
of victim policy. At a similar time to Victim Support gaining ground in the UK
as a third-sector organisation attending to victims' 'needs', a set of universal
standards for victims of crime was devolved from the Council of Europe and
the United Nations, with the intention of placing the victim of crime at the
forefront of the justice process.

European and international victim policy

The Council of Europe (1983) unveiled the 'European convention on the
compensation of victims of violent crimes' (1983), introducing the requirement
for compensation to be awarded for victims of crime as a matter of 'equity and
social solidarity'. This was followed by the 'Declaration of basic principles of
justice for victims of crime and abuse of power' (United Nations, 1985), in which
victims were appointed a set of non-statutory 'rights' that included the right to be
treated with dignity and respect, to receive redress from harm via criminal-
justice processes, and the right to be awarded compensation. Further to these
developments, in 1996 the United Nations Commission on Crime Prevention
and Criminal Justice (United Nations, 1997) passed resolution 1996/14 as a
platform for member states to create victim manuals to compliment their
criminal-justice practices. This resulted in the *Handbook on Justice for Victims*
(United Nations, 1999) and was used to interpret the 1985 Declaration. From
this point onwards the international community had a set of standards and
principles to cater for victims' 'needs' within criminal-justice practices, and
guidelines to develop victim-sensitive policies as a claimable set of 'rights'.

These broader international developments undoubtedly had an influence on
the way victim policy began to develop across Western democratic nations, and
in England and Wales the criminal-justice system underwent a similar process of
placing the victim front-and-centre of justice policy. Notably this occurred

with the publication of the *Victims' Charter* (1990), which purported to outline for the first time the oxymoron of non-statutory 'rights' for victims of crime. This document, produced in the shadows of Thatcherism, had the lasting effect of entwining citizenship with being a 'consumer' of public services, and set the political context within which this and subsequent victim policies developed (Mawby and Walklate, 1994). This *Victims' Charter* was later updated in 1996 and came to be superseded in 2001 following the publication of the Home Office's *Justice for All* white paper (see Home Office, 2001). Published under the New Labour Government, this document claimed to situate the victim at the 'centre' of the processes of criminal justice, requiring all justice agencies to play their part in this 'rebalancing' of the criminal-justice process. The configuration of this 'rebalancing' has seen a succession of initiatives introduced which built on the momentum of the previous victims' movement and extended the 'service' on offer to victims as 'consumers' of the justice process. The *Domestic Violence, Crime and Victims Act* (2004) was the main legislative device that followed, and this emphasised the victim as a key part of the justice process, with a role to play in delivering justice (HMSO, 2004). It was said to have introduced the first set of statutory 'rights' for victims' of crime, but instead placed 'obligations' on criminal-justice organisations to provide 'services' to victims via the accompanying *Code of Practice for Victims of Crime* (Ministry of Justice, 2005). More recently the newer *Code of Practice for Victims of Crime* (Ministry of Justice, 2013) sets out what victims can now *expect* from justice services, who are obliged to provide a set of minimum standards for victim provision, although criminal-justice agencies still only remain indirectly accountable if provision is not met (see: HMSO, 2004, Chapter 1, 34[1] and [2]). For victim-support movements in the European Union, formalised rights for crime victims might not be too far away, however. During 2012, the European Commission pledged their support to victims of crime by drafting a set of minimum standards that are set to transpose identifiable victim 'needs' into claimable 'rights' (European Commission, n.d.). The working framework for these rights is set out in a Directive instructing EU member states to have implemented a means of adopting them within criminal-justice policy by November 2015 (European Commission, 2001). As Weber et al. (2014) enthuse, this marks a significant move forwards towards a set of enforceable criteria to protect victims of crime. Only time will tell if these 'rights' become fully claimable in law. However, what is apparent within this policy setting is the repositioning of the victim at the centre of the justice process, offering the opportunity for the victim to have a 'voice': to have their personal testimony heard.

The rise of victim testimony

The obligations put on justice agencies to be more inclusive of victims as part of the criminal-justice process has seen an increase in policies and practices concerned with 'victim allocution' (Walklate, 2007). This will be discussed in more detail in Chapter 6, but for now it is worth noticing that this period of policy development formalised the use of the victim's voice within the justice process across Europe and the US. In the UK, for example, the opportunity for personal testimony became available through the introduction of Victim Impact Statements and/or the personal-statement scheme. These policy shifts, no matter how problematic, sensitise us to a broader range of issues that such policies may connect with. Listening to victims' voices, as Elias (1993) points out, may by implication also involve us in terms of policy aligning with voices with very particular ideological interests and intentions. In order to elucidate this more clearly, in what follows, individual and collective examples are drawn from the UK context as illustration.

Individual personal testimony as practice

In 2009 Sara Payne, the mother of a murdered school girl Sarah Payne, was appointed as a *Victims Champion* in the UK. This appointment saw Sara consult with crime victims and front-line criminal-justice services to review victim service provision (see Payne, 2009). Later in 2011, following the death of her brother Ben in 2008 to a knife crime, Brooke Kinsella was commissioned to conduct a 'fact-finding mission' into schemes aimed at tackling knife crime in the UK (see Kinsella, 2011). Both of these initiatives were commissioned by the then Home Secretaries, the findings and recommendations of which were fed directly back to the Home Office with the intention to inform policy. Both also make full use of the voice of indirect victims in the policymaking process. However, as Elias (1993) points out, they also, almost by definition, align with state justice interests and play their part in shaping views of a justice system as too lenient and in need of tougher criminal-justice policies for dedicated causes (i.e. terrorism, knife crime, and so on).

Collective personal testimony as practice

There are, however, other grass-roots organisations that self-mobilise without state sponsorship, often as a result of indirect victims losing loved ones to violent crimes. For example the Stephen Lawrence Charitable Trust (see http://www.stephenlawrence.org.uk) was formed as a result of the racist murder of Stephen Lawrence in London (as discussed in Chapter 3); the Tim Parry Johnathan Ball Foundation for Peace (see http://www.foundation4peace.org) came into being following the death of two young boys killed in Warrington as a result of an IRA terrorist attack; and Mothers Against Violence (see http://mavuk.org) was created by the mother of a young man shot and killed in Manchester. Like Victim Support, such organisations reside within the third sector and are active in campaigning and educating on issues of social justice, peace, reconciliation and crime reduction to prevent the further victimisation of others. However, unlike Victim Support and government-appointed victim ambassadors, such campaigns can often either have less accord with state crime-control agendas, or be more politically charged and promote a less structurally neutral victim image, diminishing their appeal for state sponsorship and policy influence.

Repositioning the victim

This overview points to the embedded nature of victim policy across Europe, and the United Nations advocating an enhanced role for the victim and what they have to say about their experiences (a more detailed discussion of the problematic issues these raise for victims is addressed in Chapter 6). In addition, it is possible to evidence different ways in which victim-related issues have been brought to the attention of the policy arena, either as a result of individual campaign voices or more collective campaign groups. Both of which can pose different kinds of questions about the nature and reach of their influence (leaving aside the thorny issue of the extent to which such influence might be considered 'democratic'). Moreover, although there are now established international frameworks guiding the development of victim 'needs' and 'rights', transferring such minimum standards across international jurisdictions is deeply problematic. On a practical level, it is difficult to translate minimum standards from the national to the local, as not only are such guidelines not universally commutable from one cultural context to the next, they rely on the discretion of national and/or state governments to mobilise them into legally binding statutes and policy (Sebba, 2008). However, in contrast with Western Europe and the US, the development of victim policy has been less than even in other parts of the world, and indeed the extent to which such policies have been embraced is, arguably, tainted with Western imperialism (Sebba, 2008). This is particularly the case across Asia, where the development of victim policy has been less progressive in some parts. With particular reference to India, the locus of concern in our next case study, although having inherited its penal policy from British colonial rule, the role of crime victims has not developed at anywhere near a similar pace to the UK. To explicate this further, we now turn to our fifth case study.

Case study: Bhopal industrial disaster[1]

In 1968, a US transnational corporation (TNC), Union Carbide Corporation (UCC), constructed a pesticides formulation factory in Bhopal, India, under the rubric of a subsidiary, Union Carbide India Limited (UCIL). Established during the 'green revolution' in agricultural farming in India, one of the key outputs of this plant was to create large quantities of a pesticide known as Sevin. This was made by combining Alpha Naphthol with a highly volatile chemical known as Methyl Isocyanate (MIC). MIC was originally imported into India until the late 1970s, following which UCC were licensed by the Madhya Pradesh state government to manufacture Sevin and formulate MIC in Bhopal, despite the factory being situated in close proximity to its large local population. The UCIL factory in Bhopal was a subsidiary of UCC, who held and maintained a majority (59.99 per cent) shareholder position from within the US. Using its influence and capital bargaining power with the Indian authorities, UCC held on to its majority shares in UCIL and remained under the total managerial control of UCC, led by company CEO Warren Anderson. It was under this managerial control that the Bhopal factory, its workers and the local population were to be exposed to the events of 1984.

During the 1980s, the production of pesticides became less profitable, resulting in the UCIL plant in Bhopal being stripped of resources. This, it transpired, dangerously impacted upon its already inadequate health and safety capabilities. Then, in 1983, a major $1.25 million cost-cutting exercise resulted in the layoff of half the Bhopal factory workforce, further compromising what few safety standards were in place. Due to the general inadequacy of the MIC unit, and the added aggressiveness of UCC's cost-cutting at the expense of safety, on the evening of 2 December 1984 water was accidentally leaked into MIC tank 610, causing an unstoppable 'runaway reaction'. The result was a gas leak that created the world's largest industrial disaster. Thousands of people died as a direct result of this gas leak, many more have perished from its effects since, and countless Bhopalis have endured three decades of illness and suffering as a consequence. In a show of support for the sake of publicity, Warren Anderson flew to Bhopal in 1984 and was subsequently arrested on suspicion of culpable homicide (manslaughter), causing grievous hurt, death and the poisoning of animals. Hours later he was released on bail and allowed to return to the US on the promise of returning to face criminal proceedings. Up until his death some 30 years later, in September 2014, he never returned to India and remained a fugitive of the Indian justice system for the remainder of his life.

Corporate victimisation

Thirty years after this disaster, much is known and has been written about it in relation to corporate crime (see Pearce and Tombs, 1989; 1998; 2012). For our purposes, we follow Tombs and Whyte's (2010a: 81) definition of corporate crime:

> Illegal acts or omissions, punishable by the state under administrative, civil or criminal law, which are the result of deliberate decision making or culpable negligence within a legitimate formal organization.

Walklate (1989) had previously cautioned that corporate crime has had less attention paid to it by criminologists and victimologists than other kinds of crime. Over 20 years later, Tombs and Whyte (2010b) draw the same conclusion. However, as victimologists, and as victimologists interested in what can be learned from testimony as practice, there is much to learn from this particular set of events. To do so requires an engagement with this disaster as an instance of corporate *victimisation* (see *inter alia* Walklate, 1989; Croall, 2007; Whyte, 2007; Tombs and Whyte, 2010b), the first step of which is to identify who the victims of this disaster are and what do their experiences look like.

Direct victims

The gas that leaked from MIC tank 610 was deadly. It descended upon the residents of Bhopal, exposing between 200,000 and 400,000 of its 800,000 population to lethal toxins while they were sleeping (Pearce and Tombs, 1998) and produced multiple direct victims. The noxious gas immediately caused devastating human suffering and death through violent physical illness and respiratory problems, in addition to deaths caused by stampedes of people desperately attempting to escape. The gas leak killed and maimed indiscriminately, although the numbers of people fatally hurt as a consequence varies widely, from 1,700 to 10,000 deaths or more (Pearce and Tombs, 1998). Official sources reporting in the immediate aftermath of the disaster offer conservative estimates on the numbers killed. The Indian government's first estimates ranged from 1,754 to 3,329 deaths (Pearce and Tombs, 1989), whereas a report commissioned by UCC claimed that over 3,800 lives were lost as a consequence of the gas leak, with a further 11,000 people suffering disabilities (Browning, 1993). While still substantial, these figures remain moderate compared to the unofficial consensus between researchers, activists and personal testimonies, who estimate far greater numbers killed in the aftermath. Pearce and Tombs (1989) reported soon after the disaster that somewhere in the region of 5,000 deaths were reported by researchers. Other activist groups claim that between 7,000 and 10,000 people died in the immediate aftermath (see ICJB, 2014d; Amnesty International, 2004), far exceeding those officially recorded by the Union of India and cited by UCC. Similar unpleasant estimates of 10,000 deaths and more derived from unofficial reports such as survivor testimonies (Pearce and Tombs, 1989). By 2003, Amnesty International (2004) estimated that a further 15,000 people had died as a result of the disaster, and ten years on those estimates have continued to rise to approximately a further 20,000–30,000 deaths (ICJB, 2014d).

Primary victimisation

In addition to the horrific number of deaths caused by the Bhopal disaster, approximately 60,000 people were seriously affected by the exposure to gas and more than 20,000 have been recognised by the Indian government as having legitimately suffered permanent *physical* injuries as direct victims (Pearce and Tombs, 1989). Three decades after the disaster, over 100,000 people are still suffering from serious illnesses, including abnormal levels of skin, lung and gastrointestinal cancers; physical deformity to children; genetic birth defects and miscarriages; women suffering from irregular or no menstrual cycles; impairments to the immune system; irreversible damage to the nervous system; memory loss, paralysis, and partial blindness (see Mishra et al., 2009; ICJB, 2014e). Much of this continued illness is associated with the local land and water supplies remaining contaminated from the Bhopal gas leak, and the factory itself having been left abandoned and contaminated. The resolution of these problems has been left in stasis by UCC and the Indian authorities. The former have shifted the problem away from corporate responsibility on to the Indian authorities; the latter have denied the extent of the contamination. However, illness and contamination have not been the only primary victimisation experienced by those who have survived: standards of living have been reversed, entire families have been wiped out, and, as we now go on to discuss, many people have suffered, and continue to suffer, from psychological health problems.

Psychological illness

An initial study, between February and April 1985, found the prevalence of psychological problems following the Bhopal disaster to be 22.6 per cent of the population, including changes in emotional behaviour (adjustment reaction) leading to prolonged depression (20 per cent) and emotional disturbance (16 per cent); mild depression over long periods (depressive neurosis; 37 per cent) and general anxiety disorder (anxiety neurosis; 25 per cent) (Murthy, 1990). A subsequent survey, in June 1985, found approximately 9 per cent of a population sample in Bhopal (387 people from a sample of 4,098 adults) to be suffering from a mental health disorder, the most prevalent continuing to be mild depression over long periods (neurotic depression; 51 per cent), anxiety (41 per cent) and hysteria (2 per cent) (Murthy, 1990). Other cognate studies identified psychological disorders accompanied by other complications, including behavioural issues (i.e. memory, concentration, motor speed, fatigue) and neurological problems (i.e. effects on the nervous system, vertigo, impairment to hearing, stroke, muscle weaknesses, fatigue, abnormal smell and taste, headaches), evident in both adults and children, and most prevalent in women (see: Murthy, 2002b). As such,

> These general population psychiatric epidemiological studies show that the gas-exposed population were having significantly higher prevalence rates for psychiatric disorders in comparison to the general population.
> (Murthy, 2002b: 7)

Murthy (2002a) provides a more comprehensive overview of the extent of mental health problems found in Bhopal disaster victims, but it is clear from this brief overview that there were, and continue to be, far-reaching consequences of psychological illness in the aftermath of the disaster as a form of traumatic primary victimisation.

These observations present themselves as somewhat prosaic without further elaboration – as Pearce and Tombs (1989: 117) put it, 'a simple listing of the number of dead and injured gives little idea of the overall impact of the tragedy'. Indeed a key to extending our analysis of this kind of victimisation is through the lens of structural powerlessness (Croall, 2007). This is illustrated by revisiting the role of victim movements and personal testimony to establish what more they can tell us about corporate victimisation and its consequences.

Alternative victim movements

The earlier discussion within this chapter illustrated that victim personal testimony is frequently used in practical ways to either inform state criminal-justice policy, or to campaign against crime. As such, the broader context of victim movements within Western criminal justice can be understood as being divided between campaigns that are either appropriated within state justice interests, or excluded to the margins if they adopt a position out of kilter with orthodox policymaking (Elias, 1993). Of course, there are 'alter-native movements' that do not chime with crime-control policy interests and which seek to fight against victimisation by powerful institutions (Elias, 1993). Examples include the Hillsborough Justice Campaign (see http://www.contrast.org/hillsborough) and the Justice for Mark Duggan Campaign (see http://justice4mark.com), both of which implicate state wrongdoing in the victimisation and death of loved ones, relatives and friends. Rather than looking to merely inform state policy, campaigns such as these intend to challenge it directly, and seek to rectify injustices considered to have been directly caused by state violence and 'embrace what official recognition leaves out' (Elias, 1993: 57). Such campaigns have had a high profile in the British press, driven by the voices of indirect victims. However, as Moore (2014) reminds us, the mass media are just one of many social elements that shape public events as culturally 'traumatic', and more importantly not all harmful or criminal events 'naturally' become enshrined with collective public empathy. A key vehicle for affording harmful incidents a 'newsworthy' status – or not – is their cultural and spatial proximity to the Western global media (Jewkes, 2011). Despite the scale and severity of the Bhopal disaster, its geographical location, occurring on the India subcontinent, and the structural vulnerability of those affected by it, provided the potential for it to be rendered invisible to a wider global audience, or relegated to a footnote in history. However, although 30 years have now passed since this disaster occurred, it remains firmly in the public domain. Arguably, the continued recognition of the Bhopal disaster is the result of a persistent 'alternative' victim movement that has been in 'practice' for the past 30 years and con-tinues to draw attention to, and keep the spotlight firmly fixed upon, the suffering experienced in Bhopal.

Collective personal testimony – the Bhopal Movement

The discussion above suggests that the structure and formation of victim assistance can take public, private or voluntary forms, often operating independently of the criminal-justice process and, as Elias (1986) notes, it is possible to find victim movements occupying similar spaces, albeit with different intentions. Although marginal, 'alternative' victims' movements are not necessarily totally ignored. They may perhaps be lacking in governmental support, but they attract assistance from individuals, groups and campaigns that seek to address injustices and the exploitative conditions which victims are seen to endure (Elias, 1993). For the victims of the Bhopal disaster there are several key campaign groups that live up to this 'alternative' status:

International Campaign for Justice in Bhopal (ICJB) (www.bhopal.net)
The Bhopal Medical Appeal (www.bhopal.org)
The International Campaign for Justice in Bhopal, North America (ICJB-NA) (http://www.studentsforbhopal.org)

Known generally as Transnational Social Movement Organisations (TSMOs) and collectively as the Bhopal Movement, these organisations (and others) have a long and turbulent history in campaigning for social justice in Bhopal (see Zavestoski, 2009 for a detailed history). What makes the Bhopal Movement unique, however, is that it is grounded in the collective experiences of direct and primary victimisation. It is not just a call to action by transnational activists which is shaped *around* such events (Zavestoski, 2009). For Spalek (2006), it is precisely this sense of embeddedness and commonality of experience that undergirds victim movements of this kind and gives rise to a sense of purpose and identity. As an example, the International Campaign for Justice in Bhopal (ICJB) consists of a collectivity of survivors of the disaster, volunteers, social justice, human rights and environmental groups who campaign for justice through non-violent direct action, education and outreach programmes. Elias (1986: 217) comments that some people will organise to repel or accommodate victimisation, but others 'will organize on some level for their mutual defence, if not for some fundamental change'. The type of activism practiced by ICJB is at the core of human rights advocacy present in victimology, and intends to capture the 'hearts and minds' of those oppressed by state and corporate actors to bring about fundamental changes to rights and social injustice on local and global platforms.

In looking to the ICJB (2013), a variety of personal testimonies come to the fore and illustrate why, after 30 years, the victims of the Bhopal disaster continue to fight for justice. As one woman states, this is a fight for the rights of Bhopal disaster victims, reflecting the objectives of ICJB:

> If we go and fight for our rights, then there would be better treatment for us, so this gives me more spirit to fight.
>
> (Vimla Bai, n.d. cited in ICJB, 2014c)

As Spalek (2006) continues, however, relating individual subjectivity to wider group concerns allows victims to share aspects of their identity with others, and at the same time can form part of a 'collective consciousness' that extends beyond the victim group based on other shared aspects of identity and structural vulnerability (Spalek, 2006). As a leading TSMO, the Bhopal Movement also has broader influential appeals to address international corporate liability; providing people with the right to know of harmful contamination to the places in which they live; and the unjust exploitation of poor communities by corporate entities, particularly in the global south (Zavestoski, 2009). As another victim of Bhopal states, this fight transcends Bhopal and signifies the prevention of further disasters elsewhere:

> Whatever is happening in Bhopal, should not happen anywhere, so for this we started our struggle.
>
> (Rashida Bi, n.d. cited in ICJB, 2014c)

The identities of such victim movements and their members serve to embed the experience of victimisation and fix our gaze as victimologists on issues that may not routinely be considered as part of broader victimological interests (Spalek, 2006). Moreover, two questions remain: in what ways have such movements demonstrated their testimony in practice, and what else can this teach us about the role of the victim in the global south?

Victim conflict as state 'property'

In the months that followed the Bhopal disaster, the Union of India 'sought damages on behalf of victims of Bhopal Gas Leak mass disaster' (see Supreme Court of India, 1989: 14). A deal was struck to pay $470 million in settlement directly to the central Union of India; only $200 million of which was paid from UCC, the rest being covered by corporate insurance and shareholder equity (Pearce and Tombs, 1989). Fixed settlements were paid to those people officially recognised by the Indian government as victims of the disaster: $1,000 was paid to the families of the 3,393 deceased and $500 to each of the 20,000 seriously injured (Pearce and Tombs, 1989). However, these payments only began to be distributed to victims in 1992 and it was not until 2004 that the Indian government was ordered by the courts to pay the remaining funds of approximately $270 million to a further half a million complainants (Pearce and Tombs, 2012). Within the 1989 settlement, UCC liabilities were absolved from any corporate negligence and wrongdoing, all criminal cases against them were revoked and the Madhya Pradesh state government was positioned to defend UCC in any subsequent lawsuits (Supreme Court of India, 1989). UCC were initially granted criminal and civil immunity and protection before the law in return for a rate of compensation it dictated for itself (the original claim was in the region of $3 billion). This process systematically removed the victims of Bhopal from the civil litigation process and represented their 'needs' without seeking their input. Unhappy with the outcome of the 1989 settlement, the Bhopal Movement pursued a curative petition for more satisfactory compensation and support for long-term healthcare and accountability for the contamination of their community. In 1991 and 2007 they fought and lost in their appeals (see Supreme Court of India, 1991; 2007). Following the 1991 appeal, however, the Supreme Court of India ruled that the compensation settlement was appropriate for the victims, committing UCC to building a local hospital to monitor the heath of Bhopal victims without charge as an alternative, again without consultation as to the victims' actual needs. Instead the Supreme Court of India reinstated criminal proceedings against UCC and Warren Anderson, a political move more in line with state rather than victim interests.

Although situated outwith the criminal-justice process, this tells us much about the role of the victim in the Indian justice system. We are informed by Satish (2008) that the victim of crime plays no role in the Indian justice process beyond providing a statement of complaint; the state then subsumes total responsibility for the ensuing investigation, owning its 'conflict', as Christie (1977) suggests, as state 'property'. In recognition of this, during 2003 the Malimath Committee (Malimath, 2003) undertook a review of the Indian justice process and indicated that the role and status of crime victims required much improvement to ensure they were provided with requisite support for their needs, at least commensurate with the UN minimum standards (Satish, 2008). Some of the key recommendations made by the Malimath Committee reflected the progressive role of the victim within European criminal-justice policy-making (Malimath, 2003). This included the active inclusion of the victim's opinion (or 'voice') in the criminal-justice process (see Satish, 2008). In light of such recommendations, it was not until 2009 that the *Criminal Procedure Code of India* was amended to include a formal definition of 'crime victims' and to recognise particular needs, such as compensation, healthcare and a right of appeal, that resembled some of the core components of the UN guidelines (Jaishankar, 2014). However, although indicating a positive move towards the status of victims within the Indian justice process, much like other European victim policies, these amendments fall far short of being claimable 'rights' as they are not enshrined in law. Unlike European policy, however, judges in India hold the power of their own legal discretion to award compensation to victims (Jaishankar, 2014), though the victim's voice has yet to find its place within the judicial process as suggested by the Committee (see: Malimath, 2003).

The efforts of the collective personal testimonies of the Bhopal Movement therefore reveal something valuable about the shared identity that can be derived from victimisation and the ways in which this can be collectively mobilised to campaign for victims needs/rights, no matter how unsuccessful. As illustrated in Chapter 4 and earlier in this chapter, it is not always collective victim testimonies that help illustrate wider issues of victimisation. Personal testimony can also be practiced by individual victims and illustrate harm that may not simply go on 'behind our backs' (qua Walklate, 2007). Harm may be hidden in plain sight.

Testimony, harm and trauma

The consequences of victimisation can result in a range of costs for the individual, the offender and the state, but one of the most profound costs of victimisation, which may far exceed the discomfort of financial losses, is the psychological effect of victimisation (Elias, 1986). These consequences can be felt, by both women and men, in a number of different forms (i.e. anxiety, depression, PTSD) following victimisation, requiring people to overcome their effects (i.e. guilt, stigma and trauma) in various ways (Elias, 1986). The development in professional recognition of emotional and psychological trauma (a 'trauma narrative') has been noted by Fassin and Rechtman (2009) as aiding the growth of the victim movement across Europe. The purposes and influence of victim movements are said to have benefited from the professional expert opinion of 'clinical' victimologists in what was noted in Chapter 2 as 'psychiatric victimology' (Fassin and Rechtman, 2009: 108). Coupled with the emergence and recognition of victim personal testimony beyond its pedestrian role in the judicial process, the conjoining of the professional recognition of psychological trauma in the aftermath of a disaster and the personal experiences of those who experience primary victimisation were said to be an influential force in acquiring the 'need' for victim compensation as a 'right' (Fassin and Rechtman, 2009). Indeed, Fassin (2012) has traced the significance of the way in which such links have been forged even further in defining the type of emergency response considered essential in the aftermath of a disaster that privileges psychological trauma. However, Bhopal and its aftermath reveal some additional problematic features associated with such trauma.

'Tracing' trauma

Emotional reactions to victimisation can elicit responses of passivity, aggression towards assailants, self-reconciliation or denial on behalf of victims, to name but a few (Elias, 1986). For Alexander (2012: 6), the wider mobilisation of such emotional and psychological responses to victimisation are established as 'cultural trauma', occurring

> when members of a collectivity feel they have been subjected to a horrendous event that leaves indelible marks upon their group consciousness, marking their memories forever and changing their future identity in fundamental and irrevocable ways.

However, not all traumatising events are initially 'traumatic'. As described earlier by Spalek (2006), if the shared identity of victims following harmful events undergirds the formation of victim movements, then it is the claims of victim collectivities in the recognition of such harmful events that become key to the 'cultural construction of trauma' (Alexander, 2012: 16). Thus the wider communication of victimising events as traumatic is contingent on a set of cultural processes that require convincing and meaningful translation to others as being 'traumatising' (Alexander, 2012). As noted in Chapter 2, for Alexander (2012) this cultural process includes an articulation of the harmfulness of the event; the nature and vulnerability of the victim; the proximity of the victim to the audience; and identification of the perpetrators of such harm. The 'reclassification' of events as 'traumatic' is also contingent upon their recognition in the legal and bureaucratic processes of the state. So, if the experience of being a victim has the potential to be subsumed as the property of the state (qua Christie, 1977), then what kind of political space affords trauma its legitimacy?

Individual personal testimony – self-immolation

Depicting the self-immolation of Mohamed Bouazizi in Tunisia during 2010, Didier Fassin (2011) offers an account of the body of this young street vendor as a locus of state violence, humiliation and disempowerment. Although clearly a traumatic suicidal act, Fassin (2011) suggests that rather than being psychological, this was a significant political act, leaving us – intentionally or not – with the 'traces' of other violences to pursue in its wake. We would aver that such an act should also be considered as the final exposition of a subjugated personal testimony in action, in which the body becomes a 'site of memory' within an unequal relationship with the state, depicting political violence on the physical body, or structural violence on the body politic (Fassin, 2011). In the aftermath of the Bhopal disaster we evidence a similar event that connects psychological trauma and the body to the structural powerlessness caused by corporate victimisation.

Having been exposed to lethal gas in Bhopal on the day of the disaster, Kailash Pawar (please note this story is taken from ICJB, 2014a) had fallen unconscious following attempts by his mother to save his life. When he awoke, he found himself on the back of a truck, surrounded by dead bodies being driven away from Bhopal to be burned. Kailash survived Bhopal with lifelong respiratory injuries, having lost his mother to the gas and his father as an ill recluse. In 1989, just 14 days after featuring in a news article in *India Today* (see Singh, 1989) and one month after the UCC settlement, Kailash self-immolated in protest so that the world would remember 'the continuing suffering of gas victims in Bhopal' (ICJB, 2014a). He had felt a burden to his wife, an indirect victim, as he could no longer work. He suffered as a direct victim of his injuries and experienced a secondary victimisation through state ownership of his 'conflict' and the meager compensation awarded to disaster victims. Kailash had also suffered psychologically, haunted by nightmares of the dead that surrounded him when he awoke from the gas. Following Fassin

(2011), we consider the actions of Kailash to represent a violent personal testimony in action, evidencing the more commonly known corporate victimisation
caused by UCC, but also giving affordance to other psychological and emotional
'traces' of suffering left in the wake of Bhopal.

The self-immolation of Kailash demonstrates a personal testimony that is
demanding to be heard, and makes us cognizant of the widespread prevalence
of psychological trauma that exists for the other victims of Bhopal. Further 'traces'
of primary victimisation are evident in Carlson's (2012) account *Bhopali*. Not only
have the victims of the Bhopal disaster been affected by lifelong physical
illness, there is also a strong footprint of emotional and psychological trauma
present in the form of paranoia, fear, depression, anxiety and indeed suicide.
In keeping with the value of investing in the embedded experiences of victimisation as part of a trauma narrative in victimology, Basu and Murthy (2003)
conducted interviews with direct and indirect victims, and a few of the mental
health practitioners that now work in Bhopal. The narratives of the lived
experiences of primary victimisation following the Bhopal disaster evidenced here
add to the prevalence of mental illness and attendant neurological and behavioural problems as described earlier (Basu and Murthy, 2003). Thus Basu and
Murthy (2003) raise a valuable methodological issue connecting with our
previous concerns in Chapter 4. They state,

> If figures and tables with sophisticated statistical tools are for some esoteric
> exercises to be built on the survivor's mental trauma, then the scientific
> community needs to be hit hard with narratives, which has been termed
> by them as 'fiction' or non-science.
>
> (Basu and Murthy, 2003: 1082)

Here the emotional investment of engaging with the individual 'voice' of the
victim, however constituted, is advocated as central to a more complete understanding of the effects of the aftermath of disaster; challenging official discourses
that are weighted against those in positions of structural vulnerability and
adding rich experiences to a trauma narrative concerned with choice, suffering
and power relations. Kailash's self-immolation would have been difficult to
ignore for the passer-by, but what his violent personal testimony draws
attention to is victimisation made structurally invisible: hidden in plain sight.

Invisible trauma? Thinking differently about victim responsiveness

Traumatic events may become widely recognised as such through socially
mediated processes, and can be contingent on political recognition to gain
legitimacy (Alexander, 2012). As part of this process, in what Geis (1973)
describes as 'victim responsiveness', the recognition of harm is also reliant upon
individuals or groups recognising that they have experienced victimisation and

are empowered enough to respond to it. Amongst those writing about corporate victimisation, 'victim responsiveness' has frequently featured as a recurring means of explaining how experiences of harm may go unnoticed by victims due to being part of the tapestry of their day-to-day working activities (qua Walklate, 1989; Whyte, 2010b). As Croall (2007) argues, uncovering, and indeed measuring, this type of victimisation is possible. The problem is more that it has not frequently been in the purview of victimologists (Walklate, 1989; Tombs and Whyte, 2010b). However, as we have already noted in Chapter 2, in the work of Spalek and King (2007) there is another way to consider victim responsiveness. Rather than victimological otherness being experienced 'behind our backs' (qua Walklate, 2007), it is equally possible to have victimisation hidden in plain sight through precisely the same processes that serve to afford trauma legitimacy. We can evidence this in the aftermath of the Bhopal disaster, where psychological trauma has been made structurally invisible in various ways through service provision and policymaking.

Provision and policy for psychological trauma

The first and only major study of mental health in Bhopal, conducted by Murthy (1990), identified that there was no mental health provision in the immediate aftermath of the disaster. There were no mental health professionals in any of the five medical institutions in Madhya Pradesh or Bhopal at the time of the disaster, and despite early recognition of the need for assistance there was a delay of up to two months before mental health professionals became involved (Murthy, 2002b). Most doctors working in the gas-affected area had no mental health training – noticeable in the limited perception of emotional problems of the victims and suggestions that monetary compensation would resolve the physical symptoms of patients (Murthy, 1990). Although having improved since, there is a continued lack of provision for emotional and psychological support in Bhopal. What is provided is done so by NGOs such as the Chingari Trust and the Samdhvana Trust Clinic, run by survivors of the Bhopal disaster (Basu and Murthy, 2003). However, as Kumar (1990, cited in ICJB, 2014a) notes, neither recognition of mental health problems, nor compensation for this primary victimisation, was forthcoming from UCC or the Union of India. A fundamental question is, then, with so many in the Bhopal Movement willing to use their personal testimony as action, and the self-immolation of Kailash Pawar, how has this invisibility been sustained?

The Personal Injury Evaluation (PIE) adopted by the Indian government for the receipt of compensation initially facilitated this invisibility. First it required claimants to provide medical proof of their illness (Sathyamala, 2009). Given the lack of mental health support in the aftermath of the disaster it is unlikely that this would be possible. Second, detrimental consequences of mental health for Bhopal disaster victims were not included as a compensable injury in the 1989 settlement (Sathyamala, 2009). Instead, the discourse of 'psychological factors' was used in different ways by UCC to neutralise their corporate responsibility. In its version of events, the gas leak was caused by a disgruntled but unidentified UCIL employee who had sabotaged the plant (Pearce and Tombs, 1998). Thus the implication was that it was UCC who were the tertiary victims of this disaster, through sabotage and cover-up by witnesses, caused in part by 'psychological factors' relating to UCIL employees (see Kalelkar and Little, 1988). In this UCC defence the personal testimonies depicting the cause of the disaster are thrown into question by implicating workers in collusion through their 'eyewitness accounts' (Kalelkar and Little, 1988: 2):

> Once a story is told, whether accurate or inaccurate, it tends to harden. Further, where a deliberate distortion occurs, with the passage of time, the persons involved tend to coordinate their stories better.

Whilst the experiential accounts of victimisation are a vital source of data that needs to be trusted and indulged to accord with the 'embeddedness' of the lived experience of victimisation (Basu and Murthy, 2003), the opposite is at work here. There is evidence of power relations that had begun manipulating the significance of psychological trauma just when recognition of these problems had begun to gain prominence in victim policy across the US and Europe (see Chapter 2).

Victimisation hidden in plain sight

Irrespective of all of this, the victimisation experienced by the people of Bhopal reveals something different about corporate victimisation and 'victim responsiveness'. Despite the popularity of this term to help understand the unawareness of corporate harm experienced by victims, the quick formation and longevity of the Bhopal Movement provides evidence that 'victim responsiveness' is perhaps a moot issue. This case may well evidence a form of hierarchical 'dominance' 'over the traumatized parties themselves' (Alexander, 2012: 25), or indeed may be part of an official denial (qua Cohen, 2001). However, the longevity of victim campaigning about the corporate victimisation experienced in Bhopal, and the range of issues discussed throughout this chapter, make such claims hard to sustain on their own. We could suggest that there is a paucity of statistics to accurately evidence the extent of the harm that has taken place, but we cannot say that there has been no public knowledge about the fact that victimisation has occurred. Nor can we suggest that there has been no theory, research or politics related to Bhopal either; the work of Pearce and Tombs (1989; 1998; 2012) alone mitigates this fact. Instead, if we are to understand this victimisation as being structurally invisible then perhaps it is important to appreciate its obfuscation with a different emphasis. As was discussed in Chapter 1 regarding the legacy of sexual crimes committed by Jimmy Savile, and as Davies et al. (2014) noted in a follow-up to their analysis on the invisibility of corporate crime, like other wide-scale victimisation committed by those in positions of power, such harm is not so much 'invisible' per se, it is instead hidden in plain sight.

Conclusion: hidden in plain sight?

The two parts of this chapter have offered a novel way to consider the role of personal testimony when situated as a 'practice' against corporate victimisation. The first part of the discussion documented the centring of the victim in justice processes in Western Europe and elsewhere. This provided the space to present our fifth case study, the Bhopal industrial disaster, in a part of the world where such centring has been slow to develop. This case study afforded the opportunity to develop an in-depth appreciation of testimony as practice. The second part of this discussion looked to extend the victimological imagination by considering the role of a collective 'alternative' victim movement and what could be learned from it. This was followed by tracing the trauma of an individual personal testimony in order to revisit the prevalence of psychological illness in the aftermath of disaster and illustrate how this has been made structurally invisible by the same processes that serve to afford such trauma legitimacy. Finally, it has been suggested that this represents an inversion of victim responsiveness – obscuring widespread primary victimisation by hiding it in plain sight.

However, it is also important to acknowledge that victim movements are not ideologically foolproof. For example, in finding a balance between local and global interests, Zavestoski (2009) informs us that in its early stages the Bhopal Movement came into internal conflict with itself, and split between two interests: lobbying for action against UCC and the Union of India, or providing for victims who had their 'material existence' and health changed dramatically. This struggle is articulated slightly differently by Sathyamala (2009), expressed here in terms of the inherent class interests of alternative victim movements, with both imposing values on the identity of victims and making choices for them. Nonetheless, undergirding the broader message of this chapter is the struggle against what Whyte (2007) describes as 'silencing' of victims of corporate victimisation, caused by either an officially permitted state apparatus or through entrenched corporate power imposing structural powerlessness upon marginalised and vulnerable groups. The fight not to allow the Bhopal disaster to be silenced, against the forces of state and corporate interests, has been the purview of the Bhopal Movement, leading with personal testimony as practice, for the past three decades. However, there is one more means of silencing that Whyte (2007) suggests needs to be overcome: the silencing of criminologists and victimologists in observing these issues. In this chapter we have intended to piece together the ways in which victim personal testimony as practice can be situated as both a means of social action and victimological analysis. More broadly, this adds some background noise to the relative 'silence' of the victimological imagination on these issues.

Further reading

For a varied analysis of the Bhopal disaster, we recommend the following Special Issue academic journals dedicated to the disaster: *Global Social Policy* (2009) and *Social Justice* (2014). Information on the role of the Bhopal Movement can be found at the International Campaign for Justice in Bhopal (ICJB) (see www.bhopal.net) and the Bhopal Medical Appeal (see www.bhopal.org). In addition, Carlson's (2012) *Bhopali* and Condi's (2004) *One Night in Bhopal* are excellent films/documentaries to connect the reader with the expcriential aspects of Bhopal's victims.

Note

1 Unless otherwise stated, details of this case study and other circumstances relating to the Bhopal industrial disaster throughout this chapter have been largely constructed by drawing upon the work of Pearce and Tombs (1989; 1998; 2012) and the International Campaign for Justice in Bhopal (www.bhopal.net), in addition to the BBC documentary *One Night in Bhopal* (Condi, 2004) and the independent film *Bhopali* (Carlson, 2012). Any inaccuracies are entirely our own.

References

Alexander, J. C. (2012) *Trauma: A Social Theory*. Cambridge: Polity Press.

Amnesty International. (2004) 'Clouds of injustice: Bhopal disaster 20 years on'. Available at http://www.amnesty.org/en/library/asset/ASA20/015/2004/en/fa14a821-d584-11dd-bb24-1fb85fe8fa05/asa200152004en.pdf.

Basu, A. R. and Murthy, R. S. (2003) 'Disaster and mental health: revisiting Bhopal', *Economic and Political Weekly,* March 15: 1074–82.

Browning, J. B. (1993) 'Union Carbide: disaster at Bhopal. Jackson Browning report – Union Carbide Corp'. Available at http://storage.dow.com.edgesuite.net/dow.com/Bhopal/browning.pdf.

Carlson, V. M. (2012) *Bhopali*. Oddbox Films.

Christie, N. (1977) 'Conflicts as property', *British Journal of Criminology*, 17(1): 1–15.

Cohen, S. (2001) *States of Denial: Knowing About Atrocities and Suffering*. Cambridge: Polity Press.

Condie, S, (2004) *One Night in Bhopal*. BBC Television.

Council of Europe (1983) 'European Convention on the compensation of victims of violent crimes, Strasbourg, 24.XI.1983'. Available at http://conventions.coe.int/Treaty/en/Treaties/Html/116.htm.

Criminal Justice System (1990) 'The Victim's Charter: a statement of standard services for victims of crime'. Available at http://webarchive.nationalarchives.gov.uk/20130128103514/http://www.homeoffice.gov.uk/documents/victims-charter2835.pdf?view=Binary

Croall, H. (2007) 'Victims of white-collar and corporate crime', in P. Davies, P. Francis and C. Greer (eds) *Victims, Crime and Society*. London: SAGE. pp. 50–77.

Davies, P., Francis, P., and Wyatt, T. (2014) 'Taking invisible crimes and social harm seriously', in P. Davies, P. Francis, and T. Wyatt (eds) *Invisible Crimes and Social Harms*. Basingstoke: Palgrave Macmillan.

Elias, R. (1986) *The Politics of Victimisation: Victims, Victimology, and Human Rights*. Oxford: Oxford University Press.

——(1993) *Victims Still: The Political Manipulation of Crime Victims*. London: SAGE.

European Commission (n.d.) 'Rights of the victim'. Available at http://ec.europa.eu/justice /criminal/victims/rights/index_en.htm.

——(2001) '2001/220/JHA: Council framework decision of 15 March 2001 on the standing of victims in criminal proceedings'. Available at http://eur-lex.europa.eu/Lex UriServ/LexUriServ.do?uri=CELEX:32001F0220:en:HTML.

——(2013) 'Directive 2012/29/EU of the European Parliament and of the Council of 25 October 2012 establishing minimum standards on the rights, support and protection of victims of crime, and replacing Council Framework Decision 2001/220/JHA'. Available at http://ec.europa.eu/justice/criminal/files/victims/guidance_victims_rights_directive_en.pdf.

Fassin, D. (2011) 'The trace: violence, truth and the politics of the body', *Social Research*, 78(2): 281–98.

——(2012) *Humanitarian Reason*. Berkeley: University of California Press.

Fassin, D. and Rechtman, R. (2009) *The Empire of Trauma: An Inquiry into the Condition of Victimhood*. Princeton: Princeton University Press.

Furedi, F. (2002) *Culture of Fear: Risk Taking and the Morality of Low Expectation*. London: Cassell.

Geis, G. (1973) 'Victimization patterns in white collar crime', in I. Drapkin. and E. Viano (eds) *Victimology: A New Focus, Vol. V: Exploiters and Exploited*. USA: Lexington Books.

Goodey, J. (2005) *Victims and Victimology*. London: Longmans.

HMSO (2004) 'Domestic Violence, Crime and Victims Act 2004'. London: The Stationary Office. Available at http://www.legislation.gov.uk/ukpga/2004/28/pdfs/ukpga_20040028_en.pdf.

Home Office (2001) *Justice for All*. Available at https://www.cps.gov.uk/publications/ docs/jfawhitepaper.pdf.

Home Office (2005) 'The code of practice for victims of crime'. London: The Stationary Office.

International Campaign for Justice in Bhopal (2013) 'In their words'. Available at http:// www.bhopal.net/what-happened/that-night-december-3-1984/in-their-words.

——(2014a) 'Mission statement and guiding principles'. Available at http://www.bhopal .net/about-icjb/guiding-principles.

——(2014b) 'Survivor memories – 29th anniversary'. Available at http://www.bhopal.net/ survivor-memories-29th-anniversary.

——(2014c) 'The death toll: quantifying immeasurable loss'. Available at http://www .bhopal.net/what-happened/that-night-december-3-1984/the-death-toll.

——(2014d) 'The ongoing health crisis'. Available at http://www.bhopal.net/what-happened /1990-present/ongoing-health-crisis.

Jaishankar, K. (2014) 'Rights in newly industrialized countries', in I. Vanfraechem, A. Pemberton, F. M. Ndahinda (eds) *Justice for Victims Perspectives on Rights, Transition and Reconciliation*. Oxon: Routledge. pp. 66–88.

Jewkes, Y. (2011) *Media and Crime* (2nd edition). London: SAGE.

Jupp, V., Davies, P., and Francis, P. (1999) 'The features of invisible crimes', in P. Davies, P. Francis, and V. Jupp (eds) *Invisible Crimes: Their Victims and Their Regulation*. Basingstoke: Palgrave Macmillan.

Kalelkar, A. S. and Little, A. D. (1988) 'Investigation of large-magnitude incidents: Bhopal as a case study'. Presented at *The Institution of Chemical Engineers Conference on Preventing Major Chemical Accidents*, London, England, May 1988. Available at http://storage.dow.com. edgesuite.net/dow.com/Bhopal/casestdy.pdf.

Kinsella, B. (2011) 'Tackling knife crime together – a review of local anti-knife crime projects. A report by Brooke Kinsella'. London: Home Office. Available at https://www.gov.uk/government/uploads/system/uploads/attachment_data/file/97777/tackling-knife-crime-report.pdf.

Malimath, V. S. (2003) 'Committee on Reforms of Criminal Justice System Government of India, Ministry of Home Affairs'. India: Ministry of Home Affairs. Available at http://www.mha.nic.in/hindi/sites/upload_files/mhahindi/files/pdf/criminal_justice_system.pdf.

Mawby, R. I. and Walklate, S. (1994) *Critical Victimology: International Perspectives*. London: SAGE.

Ministry of Justice (2005) 'The code of practice for victims of crime'. London: The Stationary Office. Available at https://www.gov.uk/government/uploads/system/uploads/attachment_data/file/254459/code-of-practice-victims-of-crime.pdf.

Mishra, P. K., Samarth, R. M., Pathak, N., Jain, S. K., Banerjee, S., and Maudar, K. K. (2009) 'Bhopal gas tragedy; review of clinical and experimental findings after 25 years', *International Journal of Occupational Medicine and Environmental Health*, 22(3): 193–202.

Moore, S. E. H. (2014) *Crime and the Media*. Basingstoke: Palgrave Macmillan.

Murthy, R. S. (1990) 'Bhopal', *International Journal of Mental Health*, 19(2): 30–35.

——(2002a) 'Bhopal gas leak disaster: impact on health and mental health', in J. Havenaar, J. Cwikel, and E. J. Bromet (eds) *Toxic Turmoil: Psychological and Societal Consequences of Ecological Disasters*. New York: Springer. pp. 129–48.

Murthy, R. S. (2002b) 'Mental health report: mental health impact of Bhopal gas disaster', *The Bhopal Memory Project*. Available at http://bhopal.bard.edu/resources/research.php?action=getfile&id=381523.

Payne, S. (2009) 'Redefining justice: addressing the individual needs of victims and witnesses'. London: Ministry of Justice.

Pearce, F. and Tombs, S. (1989) 'Bhopal: Union Carbide and the hubris of the capitalist technocracy', *Social Justice*, 16(2): 116–45.

——(1998) *Toxic Capitalism: Corporate Crime and the Chemical Industry*. Dartmouth: Ashgate.

——(2012) *Bhopal: Flowers at the Altar of Profit and Power*. North Somercotes: CrimeTalk Books.

Reeves, H. and Dunn, P. (2010) 'The status of victims and witnesses in the twenty-first century', in A. Bottoms, and J. V. Roberts (eds) *Hearing the Victim: Adversarial Justice, Crime, Victims and the State*. Collumpton, Devon: Willan. pp. 46–67.

Sathyamala, C. (2009) 'Learning from Bhopal: Bhopal: reflections on justice activism from a health professional', *Global Social Policy: Special Issue: The Bhopal Disaster*, 9(3): 311–27.

Satish, M. (2008) 'The role of the victim in the Indian criminal justice system', in W.-C. Chan (ed.) *Support for Victims of Crime in Asia*. Oxon: Routledge. pp. 160–73.

Sebba, L. (2008) 'Wither victim policies? A view from the crossroads', in W.-C. Chan (ed.) *Support for Victims of Crime in Asia*. Oxon: Routledge. pp. 81–112.

Singh, N. K. (1989) 'The horror continues: horror continues for Bhopal gas victims', *India Today*, 15 March 1989. Available at http://indiatoday.intoday.in/story/horror-continues-for-bhopal-gas-victims/1/323232.html.

Spalek, B. (2006) *Crime Victims: Theory, Policy and Practice*. Basingstoke: Palgrave Macmillan.

Spalek, B. and King, S. (2007) 'Farepak victims speak out'. London: Centre for Crime and Justice Studies.

Supreme Court of India (1989) 'Union Carbide Corpn. v. Union of India'. Available at http://storage.dow.com.edgesuite.net/dow.com/Bhopal/1989_Settlement.pdf.

——(1991) 'Union Carbide Cororation and others versus Union of India and others'. Available at http://storage.dow.com.edgesuite.net/dow.com/Bhopal/1991_Review_order.pdf.

——(2007) 'Bhopal Gas Peedith Mahila Udyog Sangathan & Anr. v. Union of India'. Available at http://storage.dow.com.edgesuite.net/dow.com/Bhopal/scbhopal3.pdf.

Tombs, S. and Whyte, D. (2010a) 'Crime, harm and corporate power', in J. Muncie, D. Talbot, and R. Walters (eds) *Crime: Global and Local*. Collumpton, Devon: Willan. pp. 137–72.

——(2010b) 'Reflections upon the limits of a concept: "victims" and corporate crime', *International Journal of Victimology*, 8(2): 184–99.

United Nations (1985) 'Declaration of basic principles of justice for victims of crime and abuse of power'. Available at http://www.un.org/documents/ga/res/40/a40r034.htm.

——(1996) 'Use and application of United Nations standards and norms in crime prevention and criminal justice: use and application of the basic principles of Justice for victims of crime and abuse of power'. Available at http://www.uncjin.org/Documents/6comm/16e.pdf.

——(1999) 'Handbook on justice for victims: on the use and application of the basic principles of justice for victims of crime and abuse of power'. Available at http://www.uncjin.org/Standards/9857854.pdf.

Walklate, S. (1989) *Victimology: The Victim and the Criminal Justice Process*. Oxon: Routledge.

——(2007) *Imagining the Victim of Crime*. Maidenhead, Berkshire: Open University Press.

Weber, L., Fishwick, E., and Marmo, M. (2014) *Crime, Justice and Human Rights*. Basingstoke: Palgrave Macmillan.

Whyte, D. (2007) 'Victims of corporate crime', in S. Walklate (ed.) *Handbook of Victims and Victimology*. Cullompton, Devon: Willan. pp. 446–63.

Zavestoski, S. (2009) 'The struggle for justice in Bhopal: a new/old breed of transnational social movement', *Global Social Policy: Special Issue: The Bhopal Disaster*, 9(3): 383–407.

Part III

Justice

Chapter 6

Justice as therapy?

Introduction

Chapter 2 considered the impact of crime and charted the convergence of two narratives both claiming to make sense of that impact: the victim narrative and the trauma narrative. Further evidence of the salience of these narratives has been discussed in Chapters 3, 4 and 5. Implicit in this discussion, and particularly in the previous section on testimony, have been a series of questions pertaining to the demand of victims to be at least heard if not listened to. Of course, victims as complainants have the opportunity to be heard within any criminal justice system through various mechanisms for providing evidence and/or testimony as a witness and/or complainant. Nonetheless, Chapter 2 alluded to inherent problems within these opportunities from the victim's point of view. Such opportunities, as the term 'evidence' implies, are not necessarily the means by which the victim tells 'their story'. They are the means by which the legal process is equipped to make judgements of guilt or innocence in particular cases. Indeed, even in those circumstances, such 'testimonies' can be found wanting in terms of their accuracy, as much work on eyewitness evidence demonstrates. Moreover, as discussed in Chapter 4, using victims' stories as a source of data for the victimologist adds a valuable layer of understanding to the victim experience, but still needs to be handled with care. The concept of testimony, being heard and/or listened to, from the victims' point of view can mean something different than either traditional criminal justice understandings convey or biographical data that might be of value for the victimologist can capture. Chapter 5 outlined that these 'voices' face further problems of structural invisibility when they are situated outside of the justice process. Yet 'policy has proceeded as if "testis" (the testimony of a person as a third party in a trial or law suit) can be conflated with "superstes" (a person who has lived through something and can thereby bear witness to it)' (Agamben 1999: 13). A similar conflation was noted in Chapter 2 in the contemporary allusion to 'trauma'. In this chapter we shall explore how the process commented on by Agamben has manifested itself within contemporary criminal justice policy.

Wemmers (2009: 401) reports that, 'Victims come to the criminal justice system seeking recognition and validation of what has happened to them'. However, as Chapter 1 implied, the extent to which such recognition and validation occurs is subject to much debate and is largely contingent upon what kind of victim they are and of what kind of crime. Indeed these questions become even more complex when considered in relation to victims of state or corporate crime (Kauzlarich, 2014 and Chapter 5). However, if one of the drivers for recognition and validation for the victim is the suffering that the impact of crime has caused them, then, as the discussion in Chapter 2 intimated, this too can be both difficult to predict and hugely variable. Nonetheless, as Doak (2014) reminds us, there have been consistent international efforts to ensure that victims are treated with respect and dignity. Indeed this is one way to take on board the need for recognition and validation. It is, of course, important to note that much progress has been made across a wide range of jurisdictions to provide circumstances in which those victim/witnesses deemed 'vulnerable' are handled with sensitivity. Adhering to standards of policy and practice that embrace these kinds of principles has been taken to mean a range of things, from the implementation of compensation schemes to the development of support services to how criminal justice processes themselves might operate with the victim in mind. How such standards might materialise in practice, however, remains an open question (see for example Shapland, 2010).

As noted in Chapter 5, in general terms what victims want (or 'need') from any criminal justice system is in some respects fairly straightforward: the desire to be kept informed about 'their' case, guidance about what to expect from the criminal justice system, practical advice, and sometimes also reassurance and counselling (see Goodey, 2005). There is also evidence to suggest that some victims would appreciate the opportunity to express how a crime has affected them: to say how they felt. Of course, there are different ways in which a victim may express their feelings about the impact of crime. Retribution, restitution, reparation and restoration capture a range of emotions and are all differently emphasised within different criminal justice contexts. They all connote different ways in which a victim might express their feelings. Being victimised can just as easily provoke a victim to revenge as promote forgiveness, and a criminal justice system in its policy orientation can provide the victim with different ways of giving expression to these feelings. The policy initiatives that are the focus of this chapter, in affording the opportunity to give the victim a voice, capture some aspects of the emotional facets of the justice process.

Often starting from the position that victims are the forgotten voice of the criminal justice system (a process that has systematically stolen their 'conflicts' from them, qua Christie, 1977 and as illustrated in Chapter 5), initiatives that focus on giving victims a voice in the criminal justice system stem from a commitment that justice can be done better: that is, justice can be more sensitively nuanced to take account of victims' feelings. This vision of justice takes as a given that emotions have always been central to the workings of the criminal justice system (Karstedt, 2002) but that the emotionality of the system has been focused on exploring the state of mind of the defendant, or capturing the imagination of the jury, rather than taking account of what the process means for the victim and does to the victim. Focusing on the victim in this way needs to be understood against the backcloth of what is referred to as 'therapeutic jurisprudence'. Such a vision of the justice system is not without its critics and the debates that this has generated need not be of concern here. However, thinking about the potential ways in which justice might have a therapeutic element to it draws attention to the central role that emotions have within the criminal justice process for all parties within it. It also facilitates one way of considering how that process can either enhance or diminish an individual's sense of well-being. Doak (2011: 439) observes that 'there are more effective means of assisting the process of emotional catharsis and addressing mental health issues than reliance on the criminal justice system', and this point is in many ways beyond dispute. Nonetheless, recent policy agendas across the globe have moved in the direction of affording the victim a voice and this movement gels with an embrace of thinking about the potential for justice to be therapeutic. These moves are evidenced in two ways. First by the desire to offer the victim a more structured opportunity to participate in the criminal justice system so that they can voice the impact that a crime has had on them: victim impact statements. Victim impact statements give victims an opportunity to present their account of what has happened to them: to tell their story either during the evidence-gathering process or as a part of the court proceedings. Second by considering the ways in which a more structured opportunity might be made available for the offender to offer an apology to the victims and for the victim to offer forgiveness to the offender: restorative justice. Braithwaite (2002: 564) comments:

> The restorative method is to discuss consequences of injustices and to acknowledge them appropriately as a starting point toward healing the hurts of injustice and transforming the conditions that allowed injustice to flourish.

So restorative justice initiatives offer a space in which victims can present their version of events without being subjected to cross-examination or answering questions within the boundaries set by the questioner in the context of the courtroom. Each of these policy initiatives afford the victim a voice and in so doing may also provide the opportunity of healing for the victim – one of the central tenets of therapeutic jurisprudence. This shared focus on giving the victim a voice, and the potential for that process to repair some of the harm done by crime, underpins the question with which this chapter is concerned: justice as therapy? In what follows we shall discuss each of the policy directions suggested above (victim impact statements and restorative justice) in turn, before turning our attention to how and under what conditions they either give a voice to the victim of crime or provide the opportunity for healing to take place.

Victim impact statements

There are different ways in which a victim (of crime) might be afforded the space to participate in any criminal justice system (Edwards, 2004). In reviewing the various structural roles that a victim might be offered, Wemmers (2005: 130) concluded that overall the available evidence suggested, as far as sentencing is concerned, that victims were largely in favour of judges retaining full control over sentencing decisions. Such evidence notwithstanding, it is the case that many common-law countries have introduced the opportunity for the victim to provide the court with information about the impact of the crime as a means of participating in the criminal justice process (see, for example, Roberts and Manikis, 2013: 245–46). The question is, at what point, and under what conditions, might such participation occur? There are a number of different ways issues such as these might be addressed. For the purposes of this chapter we have chosen to introduce these questions, and the debates that victim participation generates, in the first part of our sixth case study.

Case study: massacre in flat 12, London, June 2008

In June 2008 two French students, Laurent Bonomo and Gabriel Ferez were tied up and murdered in their flat in South East London. Between them, they were stabbed 243 times and then their flat was set on fire. The apparent motive for this crime was burglary, though little of great value was taken from the flat. As a crime, its particularly violent nature, and the fact that the victims were French nationals studying in London as exchange students, meant that it made the headlines in the newspapers in both France and the UK, and was subsequently followed in some detail. When the perpetrators were brought to trial, the parents of these two young men were given the opportunity to present a statement to the court addressing the impact that this crime had had on them and their families. These statements were published in full in *The Daily Mail* in 2009. What follows is an analysis of them. (For an overview of the role of victim statements at sentencing see Erez and Roberts, 2014.)

Victim impact statement: Guy Bonomo

Guy Bonomo, Laurent's father, presented this victim impact statement to the court. In it he speaks directly to the defendants. His key question is: Why? Why did you do this to our children? Why have you not told the truth to the court? Why do you not feel sorry for what you have done? These questions are couched in strong words: 'atrocity', 'lack of remorse' and 'conscience', clearly conveying that without answers he, as a parent 'cannot move on and find peace'. He goes on to tell the court something about his son. He was a 'fantastic boy', clearly loved very much by all who knew him: his family, younger sister and wider relations. All of whom Bonomo says have been hugely affected by his son's murder: in an event that has left him 'tormented by the images of his suffering'. He ends in almost a begging tone by appealing to the defendant to say why these things happened.

Guy Bonomo's full victim impact statement is available at http://www. dailymail.co.uk/news/article-1190846/Laurent-Bonomos-fathers-heartbreaking -victim-impact-statement-I-bear-think-evil-walk-streets-again.html.

Victim impact statement: Françoise Villemont

Françoise Villemont, the mother of Gabriel Ferez, presented her victim impact statement to the court. Interestingly, she has little to say or ask of the defendants but uses very strong terms to describe what happened: a 'barbaric act', 'inexcusable', 'indescribable', 'gratuitous torture' from which her family's life has been 'shattered forever'. She too tells the court something of her son: a 'sociable boy', 'kind', 'sensitive', the kind of young man who 'loved life' and offered all who came into contact with him an 'everyday happiness'.

Françoise Villemont's full victim impact statement is available at http:// www.dailymail.co.uk/news/article-1190976/Gabriel-Ferezs-mothers-victim -impact-statement-full.html.

The text above comprises selected extracts from each of these victim impact statements. However, just from these extracts we are exposed to the distress, pain and suffering that these parents have gone through, and were continuing to go through at the time of the trial. This is perhaps not very surprising. There are, however, some other issues in these extracts that are worthy of further exploration.

Statements of the kind referred to above represent one way of giving a voice to the victim, in this case the victims' family, at one point in the criminal justice system. In the UK this kind of statement, in cases of murder and manslaughter, can be presented to the court. The *Victims' Advocates Scheme* offers the families of those bereaved in such cases the opportunity to present a statement to the court outlining the impact that that event had on them (a Family Impact Statement) once a conviction has been secured for the crime and before sentencing has been pronounced. The two families referred to above did this. In an initial evaluation of this scheme. Sweeting et al. (2008) suggested that families welcomed these statements as an opportunity to have their voice heard in court and, as a result, felt a sense of positive and active involvement in the trial. They also reported the process to be therapeutic. Indeed, in the extracts above it is possible to discern some resonance with these findings. At a minimum, Guy Bonomo had the chance to ask the defendants to explain to him why they had done what they had. This is the kind of question that many victims have, and the opportunity to express it directly to those responsible is considered to be an important process for them. However, there is something more to be said about the extracts above.

Memorialising the dead?

In each extract above we can see the desire on the part of each parent to present their child as a whole person: as someone with hopes, aspirations, friends, not just a victim or a damaged body. Rock (2010: 216) comments on the importance (for the families of the bereaved) of memorialisation and 'normalisation of the dead', and these practices are evident above. At the same time, each of these statements is also (understandably) deeply emotional and it is at this juncture that some tensions emerge. Rock (2010: 219) also observed that other court members displayed 'civil inattention' whilst such statements were being made. This observation is supported in the work of Booth (2012), who, in a detailed study of eighteen sentencing hearings in the New South Wales Supreme Court, observed the different points at which victim participation in the form of the oral presentation of victim impact statements was 'cooled out'. In other words, the potential conflict between the expressive (emotional) function of the victim impact statement and the legal focus of sentencing was managed so that the role of the latter was not taken over by the presence of the former. Indeed it should be noted that despite moves to offer participation in the form of advocates in Ohio in the United States, few of the families of the homicide victims in the study reported by Englebrecht et al. (2014) could recall much detail about what the role of the advocate actually was. So if, for all practical purposes, the end product of these kind of developments is patchy and subject to the institutional sensitivities of the court personnel, what function do victim impact statements serve in cases of this kind, or indeed more generally?

Participation?

Roberts and Manikis (2013) observe that the opportunity for a victim to present the impact that a crime has had on them to the court can occur at junctures other than the point of sentencing (see also the overview by Booth and Carrington, 2007). In England and Wales this takes the form of a victim personal statement. This can be taken at the time of any offence and can form part of the papers associated with a particular crime which are presented to the court. The purpose this scheme is to offer an (optional) opportunity to the victim of crime to relate to all the agencies of the criminal justice system how a crime has affected them, and to provide the system with more information about that impact. In an early assessment of this scheme, Tapley (2005: 42) reported that 'Victim Personal Statements were not being offered to victims on a consistent and regular basis' and Graham et al. (2004), in a more qualitative evaluation, pointed to problems in victims' understanding of the scheme. In a more recent review, Roberts and Manikis (2011), using data from the *Witness and Victim Experience Survey*, found that from 2007 to 2010 only 42 per cent of victims/witnesses recall being offered the opportunity to make a personal statement, and of these 55 per cent actually made a statement, with 67 per cent of them recalling it having been taken into account. This study also found significant variations in the use of this scheme by type of crime and geography. More recent work, also by Roberts and Manikis (2013: 258, *our insert*), concludes optimistically that,

> greater participation in the VPS (victim personal statement) programme would increase overall victim welfare in this country. This will come about if a greater effort is made to inform crime victims of the opportunity to depose a statement in the first place.

Moreover, work reported by Mastroncinque (2014) suggests that offence type is a factor in whether or not victims are notified about making such a statement, and such notification practices influence their subsequent willingness to do so. These findings add to, and endorse, the assessment made by Walklate (2007: 119) that,

> there are clearly issues here for practitioners to consider that centre on such questions as to who takes the statement, how is it done, where is it done, and how it is brought to the attention to the court.

Emotionally intelligent?

So, if at one end of the spectrum families of murder victims receive 'civil inattention' (qua Rock) and are 'cooled out' (qua Booth), and at the other end of the spectrum there are other barriers to victims participating effectively in an impact statement designed to be part of the papers presented to the court, to what extent do policy moves of this kind equate with hearing victims' voices, and in what sense? Of course, as Snell and Tombs (2011) astutely observe, and as we have demonstrated in Chapter 5, victims of corporate crime have no space to be heard since their victimisation more often than not falls outside of the remit of real crime (see also Croall, 2014). In this sense, the space to be heard that is afforded to the victim of 'conventional' crime is considerable. However, if in offering that space victims are either not informed about such an opportunity, choose not to take it, or indeed if they do take it and the process itself leaves much to be desired, what do such opportunities amount to in real terms?

Therapeutic?

Erez (1999: 551) observed some time ago now that 'Proceedings that provide victims with a voice or "process control" enhance their satisfaction with justice and a sense of fair treatment'. This in itself, in her view, justified the presence of a therapeutic jurisprudence and/or initiatives with some therapeutic intent. Concerns with victim satisfaction have indeed been part of the rationale for the introduction of such schemes: a need to ensure and enhance ongoing victim engagement with the criminal justice system in the interests of the justice system as a whole, over and above providing the court with more detailed information about the impact of a crime. Additionally, Booth (2012) comments that the policy moves in this direction need also to be situated within wider changes in societal sensibilities about the impact of crime and the role of the law in perpetuating or alleviating that impact. Moreover, Erez and Roberts (2010) suggest that whilst victim impact statements have a communicative function, they also have an expressive function that can be validated in the courtroom if used appropriately. Such improvements in use and practice may avoid the tendency for victims to be 'ignored as comprehensively as ever' (Sanders, 1999: 4). However, in adding some further detail to the observations made by Booth (2012), it is important to note two other tendencies underlying this kind of policy shift. One is the historical coincidence between this kind of policy initiative and the movement in thinking about victimhood from secondary victimisation to trauma (as highlighted in Chapter 2). The second is the emergence of what Sherman (2003) has called concerns with 'emotionally intelligent justice'. This version of justice is concerned not so much with the emotional sensitivities of criminal justice institutions and their actors (which can explain some of the difficulties associated with victim impact statements and their 'fit' with the court and its culture) – Sherman's (2003) observation returns us to the question of doing justice differently. It is at this juncture that thinking about justice as therapy leads to a consideration of the problems and possibilities for restorative justice.

Thinking about restorative justice

Goodey (2005) intimates that restorative justice is more often than not presented as victim-centred justice. Indeed United Nations resolutions and those passed by the Council of Europe imply almost a paradigm shift in criminal justice thinking towards this policy initiative, so much so that in 2002 McEvoy et al. could comment on the 'swagger' that such policies seemed to have, especially in acquiring political embrace and funding when other policies were being somewhat less successful. Indeed some would argue that it is a moot point as to the extent to which this kind of justice is victim-centred at all since one of its central concerns is to find a more constructive way of reintegrating the offender rather than ostracising them (Braithwaite, 1989), albeit by 'the bringing together of victims and offenders' (Hudson, 2003: 178). It is perhaps only as a consequence that the end product of this process might repair some harm done to the victim. Nonetheless, restorative justice initiatives have developed across a wide range of jurisdictions and, as we shall see in Chapter 7, in some contexts provide the bedrock for practices of reconciliation in post-conflict societies.

Such developments have continued apace, despite the evidence that what is actually meant by restorative justice is highly contested. Indeed Miers (2004) refers to it as an elastic concept. It is a concept that has become a catch-all category for a whole range of different policy initiatives that loosely involve the victim and/or require the offender to make amends for their offence in some way. In a similar vein, Strang et al. (2013) point to a diverse range of theoretical perspectives laying claim to the origins of this policy direction. Routinely its increasing popularity has been attributed to the work of Braithwaite (1989), but it is also notable that Collins' (2004) work on interaction rituals has provided a further conduit for thinking about the value of restorative justice from the victims' point of view (see for example Rossner, 2011; 2013). Indeed, it is the question of what this kind of engagement with the criminal justice process can do, or not do, for victims that is of interest here (for a useful general evaluation of the limits of restorative justice see Daly, 2006). As a result, what follows does not constitute an overall evaluation of restorative justice. The reader is directed to a wide range of handbooks on restorative justice that do this more or less effectively (see *inter alia* Johnstone and Van Ness, 2007; Sullivan and Tift, 2006). Here we are centrally concerned with the role and nature of the victims' voice in restorative justice.

In discussing restorative justice as a victim-centred approach, Braithwaite (2002: 570) suggests five standards that might meet with such a focus: remorse over injustice, apology, censure of the act, forgiveness of the person, and mercy. It is self-evident that all of these demand emotional work on the part of all participants, including the victim. In offering an overview of the capacity for restorative justice to offer victims emotional redress, Doak (2011: 442) suggests there is little evidence that it can do this and observes that, 'Specific issues of emotional and psychological well-being are often conflated in the literature with more general inquiries as to the overall levels of satisfaction'. Here, drawing on the work of Zehr (2001), we shall endeavour to add some flesh to these anecdotal bones in the second part of our case study for this chapter.

Transcending: Reflections of Crime Victims: Portraits and Interviews, by Howard Zehr (2001)

In this book Zehr presents the stories of 39 victims of crime in their own words, accompanied by photographs. They are the stories of ordinary people who have found a way to come to terms with extraordinary and exceptional experiences of serious, violent crime. These people were primary victims and the use of the word 'trauma' to describe what happened to them may well be appropriate (see also the discussion in Chapter 2). These stories are very varied but they are all deeply moving. Each of these individuals gives voice to the full range of feelings any individual might have in response to challenging, tragic circumstances, from revenge to forgiveness. They present themselves as neither victims nor survivors but a complex mix of these all at the same time as they move forward in their lives with a view to coming to terms with what happened to them. Zehr (2001) found it difficult to find a word that would encompass the experiences of all of these people. He settled for 'transcending': 'rising above, or going beyond the limits, triumphing over negative or restrictive aspects, extending notably beyond ordinary limits' (Zehr, 2001: 2). For example, Wilma Derksen, one of Zehr's participants, whose daughter was kidnapped, murdered, and her killer never found, has this to say:

> Even though the killer has never been found, I think I have experienced justice ... Justice is, for the lack of better words, the healing of the soul ... We as victims need truth, judgement of the wrongdoing, validation and vindication ... I realize that a trial doesn't guarantee these things.
>
> (Zehr, 2001: 116)

And Ellen Halbert, another participant who was beaten and raped by a stranger in her own home and left for dead says:

> Rage was going to destroy me if I didn't forgive this man. I'm a big believer in forgiveness but I don't believe that I have to go somewhere and say 'I forgive you.' ... It's something that you have to do for yourself.
>
> (Zehr, 2001: 170)

Janet Bakke, abused as a child by her stepfather, when given the opportunity to question him, adds:

> I got to hold him accountable to *me* not the justice system, not his case management officer. And when he said 'You didn't put me here; I put myself here', it was the most powerful thing he could have said because he finally admitted it.
>
> (Zehr, 2001: 14)

We return to the themes addressed in each of these extracts below, but for now it is worth noting that the common thread that ties all of these stories together is optimism. All of these individuals have risen above their experiences; they have not forgotten them, but have reached different points along a road in which self-blame and vindictiveness no longer seem to drive their sense of self and self-identity.

In the conclusion to this book, Zehr offers his own observations on the stories that he brought together. There he suggests that,

> The cycle of victimisation is comprehensive. I often visualise it as three overlapping circles: a crisis of self-image (who am I really?), a crisis of meaning (what do I believe?), and a crisis of relationship (whom can I trust?).
>
> (Zehr, 2001: 188)

These three crises touch upon taken-for-granted assumptions that we all hold dear: that we have some control over our lives, that social life is ordered and predictable, and that we are accepted and can accept others. This choir of voices, as Zehr refers to them, makes good music, and that music asks us to listen to it carefully since it raises some difficult questions for those who would put victims' voices at the heart of the criminal-justice process. It is music that also asks some hard questions about restorative justice in terms of who might benefit from it, for what kinds of crimes, and under what circumstances. Whilst the choir might make music as one voice, Zehr's collection illustrates that responding to each of these voices individually is complex and challenging. However, what this collection also ensures is some thoughtful consideration concerning how restorative justice might deal with the complex array of victims' emotions revealed within it. The first three extracts from Zehr's book draw our attention to three main themes that occur within the wider literature on the emotional role of restorative justice for victims: the opportunity for validation, the opportunity to receive an apology, or at least admit responsibility to the victim, and the opportunity for forgiveness. These three themes inform the discussion that follows.

Victim validation

Chapter 2 commented on the ways in which the criminal justice process denies the opportunity for the victim/complainant to tell their story, and Chapter 5 evidenced how victims' stories can be silenced despite their prominence outwith the justice system. The way in which a case proceeds through the system does not lend itself easily to the kind of free narrative that occurs between people when they are offering accounts of past events. Restorative justice affords both the victim and the offender the opportunity to do that, to speak in their own words at their own pace about what happened and how they felt about it. This resonates, as Doak (2011: 442) observes, with the 'talking therapies' in which talking about traumatic events in one's life, like violent crime, becomes a means whereby individuals are encouraged to deal with them. Being able to offer accounts of what happened in this way affords the opportunity of validation for the victim: their voice being heard in their own terms, and thereby being acknowledged. Thus there is some evidence to suggest that being made aware that they were not to blame for what happened to them (qua Janet above) has significant positive outcomes for victims. Indeed Doak (2011: 444) lends some support to the view that restorative justice initiatives are better equipped to offer some kind of therapy than court-based initiatives. Moreover, a separate though connected outcome also seems to be improved levels of satisfaction with the justice process on the part of victims who participate with restorative justice in this way. However, little is known about the longer-term emotional impact that being able to offer their version of events has for the victim. Indeed, as in the case of Wilma quoted above, some of this kind of validation can come from the wider community and friends, as much as it can be generated by a criminal-justice response. Having a space to tell your story in this kind of way can, however, be impeded by other structural factors, as in cases of domestic violence, for example (see Daly and Stubbs, 2006), and the effect of these kinds of structural barriers is an issue we shall return to in the conclusion.

Apologies

Apologies are complex interaction processes (Tavuchis, 1991). In the context of restorative justice they are frequently intertwined with forgiveness, though the first does not necessarily lead to the second. Hence it is useful to consider them as separate possibilities. Scheff (1998) defines an apology as symbolic reparation that can occur when the victim and offender meet face to face and thereby can offer an opportunity for some emotional healing. In the case of Janet, above, the implied apology in her offender taking responsibility for his actions, whilst not wholly believed by her, was an important moment for her to move on. Janet's reaction in this respect raises important and interesting questions about the nature and role of apologies.

Dhami (2012: 46) observes that, for some, apologies are central to restorative justice and whilst an apology appears to be one of the commonly recurring outcomes of restorative justice (see *inter alia* Bonta et al., 1998; Shapland et al., 2006) Umbreit (1995) reports it as being important for victims, though what this means precisely is unclear. Daly (2006: 139) makes a distinction between 'ideal typical apologies' where an offender might be forgiven by their victim and what she calls 'sincere apologies', where the two parties might reach some mutual understanding about what has happened for which the offender is truly sorry but in which forgiveness does not necessarily occur. In discussing what an apology might look like, Dhami (2012: 47) reports that they include,

> (1) admitting responsibility for the behaviour and outcomes, (2) acknowledging the harm done and that it was wrong, (3) expressing regret or remorse for the harm done, (4) offering to repair the harm or make amends, (5) promising not to repeat the behaviour in the future.

She goes on to report that an empirical examination of the role of apologies in a mediation scheme found that in just over a third of cases examined, perpetrators said they were sorry to the victim, which in most cases was accepted by the victim and was related to victim satisfaction with the outcome (Dhami, 2012). Interestingly, however, Dhami (2012: 57) also reports that the giving of an apology and the receipt of forgiveness were unrelated. So what actually counts as an apology, and the effect that it has, is neither simple nor straightforward. Indeed, if we add to these observations those made by Tavuchis (1991: 50) on the presence of third parties in apologies then we have a sense of the complexity involved:

Given the fact that third parties always introduce, represent, or develop a third set of interests once they enter into the proceedings, apologies in such circumstances, if forthcoming, are likely in one way or another to become subject to standards the disputants themselves might not have otherwise applied.

So whilst apologies might be a 'magic turning point that permit the conflicting parties to reconcile' (Brook and Warsharki-Brook, 2010: 516), little is really known about how and under what conditions this might happen and what, if any, might be the lasting effects of such an interchange. In a systematic review of restorative-justice projects, Strang et al. (2013: 42) report moderate success for restorative-justice conferences in affording the kind of emotional satisfaction sought by victims and acting as a forum in which apologies might take place. Tempering these findings, Doak (2011: 447) points to the importance of issues not only relating to specific cases that may impact upon the effectiveness of an apology but also factors pertaining to the underlying relationship between the victim and offender alongside cultural factors. He concludes that care needs to be taken in talking about apologies in restorative justice since they may gloss more fundamental questions associated with victim safety (see also Daly and Stubbs, 2006). Nonetheless, Takahashi (2005: 26) suggests, 'An apology cannot undo what has been done, but a sincere apology with remorse might increase the victim's empathy for the wrongdoer and open the door to forgiveness'. So what of forgiveness?

Forgiveness

As the foregoing discussion intimates, the relationship between apology and forgiveness can be a complicated one. Interestingly, Ellen, quoted above, suggests that you do not have to go somewhere to offer forgiveness, it is something that you do for yourself. Indeed Doak (2011: 447) endorses this and argues that forgiveness and apologies, in terms of theory and evidence, suffer from similar problems. Yet Rossner (2013: 4) comments:

> Victims who meet their offender and receive an apology are, more often than not, more forgiving, feel more sympathetic towards the offender, and are less likely to desire physical revenge.

It is possible that what underpins these differently emphasised conclusions is a conflation between what Blumstein (2010) has referred to as forgiveness as a sentiment and forgiveness as performance. Indeed there is evidence to suggest that restorative-justice thinking on this issue has been influenced by the work of Retzinger and Scheff (1996). They conceived of an apology/forgiveness as a transaction that linked the two together. This may not, in fact, be supported empirically or experientially, as the victim story cited above illustrates. Thus restorative justice projects might report victim expression of forgiveness (as a performative action) that may not equate with a change in sentiment for them as individuals. Indeed forgiveness as a sentiment may continue to coexist with other emotions until such time, as Ellen goes on to suggests above, a victim decides to forgive for *themselves* rather than as a product of any other intervention. At that juncture, a process of healing may well have begun for the victim, but when this happens, how it might be measured, what its relationship is with apologies, and what in fact forgiveness actually means for the victim or offender, are all largely under-explored issues within restorative justice.

To summarise, Braithwaite (2014: 7) states:

> Restorative justice reduces victim fear, post-traumatic stress symptoms, victim anger, vengefulness, victim beliefs that victim rights have been violated and increases victim feelings of personal safety and their belief that justice has been done.

Yet, as the discussion above implies, all of these claims are neither simple nor straightforward. In assessing the therapeutic potential for restorative justice, understanding the processes of restorative justice, its value and impacts for victims, and even its conceptual armoury, have all suffered from conflating issues of improved satisfaction with evidence of emotional healing. This has led Doak (2011: 451) to conclude that as yet we do not know how and under what conditions restorative justice will be therapeutic and when it may well prove to be the opposite. Arguably this is a result of not whether or not restorative justice has the inherent capacity to afford this kind of therapeutic space for victims, but is more a result of the fact that, despite the rhetoric, victims have not been at the centre of the emergence of restorative justice, or the prime focus of its evaluation. As an illustration of this last point, in a recent systematic evaluation study, Strang et al. (2013: 33) report:

> In all these studies, primary attention was focused on offender effects, especially on re-offending, rather than victim effects … indeed, there will never be any official record of victims who do not come to the attention of the police or where the identification of complainants/victims in a case is highly arbitrary.

For these kinds of reasons alone the information available on the emotional efficacy of restorative justice for victims is likely to be limited. Moreover, neither is there sufficient knowledge about how restorative justice works, as a process, for either victims or offenders. However, there seems to be some promise that using Collins' (2004) notion of interaction rituals may well give some better insight into these processes (see for example Rossner, 2011). The question remains, where does all this leave the notion of justice as therapy?

Conclusion: justice as therapy?

It is beyond dispute that much policy activity and effort, across a wide range of jurisdictions, have been centred on putting in place the kinds of policy initiatives discussed above. Moreover, that activity has in part been fuelled by a concern to make good the harm done by crime. In this respect, concerns about the victim have featured in a number of different ways. The effect of these concerns can be found in the evidence that exists supporting the view that through the validation of their experiences, receiving apologies, making space for forgiveness, and/or providing at a more prosaic level the opportunity to express how a crime has affected them, have beneficial outcomes for victims. In this sense, such justice practices can provide the opportunity for some repair work to take place. Justice can be therapeutic. However, that evidence, such as it is, also suggests that who benefits, for what kind of crime, and how that happens, is still uncertain and in some respects arbitrary. In other words it depends on who has the appropriate information, whether or not that information is appropriately received and how, if at all, it is then acted upon. It is in the spaces that this uncertainty provides that the scope exists for notions of the ideal victim, the deserving/undeserving victim and the hierarchy of victimisation (all discussed in Chapter 1) to perpetuate. In this respect the question mark that accompanies the title to this chapter – Justice as therapy? – still carries some weight. However, in summarising the issues presented here, the presence of this question mark needs further elaboration.

From this review there is evidence to support the observations made by Booth (2012). She connects the kinds of policy initiatives under discussion here to the wider context of changing social sensibilities. Increasing awareness of the impact of crime, coincident with the growth of the criminal victimisation survey as a source of information about crime, taken alongside a discourse that gives voice to the ways in which psychologically stressful events take their toll on people (trauma) and the development of support agencies in recognition of that toll, taken together provide the fertile ground for such policy directions to take root. In many ways, forging these interconnections is not a new observation. However, subsumed within this observation are (at least) two other issues. The first returns us to the observation made by Agamben (1999) quoted at the beginning of this chapter: the conflation of testis with superstes. This observation, in this context, asks us to engage in a fundamental reflection about what is meant by justice. It is without doubt that justice can be practiced more sensitively. Indeed in the study reported by Booth (2012) there is evidence to suggest that the court practitioners made every effort to do this. However sensitive justice does not equate with what might be called outcome justice. Sensitive justice might result in victims feeling more satisfied with their experiences of the criminal-justice process (one of the more consistent findings emanating from the research reviewed here), but that does not translate easily into apologies, forgiveness or the subject matter of the next chapter: reconciliation.

Fraser (2008) raises this question in a different context in which she asks whether or not acknowledgement equals justice. Here we might substitute validation for acknowledgement to capture aspects of the same issue. In many respects the answer to this question is obvious: No. So the conflation of testis with superstes (qua Agamben) results in presumptions around healing and acknowledgement not necessarily borne by social reality. In particular it renders invisible the wider context of victims' lives in which validation and healing can occur (acknowledgement) with family, friends and so on. At the same time, in terms of practice, this conflation evens out questions of structural inequalities (age, class, ethnicity, gender and so on) in which presumptions of (legitimate) victimhood can be sustained. Thus the question remains, if justice is to be construed as therapy: for whom and under what conditions?

The second issue subsumed by the observations made by Booth (2012) is the cultural conditions in which the kinds of changes in social sensibilities to which she refers are promoted. It is worth noting that the kinds of policy initiatives discussed here have taken root as neo-liberal policies (particularly within the English-speaking world) across economic agendas more broadly. These policies, despite the ebbs and flows of particular economies at particular points in time, have made increasing demands on criminal justice systems to do more with less (see *inter alia* Garland, 2001; Simon, 2007). This goes some way to explain the focus on better offender management within restorative justice, for example, rather than better victim management. Moreover, as the demands of neo-liberalism have taken hold, so has the need to ensure that the legitimacy of, and support for, justice is maintained. It is in this respect that Fraser's (2011) analysis of the 'cunning of history' fits with the shift towards victim-centred justice and/or justice as therapy with some resonance. Put simply, neo-liberal capitalism can accommodate identity politics and provide the conditions under which the conflations observed here and in Chapter 2 provide the platform for the increasing presence of victim voices. However, this is the case for only some victim voices. The case studies used to inform Chapters 3 and 5 clearly illustrate who, and under what conditions such voices may or may not be heard. The connections between these developments and the space for the emergence of the role of the cultural under particular economic conditions are evident and will be developed more fully in the conclusion to this book.

Further reading

There is a vast range of material on both victim impact statements and restorative justice. As a backcloth to that material, the work of Tavuchis (1991), *Mea Culpa: A Sociology of Apology and Reconciliation*, provides a provocative conceptual and critical agenda for thinking about these topics. In a similar vein, though rooted in more concrete research findings, the collection edited by Bottoms and Roberts (2010), *Hearing the Victim: Adversarial Justice, Crime Victims and the State*, makes for interesting reading. For a different collection of readings focused on restorative justice, see Sullivan and Tift (2006), *Routledge International Handbook of Restorative Justice*, and for a flavour of the kind of work developed by John Braithwaite under the umbrella of restorative justice take a look at the peace-building compared literature available from www.regnet .anu.edu.au. This literature affords an interesting link between the issues discussed in this chapter and the one that follows.

References

Agamben, G. (1999) *The Remnants of Auschwitz*. Brooklyn, NY: Zone Books.

Blumstein, J. (2010) 'Forgiveness, commemoration, and restorative justice: the role of moral emotions', *Metaphilosophy* 41(4): 582–617.

Bonta, J., Wallace-Capretta, S., and Rooney, J. (1998) 'Restorative justice: an evaluation of the restorative resolutions project (User report 1998–2005)'. Ottawa: Solicitor General Canada.

Booth, T. (2012) '"Cooling out" victims of crime: managing victims' participation in the sentencing process in a superior sentencing court', *Australian and New Zealand Journal of Criminology*, 445(2): 214–30.

Booth, T. and Carrington, K. (2007) 'A comparative analysis of the victim policies across the Anglo speaking world', in S. Walklate (ed.) *Handbook of Victims and Victimology*, London: Routledge-Willan. pp. 380–416.

Bottoms, A. and Roberts, J. V. (eds) (2010) *Hearing the Victim: Adversarial Justice, Crime Victims, and the State*. Cullompton: Willan.

Braithwaite, J. (1989) *Crime, Shame and Reintegration*. Cambridge: Cambridge University Press.

——(2002) 'Setting standards for restorative justice', *British Journal of Criminology*, 42(3): 563–77.

——(2014) 'Restorative justice and responsive regulation: The question of evidence'. Regnet Research Pater 2014/51. ANU. Available at www.regnet.anu.edu.au.

Brook, E. and Warsharki-Brook, S. (2010) 'The healing nature of apology and its contribution toward emotional reparation and closure in restorative justice encounters', in S. G. Shoham, P. Knepper, and M. Kett (eds) *International Handbook of Victimology*. Boca Raton, FL: CRC Press. pp. 511–36.

Christie, N. (1977) 'Conflicts as property', *British Journal of Criminology*, 17: 1–15.

Collins, R. (2004) *Interaction Ritual Chains*. Princeton, NJ: Princeton University Press.

Croall, H. (2014) 'Victims of corporate crime', in G. Bruinsma and D. Weisburd (eds) *Encyclopedia of Criminology and Criminal Justice*. New York: Springer. pp. 5480–90.

Daly, K. (2006) 'The limits of restorative justice', in D. Sullivan and L. Tift. (eds) *Routledge International Handbook of Restorative Justice*. Abingdon, Oxon: Routledge. pp. 34–46.

Daly, K. and Stubbs, J. (2006) 'Feminist engagement with restorative justice', *Theoretical Criminology*, 10: 9–28.

Dhami, M. (2012) 'Offer and acceptance of apology in victim-offender mediation', *Critical Criminology*, 20: 45–60.

Doak, J. (2011) 'Honing the stone: refining restorative justice as a vehicle for emotional redress', *Contemporary Justice Review*, 14(4): 439–56.

——(2014) 'Victims' rights in the criminal justice system', in G. Bruinsma and D. Weisburd (eds) *Encyclopedia of Criminology and Criminal Justice*. New York: Springer. pp. 5497–5507.

Edwards, I. (2004) 'An ambiguous participant: the crime victim and criminal justice decision-making', *British Journal of Criminology*, 44(6): 946–67.

Englebrecht, M. (2014) 'The struggle for "ownership of conflict": an exploration of victim participation and voice in the criminal justice system', *Criminal Justice Review*, 36(2): 129–51.

Erez, E. (1999) 'Who's afraid of the big bad victim? Victim impact statements as victim empowerment and enhancement of justice', *Criminal Law Review*, 20: 545–56.

Erez, E. and Roberts, J. V. (2010) 'Communication at sentencing: the expressive function of victim impact statements', in A. Bottoms and J. V. Roberts (eds) *Hearing the Victim: Adversarial Justice, Crime Victims and the State*. Cullompton, Devon: Willan. pp. 323–54.

Erez, E. and Roberts, J. (2014) 'Victim input at sentencing', in G. Bruinsma and D. Weisburd (eds) *Encyclopedia of Criminology and Criminal Justice*. New York: Springer. pp. 5425–34.

Fraser, N. (2008) *Scales of Justice: Reimagining Political Space in a Globalizing World*. Cambridge: Polity.

——(2011) 'Feminism, capitalism and the cunning of history', *New Left Review*, 56.

Garland, D. (2001) *The Culture of Control*. Oxford: Polity.

Goodey, J. (2005) *Victims and Victimology*. London: Longmans.

Graham, J., Woodfield, K., Tibble, M., and Kitchen, S. (2004) 'Testaments of harm: a qualitative evaluation of the victim personal statement scheme'. National Centre for Social Research, May.

Hudson, S. (2003) *Justice in the Risk Society*. London: Sage.

Johnstone, G. and Van Ness, D. W. (eds) (2007) *Handbook of Restorative Justice*. Cullompton, Devon: Willan.

Karstedt, S. (2002) 'Emotions and criminal justice', *Theoretical Criminology*, 6(3): 299–318.

Kauzlarich, D. (2014) 'Victims of state crime', in G. Bruinsma and D. Weisburd (eds) *Encyclopedia of Criminology and Criminal Justice*. New York: Springer. pp. 5490–97.

Mastroncinque, J. M. (2014) 'Victim personal statements: an analysis of notification and utilization', *Criminology and Criminal Justice*, 14(2): 216–34.

McEvoy, K., Mika, H., and Hudson, B. (2002) 'Introduction: practice, performance and prospects for restorative justice', *British Journal of Criminology*, 42(3): 469–75.

Miers, D. (2004) 'Situating and researching restorative justice in Great Britain', *Punishment and Society*, 6(1): 23–46.

Retzinger, S. and Scheff, T. (1996) 'Strategy for community conferences: emotions and social bonds', in B. Galaway and J. Hudson (eds) *Restorative Justice: International Perspectives*. London: SAGE. pp. 315–36.

Roberts, J. V. and Manikis, M. (2011) 'Victim personal statements at sentencing: a review of the empirical research'. London: Office of the Commissioner for Victims and Witnesses of England and Wales.

——(2013) 'Victim personal statements in England and Wales: latest and last trends from the Witness and Victim Experience Survey', *Criminology and Criminal Justice*, 13(3): 245–61.

Rock, P. (2010) '"Hearing the victim": the delivery of impact statements as ritual behaviour in four London trials for murder and manslaughter', in A. Bottoms and J. V. Roberts (eds) *Hearing the Victim: Adversarial Justice, Crime Victims, and the State*. Cullompton, Devon: Willan. pp. 212–23.

Rossner, M. (2011) 'Emotions and interaction ritual: a micro analysis of restorative justice', *British Journal of Criminology*, 51(1): 95–119.

——(2013) *Just Emotions: Rituals of Restorative Justice*. Oxford: Oxford University Press.

Sanders, A. (1999) 'Taking account of victims in the criminal justice system: a review of the literature'. Scottish Office Central Research Unit: Social Work Findings No. 32.

Scheff, T. (1998) 'Community conferences: shame and anger is therapeutic jurisprudence', *Revista Juridica,* Universidad Puerto Rico, 67: 97–119.

Shapland, J., Atkinson, A., Atkinson, H., Chapman, B. et al. (2006) 'Restorative justice in practice: the second report from the evaluation of three schemes'. Sheffield: Centre for Criminological Research, University of Sheffield.

Shapland, J. (2010) 'Victims and criminal justice in Europe', in S. G. Shoham, P. Knepper, and M. Kett. (eds) *International Handbook of Victimology.* Boca Raton, FL: CRC Press. pp. 347–72.

Sherman, L. W. (2003) 'Reason for emotion: reinventing justice with theories, innovations and research', *Criminology,* 41: 1–37.

Simon, J. (2007) *Governing Through Crime.* Oxford: Oxford University Press.

Snell, K. and Tombs, S. (2011) 'How do you get your voice heard when no-one will let you? Victimization at work', *Criminology and Criminal Justice,* 11(3): 207–24.

Strang, H., Sherman, L. W., Mayo-Wilson, E., Woods, D., and Ariel, B. (2013) 'Restorative Justice Conferencing (RJC) using face-to-face meetings of offenders and victims: effects on offender recidivism and victim satisfaction: a systematic review'. *Campbell Systematic Reviews,* 2013: 9, doi: 10.4073/csr.2013.10.

Sullivan, D. and Tift, L. (eds) (2006) *Routledge International Handbook of Restorative Justice.* Abingdon, Oxon: Routledge.

Sweeting, A., Owen, R., Turley, C., Rock, P. Garia-Sanche, M., Wilson, L., and Khan, U. (2008) 'Evaluation of the victims' advocate scheme pilots'. Ministry of Justice Series 17/08. London: Ministry of Justice.

Takahashi, Y. (2005) 'Toward a balancing approach: the use of apology in Japanese society', *International Review of Victimology,* 12: 23–45.

Tapley, J. (2005) 'Public confidence costs – criminal justice from a victim's perspective', *British Journal of Community Justice,* 3(2): 39–50.

Tavuchis, N. (1991) *Mea Culpa: A Sociology of Apology and Reconciliation.* Stanford: Stanford University Press.

Umbreit, M. S. (1995) *Mediation of Criminal Conflict: An Assessment of Programs in Four Canadian Provinces.* St. Paul: University of Minnesota.

Walklate, S. (2007) *Imagining the Victim of Crime.* Maidenhead, Berkshire: Open University Press.

Wemmers, J. (2005) 'Victim policy transfer: learning from each other', *European Journal on Criminal Policy and Research,* 11(1): 121–33.

——(2009) 'Where do they belong? Giving victims a place in the criminal justice process', *Criminal Law Forum,* 20: 395–416.

Zehr, H. (2001) *Transcending: Reflections of Crime Victims.* Intercourse, PA: Good Books.

Chapter 7

Justice as reconciliation?

Introduction

Tavuchis (1991: 69) suggests that reconciliation is the transcendent product of the 'tension between sorrow and forgiveness'. Following on from the discussion in Chapter 6, which highlighted the contested nature of apologies, forgiveness, and restorative justice for the victim, this chapter considers the possibilities for reconciliation. As with the topics discussed in Chapter 6, and as will be illustrated here, reconciliation can occur in different ways and at different levels. In addition, rather like restorative justice, what is understood by reconciliation is difficult to assess. A brief excursion into any English dictionary provides a flavour of the different meanings that can be attached to this term: meanings which become increasingly difficult to unravel when situated within the policy context. Indeed Androff (2012: 77) goes so far as to say that 'Reconciliation is as popular a concept as it is unclear' and adds that, 'despite this conceptual confusion, the term abounds in social science and post-conflict projects around the world' (Androff, 2012: 78). The *desire* for reconciliation in post-conflict contexts is frequently beyond dispute. That previously warring parties should set aside their differences and move on also lends a spiritual dimension to this concept. However, what it actually means for whom, under what conditions, and how it might assist in aiding victims in particular in coming to terms with what has happened to them is, as we shall see, neither simple nor straightforward. Indeed, for some reconciliation can be a dirty word (see McEvoy, 2007; McEvoy et al., 2006). In trying to capture some of this conceptual complexity Parmentier and Sullo (2011: 337–38) point to a number of issues that frame how reconciliation can be conceived and operationalised.

First, it is evident that reconciliation can operate at different levels: the individual, the interpersonal, the communal and the national. Second, these different levels of reconciliation may interact, or fail to interact, with each other in different ways (qua the observation made by Tavuchis that reconciliation is the product of the tension between sorrow and forgiveness). Third, in some versions of reconciliation its relationship with forgiveness is seen as a prerequisite, heightening its spiritual component. This is the view adopted by Tutu (1999).

Though as Androff (2012) observes there is no necessary relationship between forgiveness and reconciliation, for either individuals or nation states. Fourth, many iterations of reconciliation programmes assume the importance of re-establishing how things once were. Fifth, there is some confusion as to whether or not reconciliation is a process, an outcome or both. Finally, whether a process or an outcome, there is some dispute as to whether or not reconciliation can be understood or even achieved as a 'top down' strategy if it fails to take account of 'bottom up' views. Taken together, these issues suggest a degree of conceptual and practical confusion about reconciliation, so much so that Parmentier and Sullo (2011: 338) suggest that it has become an 'all-encompassing concept ... void of any concrete sense'. So it is perhaps fair to say that it shares not only a lack of clarity with restorative justice but also its elasticity (Miers, 2004). This brief overview suggests a concept with multilayered and multifaceted meanings, understandings of which exist on a context-dependent continuum, from a one-off event to more systematic victimisations. Taken together, these issues raise the question of whose reconciliation: how and under what conditions does reconciliation have meaning, and for whom?

So reconciliation is a contested concept, yet, as a concept and a policy imperative, it has gained real purchase over the last 50 years. It is possible to trace the contemporary concern with reconciliation to the Nuremberg and Tokyo trials after the Second World War. These initiatives set the tone of the establishment of similar International Criminal Tribunals to deal with Serbian leaders after the events in Yugoslavia in 1993 and the Rwandan genocide of 1994. The recourse to defining the actions that resulted in these tribunals as 'criminal', 'war crimes' or 'atrocity crimes' arguably masked the political sleights of hand (as alluded to by Krever, 2014, and illustrated in relation to the Iraq war in Chapter 3) that lay behind the establishment of these tribunals and their implicit understanding of who was to be considered responsible. They also carried with them certain presumptions that such processes make possible the establishment of the truth of what happened, deliver justice for the victims, and deal with the offenders appropriately (see Doak, 2011: 264). In so doing these same processes fail to recognise, in some instances, where some of the responsibility for the events that took place lay (for example, in the case of Rwanda, as suggested in Chapter 3 – see also Cameron, 2013). Thus what can lie behind these kinds of interventions are presumptions about innocence, blame and responsibility that have a particular purchase on the victims who are seen and not seen (McEvoy and McConnachie, 2012). This is an issue that will be returned to later in this chapter.

A convincing case has also been made that situates the practical translation of reconciliation into particular policy initiatives within what Pupavac (2004) has termed the drive for international therapeutic governance. In this drive, 'War crimes tribunals and truth and reconciliation commissions are championed as political therapy, facilitating closure for traumatized nations' (Pupavac, 2004: 378): an analysis differently focused but not overly dissimilar to that offered by Fassin

(2012) in his explication of humanitarian reason. Thus in the background there are clearly discernible connections to be made between the concerns of Chapter 6 (justice as therapy) and the focus of attention here. One of the major conceptual and policy bridges between these two chapters is restorative justice. Though here the focus is on the more extraordinary criminal acts and/or crime perpetrated by states or between states, rather than being concerned with more mundane and 'ordinary' interpersonal crime. This chapter then affords a useful extension to our understanding of the victimisation of collectives discussed in Chapter 5. There, using the case study of Bhopal, some insight was gained concerning the impact of, and response to, those events in which financial reconciliation, such as it was, largely took place out of court and fell far short of the needs of victims. Here we address the recourse to the courts for cases of mass victimisation.

In this recourse to the courts, it is possible to identify three interconnected policy developments in which claims are made both to address victims' voices and for reconciliation. These are *truth commissions*, the *International Criminal Court*, and practices associated with *transitional justice*. It should be noted that these are by no means mutually exclusive initiatives. In the aftermath of any particular event they can be implemented as a package or separately. However, in many respects, as Doak (2011) avers, as initiatives they reflect a tendency to conflate individual reconciliation with societal reconciliation, echoing the conceptual fuzziness discussed above and revealing much about where victims' voices actually fit within them.

Tavuchis (1991) reminds us that apologies can take many forms, from the one to the many, from the many to the one, and so on. Logically, so it is with reconciliation. As was discussed in Chapter 6, for those victims who took the opportunity to make an impact statement to the court, many of them found that opportunity therapeutic. It afforded them the chance to not only voice their feelings but also, in the case of the families of murder victims, to 'normalise' their family members. In a similar vein in the context of reconciliation, Schotsmans (2011: 367) suggests that in order for reconciliation to work for victims they need security (to deal with the past), acknowledgement, the perpetrator being called to account, to know the truth, and to be offered some kind of reparation. Braithwaite (2011: 133), quoting a summary of the work of Maria Ericson, embellishes this by talking of the need for 'remembrance and mourning, telling the story of one's own trauma, reconnection with ordinary life'. None of which in his analysis requires the establishment of 'the truth'. Putting the victim at the centre of reconciliation resonates, then, with Sherman's (2003) 'emotionally sensitive justice', discussed in Chapter 6. If we add to this the multifaceted and multilayered nature of reconciliation, our analysis of the possibilities for justice as reconciliation can reach from the local to the regional and the global. By way of facilitating this we shall consider, as a case study, the challenges posed for reconciliation at a relatively local level following on from the actions of a single perpetrator. This was a one-off event that nonetheless had features of mass victimisation. We shall consider the questions posed by the actions of Anders Breivik in Oslo and Utoya on 22 July 2011.

Case Study: Oslo and Utoya, 2011

On 22 July 2011, Anders Breivik, pictured below at his trial in April 2012, killed 77 people, 8 by setting off a nail bomb in Oslo, and a further 69 in a shooting spree on the island of Utoya, some 40 kilometres from Oslo. The latter were primarily young people attending a Labour summer camp. Norway has a population of around five million people so, given that the young people at the summer camp came from all over the country, the loss that these actions entailed was far reaching. The picture below, of Breivik offering up a Nazi salute at the start of his trial, appeared on the front page of many newspapers across the globe. It is a powerful image reaching deep into the legacy of the Second World War for European sensibilities and beyond. In so doing it arguably also captures the problems and possibilities for a multilayered appreciation of reconciliation with which we are concerned here. This case study facilitates unwrapping some of those layers.

Who is the offender?

Of course, these events, and the wider reaction to them, need to be set in context. When news first broke about them, there was an almost automatic

Figure 7.1 Anders Behring Breivik trial, Oslo Court House, Norway – 16 April 2012. KeystoneUSA-Zuma/REX. Thanks to Rex Features for their kind permission to reproduce the image in this book.

assumption that this was a terrorist attack fuelled by Al Qaeda both in Norway and elsewhere (Asprem, 2011; Holgersen, 2012); giving rise to our observation in Chapter 3 regarding oppositional forces at work between the Orient and the Occident in the 'war on terrorism'. However, it quickly transpired that this was not the case. Breivik is Norwegian: white, blond haired, and from a middle-class background. He is from the country that determines the Nobel Peace Prize. Hence, his physical appearance as he offers up the Nazi salute taps into historical images associated with the Second World War, of perpetrators and victims, and certainly did not fit with contemporary images of terrorism or terrorists as discussed in relation to John Tulloch's experiences in Chapter 4. However, the fear his actions generated were nonetheless powerful. The reporting of these events was frequently coupled with the bloodied image of a mature, white woman staring into space, who it transpires was Sissel Wilsgaard, an employee of the Norwegian Department of Justice (an image not dissimilar to that of John Tulloch in the aftermath of 7/7). Taken together, these images convey messages of horror, albeit at different levels, one historical and one immediate to the event, but they both travelled through time and space, both raising questions about victim and offender.

Bringing the offender to trial: acknowledging the victims

In this particular case, unlike so many other similar events around the globe, the perpetrator was brought to trial, affording the opportunity for victims' voices to be heard. Indeed Wilsgaard described in detail at his trial the physical and psychological wounds that Breivik inflicted on her and others. Breivik, for his part, was declared fit to stand trial and remained largely impassive as the evidence against him was presented. There has been much speculation about, and detailed analysis of, Breivik's motivation for his actions. Simonsen (2012: 203) concludes that, 'Breivik slaughtered fellow Norwegians whom he considered too tolerant of 'intruding' strangers, people who, according to him, had betrayed the national cause'. In some respects, then, it is possible to forge links between this case study and the discussion of hate crime in Chapter 3; those who were victimised were seen by Breivik as culpable for the directed violence that they received. Breivik was sentenced to 21 years in detention in August 2012. The end product of which, following Schotsmans (2011) above, was that the victims were acknowledged and the offender called to account, the latter being unusual for events of this kind.

Democracy, social harmony and reconciliation

This particular example affords the opportunity of situating all of the above in the wider cultural context of Norway. Norway is a country with a reputation for its humanity and charity. Indeed, in the immediate aftermath of these events it is notable that the then Norwegian Prime Minister, Jens Stoltenberg, stated that the attacks were to be met with 'more openness and more democracy'.

This stands in stark contrast to the draconian responses set in place by George Bush and Tony Blair after 9/11 and the bombings in London on 7/7 respectively. Moreover there is evidence to suggest that many Norwegians took to the streets in support of 'more democracy' in the aftermath of these events. This kind of stance towards high-profile and potentially traumatic events is not new to Norway. A similar stance was adopted in response to a case of child-on-child murder in the early 1990s, again in stark contrast to the view taken on a very similar kind of case in the UK (see Green, 2008 for a full discussion of this). For the purposes of the discussion here, the wider Norwegian response to these events is suggestive of the important interplay between individual capacity for reconciliation and the wider societal embrace of reconciliation as a way of maintaining social harmony. By implication this takes reconciliation to be a social process rather than necessarily an individual outcome, but a process that is always in the making (qua the statement of the Norwegian Prime Minister). Whilst, on a larger scale, these events ensured some nuanced attention was paid to the rise of right-wing politics in Europe, overall the response to them is illuminating for what *did not* happen as much as what *did* take place. As Quinney (1972: 315) observed, 'social harm, no matter how abstract, is a reality decided upon by those in power'. The restrained response by those in power is noteworthy. This case study perhaps also illustrates that the same might also be said about the conditions under which social harms are responded to.

This discussion of the events in Norway in 2011 has sensitised us to the importance of thinking about reconciliation as a socially embedded value and process set in a particular local cultural context. In the discussion that follows, the possibilities for reconciliation are situated not as a response to geographically bounded one-off events for which an individual perpetrator can be called to account, but in circumstances where the international community have been driven to call an individual, or group of individuals, to account (the International Criminal Court); where there have been long-standing conflictual relationships within a society (the Truth and Reconciliation Commission in South Africa, for example); alongside the emergence of what is known as *transitional justice*. These different interventions are often grouped together under the heading of 'post-conflict justice', which affords a second link between the concerns of this chapter and those of Chapter 3 (in Iraq, justice of this sort is wholly absent). Indeed Arne and Alidu (2010) comment on the mutually dependent relationship between the policies under discussion here, with McEvoy and Mallinder (2012) adding that their victim-centredness acts as a source of self-legitimation for their initiation, adoption and development. The question remains what each of these interventions might accomplish, either for the victim or in terms of reconciliation.

Post-conflict justice: the International Criminal Court

Doak (2011) suggests that there is much to be gained from comparing the role of the International Criminal Court with domestic justice frameworks from a

victims' perspective. As such, the key features of engagement with such proceedings can be considered to be: whether or not there is an opportunity for
the victim to give their version of events, whether or not the 'truth' of what
happened has been established and acknowledged, whether 'justice' has been
delivered, and whether or not there has been an opportunity for what Doak
(2011: 269) calls a 'deliberative encounter' between the victim and the offender.
Indeed, in all of these respects much has been expected from the International
Criminal Court (ICC), established under the Statute of Rome in 1998. It has as its
prime focus the crimes of genocide, war crimes and crimes against humanity, and
Groenhuijsen (2014: 40) reports that in affording the victim the rights to participation, representation and protection, 'the model of the ICC looks virtually
perfect'. However, perfect models do not necessarily translate into perfect
practice. Indeed, in an early empirical investigation of the practices of the ICC in
respect of victims, Wemmers (2009) reports a range of ambiguous experiences.
Moreover, whilst sympathetic to the potential of the ICC, De Brouwer (2009)
suggests that its inception is not overly positive, particularly in relation to its
handling of sexual violence. Indeed she concludes that, 'impunity for sexual
violence remains; impunity for crimes that have historically been overlooked and
which are under-prosecuted in every corner of the world' (De Brouwer, 2009:
200–201). This is indeed a powerful indictment, from which it can be deduced
that whilst such international courts create 'new' crimes (Campbell, 2004) and
as a consequence 'new' categories of victims, they appear to fall short in
meeting the potential for victim-centred justice as outlined by Doak (2011).

   The failures to which De Brouwer (2009) refers are in some respects a result
of how the principles of participation, representation and protection have been
operationalised. Garbett's (2013) analysis of the *Prosecutor versus Lubanga* case
illustrates how this comes about. In analysing court transcripts of the victims'
narratives in this case, she concludes that not only does the individualised
model of victim participation adopted by the proceeding render it impossible
for the court to conceive of collective harms (as one might reasonably expect for a
court designed to address such issues as genocide) but also that the judgement
emanating from this particular case was marked by three absences:

> its clarification of the truth and the role of victim participants in the pro-
> cess: the form of the participation of the victim participants, the nature of
> the harms of the events under adjudication, and the victim participants'
> contribution to the legal outcome.
>
> (Garbett, 2013: 206)

Indeed, in some respects parallel with domestic courts, it is the advocates who
are heard in the ICC, not the victims (Doak, 2011). These practices of silencing
arguably contribute to the political sleights of hand commented on by Krever
(2014) and they certainly deny what, it would seem, many victims want.
Rothe (2014: 244) adds, 'many victims of mass crimes want to not only tell

their stories but to ensure a historical record of the events', and 'When victims are omitted from this process, it fails to fulfil a potential resource of restoration and holistic version of the "truth" which many victims desire'.

Thus Garbett (2013: 209) concludes that whilst the ICC offers the opportunity for victims to speak about what has happened to them, whether or not they are heard remains a moot point. Of course, in many respects the operations and practices of the ICC are still in their early days and an optimistic assessment might focus on its potential for future development. Indeed, as Doak (2011: 298) observes, recognition of victims' desires and providing the mechanisms through which such desires might be fulfilled are not easily matched together in the face of mass genocide, torture and other atrocities. We have, indeed, provided a convincing account of this in relation to Iraq in Chapter 3, and this is a point we shall return to in the conclusion to this chapter.

Post-conflict justice: truth and reconciliation commissions

Since the first *Commission on the Disappeared*, established in Argentina in 1983, truth and reconciliation commissions have become an accepted way of engaging in re-establishing some consensus on post-conflict societies (Hirsch, 2013). Indeed, since 1983 the number of such commissions has grown and they have ranged from dealing with very localised issues, like that set up to address the consequences of the Greensboro Massacre (North Carolina) in 1979 (Androff, 2010), to those established to address the consequences of national and/or regional conflicts. One of the most widely known, and arguably most researched, was the one that was established to deal with the legacies of apartheid in South Africa. Established in 1995, it was headed by Archbishop Desmond Tutu and his own analysis of the process – *No Future without Forgiveness* – provides an illuminating analysis of the difficulties that the commission faced. What is of particular interest here is the extent to which such commissions meet with their espoused principle, using the example of South Africa,

> to promote national unity and reconciliation in a spirit of understanding which transcends the conflicts and divisions of the past through investigating and establishing as complete a picture as possible of the nature, causes and extent of gross violations of human rights committed in the past conflict.
>
> (Hamber, 2002: 61)

Victims' voices were, and are, considered essential to this process, so whilst the discussion that follows focuses attention primarily on how this was manifested in South Africa, the questions that it raises for victims are pertinent to other such commissions.

For Hamber (2002), the purpose of the South African Truth and Reconciliation Commission (TRC) was threefold. It was important for the historical record to establish an account of what took place under the apartheid regime, it was important to provide a space for victims of the regime to offer an account of what had happened to them, and in the light of such accounts, the commission was to assign responsibility for what had happened. Indeed, offenders were to be given full amnesty in the face of full disclosure of their actions, though certain conditions had to be met for this to take place. Central to this was the role afforded to the victim in the search for the truth. Peacock (2011: 320) reveals that the TRC conceptualised five kinds of truth: factual or forensic truth, other corroborated evidential truth, personal truth through victim narrative, social truth established through dialogue or debate, and healing or restorative truth established by citizen relationships. Whilst Peacock (2011) suggests that, despite the inherent problems associated with these understandings of truth and their reliance on the honesty of those testifying to the commission, the TRC did break the silence around the role of the state and its security forces in torture, murder, detention and so on of its political opponents, which acted as an important stepping stone towards democracy. However, it is also the case that, as Hamber (2002) suggests, the TRC started a process it was unable to complete, with victims feeling let down in terms of reparations received and a comprehensive establishment of 'the truth'. Indeed it was evident that of the 21,296 statements of gross violations of human rights received by the TRC, only about 8 per cent were given the opportunity of a public hearing (Peacock, 2011: 326). Thus it is the case that victims entered this process with different/ competing understandings of what telling their story might mean, which led Hamber (2002: 66) to conclude that, 'individual needs such as long-term healing and the desire for justice were subordinated to the collective drive to "reconcile"'. Indeed, in a later qualitative analysis of the relationship between truth and reconciliation, Clark (2012: 202) suggests,

> there is nothing inherently 'victim friendly' about TRCs. The nature of its mandate, the resources at its disposal, how well it is equipped to address victims' multiple needs; all of these factors will help to determine how victim focused a particular TRC actually is.

Indeed Clark (2012) goes on to argue that the factors outlined above are more important to the success of a TRC than the establishment of the 'truth' itself. So, taken together these observations support the view that it is a moot point whether or not presenting a victim's narrative to a truth commission can be healing (Horne, 2013), the South African TRC mantra of 'revealing is healing' notwithstanding. Moreover, Moon (2009: 78) usefully reminds us that in the context of South Africa the healing of wounds was in reality the test bed for the post-apartheid government, 'the successful performance of which would form the basis of its future claim to govern'. Thus, in Moon's (2009) analysis, the South African TRC stands as an example, par excellence, of the global assumption that war-torn societies are traumatised and that the first duty of government (and others) is the psychiatric care of its population (Fassin 2012).

Clark's (2012: 193) construction of a 'truth reconciliation dyad' offers a useful framework for thinking critically not only about the kind of truth that TRC's can effectively provide the space for, and what impact that might have (see also Braithwaite, 2011, on partial truth and the longue duree), but how both of these may or may not effectively contribute to reconciliation. Embedded in these issues it is also important to note the question of whose voices were/are heard and how they were/are listened to. Kashyap (2009) offers an interesting gendered analysis of the TRC, and de Ycaza (2013: 210), in assessing the Liberian Truth Commission, adds,

> If the needs of victims and past abuses are not addressed in any significant way, there is a likelihood of recidivism and return to conflict. The TRC is the first step in a process of healing and reconciling the past in order to help the country of Liberia move forward.

So, despite the conceptual fuzziness associated with reconciliation discussed at the beginning of this chapter, it is evident that the links between reconciliation and truth commissions have become deeply embedded, even in the face of the ambivalent evidence of victims' experiences with such commissions. In a balanced assessment of this evidence, Doak (2011: 286) concludes that truth commissions do not necessary result in justice, substantive or procedural, since they often fail to call the offenders to account (unlike in the case study used earlier in this chapter) and consequently only superficially give the victim a voice – a conclusion echoed in Androff's (2010) observations concerning the lack of engagement of perpetrators in the Greensboro TRC. Nonetheless, it is important to note, as Tutu (1999: 184) does, the South African TRC was 'good in parts' and as a result of its presence it was no longer possible to say 'we did not know' (Tutu, 1999: 171). Whilst for the purposes of this book this latter observation affords an interesting connection with witnessing, discussed in Chapter 4 (and returned to in Chapter 8), it also affords an important insight into the variable nature of 'truth' required for such witnessing. This variation is likely to be intimately connected with the question of whose interests such commissions are intended to serve: the victim, the community, the state, or the international community? All of these issues connect with, and feed into, the questions with which this section began: what is meant by reconciliation and whose interest does it serve?

Hamber (2002) suggests that the TRC in South Africa operated with five different understandings of reconciliation: community building, human rights, religious, inter-communal and non-racial, though the concept itself was never defined in its proceedings or documentation. Following on from this, Verdoo-laege (2008) suggests that it is possible to identify a 'regime of reconciliation' within the practices of the South African TRC in which she identifies 'ideal' and 'non-ideal' testifiers that resonates well with traditional conceptions of ideal and non-ideal victims (see Christie, 1986 and Chapter 1). Both analyses lend further weight to the view that reconciliation is multilayered and multi-faceted. They also point to important and unresolved questions about victim expectations, participation, and perhaps more fundamentally whether or not the opportunity of voice afforded to victims equates with capacity for agency. However, if we add to this the moral imperative to move in the direction of reconciliation as an international norm required of post-conflict societies, it is possible to conceive of a moral economy of reconciliation in which, at the end of the day, the role of victims' voices is incidentally constituted. Nonetheless, moves towards transitional justice, and the literature associated with these kinds of developments, assumes a relationship between truth and reconciliation (Clark, 2011) and it is to a consideration of the role of the victim in transitional justice that we shall now turn.

Post-conflict societies: transitional justice

The United Nations (2010: 3) defines transitional justice in the following way,

> Transitional justice consists of both judicial and non-judicial processes and mechanisms, including prosecution initiatives, truth-seeking, reparations programmes, institutional reform or an appropriate combination thereof ... transitional justice can contribute to achieving the broader objectives of prevention of further conflict, peacebuilding and reconciliation.

So, as this definition implies, transitional justice can embrace international criminal courts and truth commissions, as discussed above, but can also include other interventions designed to contribute to peace-building more generally: amnesties, specific reparations, commemorative projects, along with the development of internationally recognised ways of conducting and enforcing the law. This definition adds some weight to the concerns expressed by McEvoy (2007) that the increasing dominance of 'legalism' in transitional justice detracts from other ways of practising transitional justice and thereby plays into the further promulgation of Western liberal democratic ideals suggested by some critics (Andrieu, 2010).

Whilst the United Nations' definition might well be contested, it is nevertheless the case that putting in place mechanisms associated with the ideals of transitional justice has become a powerful signifier of a society's capacity to deal with the worst kinds of human rights violations and to move on in the aftermath of them. All of which, to a greater or less extent, seek to afford recognition to victims (De Greiff, 2010: 42). Recognition that is predicated on assumptions of what it is that victims might want/need under these kinds of conditions. Doak (2011: 297) suggests this is one area about which little is known. However, somewhat to the contrary, Danieli (2006: 343) claims, on the basis of interviews with survivors from a range of different traumatic contexts, victims need: the re-establishment of their equal status through reparation; the removal of their stigmatisation through memorialisation and/or commemoration; the repair of damage done by apologies/complete historical records and so on; and a commitment from the international community to provide justice and redress through various judicial and non-judicial means (some of which have been discussed above). These add an international dimension to the 'needs' of victims outlined in Chapter 5, as differently constituted from conventional victims of 'crime'. In some respects, Danieli (2006) is offering an ideal list since it is clearly evident that the extent to which such outcomes are achieved, or are indeed achievable, is hugely variable (as can be inferred from the discussion above) and contingent both upon the commitment of the individual post-conflict government concerned and the nature of the support offered from the wider international community. A good case in point is the ambivalent commitment to justice and reconciliation evidenced in the case of Rwanda (see *inter alia* Waldorf, 2006). Nonetheless, central to all of the above is 'recognition of the victim'.

Victim recognition?

Greiff (2010) suggests that 'recognition' is a complex process. In the first instance recognition demands acknowledging that victims are both subjects and objects. This means that as individuals they have agency (can make choices) but as victims they have been made into objects (denied choices) as a result of the actions of others. It is this latter aspect of their experiences that victims want recognised: that they have been intentionally harmed by others. Resonant with the observations of Danieli (2006), this kind of recognition demands more than truth-telling – it demands a reinstatement of equal citizenship. So whilst truth-telling is important (qua truth and reconciliation commissions, discussed above) arguably in the absence of reparation and changes in institutional practices, it may not amount to much in real terms for the victim. Here Greiff (2010) is offering a holistic, rather than a partial, understanding of transitional justice that places the victim at its heart, yet the questions remain: who is this victim, how are they constituted, what kind of recognition do they seek?

Who is the victim? What kind of recognition?

In a study published in 2003, Cairns and Mallett produce some interesting findings on the disjunction between the extent to which people in Northern Ireland perceived themselves to be 'victims' of 'the troubles' and the assumptions of the policy initiatives designed to respond to their victimhood. Indeed many studies of transitional justice have little to say about victims, or the impact of these kinds of initiatives on them, although that picture is changing. Robins (2012), in a detailed investigation of transitional justice in Timor-Leste, offers some insight into these kinds of questions. The results of his investigation reveal that for 61 per cent of the families who took part, their greatest need was for economic support. The loss of a breadwinner during the conflict clearly made poor families poorer. Whilst this was the most commonly understood form of recognition, Robins (2012: 94) reports that when pressed, 69 per cent wanted some kind of memorial to those who were missing or dead (this was also expressed uniformly in the study by Cairns and Mallett, 2003). This was particularly the case for those families in which no body had been found. As Robins (2012: 95) states in relation to this, 'The most important cultural element of the needs expressed was the performance of rituals that would permit the spirits of the dead to rest in peace'. It is in this latter respect that truth seemed to be particularly pertinent. To know the truth of what happened to a family member so that such rituals could be effectively performed was important. Taken together, Robins (2012: 96) avers that, 'For most families, justice was perceived as recognition and compensation, or receiving an answer regarding the fate of a loved one and the return of remains'.

It is also evident from this study that the locally constituted Commission for Reception, Truth, and Reconciliation, had little contact with victims. Thus its processes and recommendations were largely irrelevant to them. Robins (2012) suggests that this initiative was flawed; in part because of the size of the task it faced but also because it failed to implement its own recommended programme of reparations. In addition it was driven by an agenda that did not match with the victims' expressed needs. Moreover, the victims in this study were engaging in their own processes of memorialisation and story-telling in tune with the traditions of their rural communities: perhaps evidence of a desire for a private truth rather than the public one desired by the state. These are processes perhaps not too dissimilar from those observed by Simic and Daly (2011) in their analysis of the 'One Pair of Shoes, One Life' demonstration post the genocide in Srebrenica. Of course, the commission established in Timor-Leste did have contact with some victims. However, they were primarily from urban areas, and their agendas, Robins (2012) suggests, were different from those in the poor, rural areas.

These observations, taken together, offer some insight into the questions posed above: who is this victim, how are they constituted, what kind of recognition do they seek? The victim and the nature of their victimhood cannot be assumed to be a direct consequence of what has happened to them. For example, Jones et al. (2012: 561), in testing their model of reconciliation in Bosnia, report:

> Trauma was negatively correlated with trust/reconciliation, whereas dialogue and active responsibility were positively correlated with trust/reconciliation. These findings suggest that as people's degree of trauma increased, it is more likely that their perceptions of the possibilities for trust/reconciliation would decrease.

Whilst there is no necessary relationship between data based on groups as a predictor of how an individual might respond to their individual circumstances, the point is well made in respect of the potential tensions between a political desire for reconciliation and the likelihood of support for such policies. All of which might well be contingent on the kind of recognition being sought and the socio-cultural and economic status of that recognition. This kind of insight is developed further in the observations on the processes of reconciliation in Serbia offered by Nicolic-Ristanovic (2006).

Whilst Nicolic-Ristanovic (2006) discusses the processes in Serbia primarily as truth and reconciliation processes rather than transitional justice per se, it is evident from what she documents that there were a wide range of engagements in this 'truth process' in Serbia, involving not only the state but also other non-governmental organisations, including the Victimology Society of Serbia itself. This analysis centres on the importance of understanding the socio-economic and historical context of the Serbian sense of victimisation, which for many individuals would include the destruction caused by NATO and the economic impact of sanctions imposed by the United Nations. Against this backcloth she lists features of victimisation in Serbia: the presence of different perpetrators, multiple victimisations by different perpetrators, conflict between the Serbs themselves, men recruited as child soldiers, alongside widespread structural victimisation. Thus she states, 'This means that among the population of Serbia there are both victims and perpetrators of crimes/gross violations of human rights, with these groups overlapping' (Nikolic-Ristanovic 2006: 373). To recognise this level of complexity required responses that would challenge the denial of the wide-ranging nature and sources of victimisation, including those committed by Serbs on other Serbs. It is at this juncture that the difficulties faced by the transitional justice desire to centre the victim surface in rather profound ways. As Nicolic-Ristanovic (2006) states, ease with which hierarchies of victimisation were constructed, particularly in public discourses in Serbia, was remarkable.

A hierarchy of recognition?

The notion of a hierarchy of victimisation was discussed in Chapter 1. Thinking about victimisation in this way includes some and not others as having a legitimate claim to victim status. In a society dealing with post-conflict in which some, or indeed all, of the conflict and victimisations that occurred were generated as a result of internal divisions, who is the victim and is accorded victim status is particularly problematic. This point is taken up by McEvoy and McConnachie (2012: 532); citing examples from Northern Ireland, Argentina and South Africa, they suggest that a hierarchy of victimhood that implicitly distinguishes between 'good' and 'bad' victims 'often maps into both subjective views on the "justifiability" of the suffering that was visited upon such victims and the strategies and tactics deployed by such victims in the transition and their attitudes to dealing with the past'. Since 'good' victims are often presumed also to be 'innocent', they go on to observe that 'Designation of deserving victimhood becomes an easy shorthand for *blaming* those deemed responsible for past horrors as well as absolving those deemed *blameless*' (McEvoy and McConnachie, 2012: 533). Our discussion on the 2003 Iraq War in Chapter 3 can easily be conceived of in the same way. Further to this, Madlingozi (2014: 185) goes on to observe the presence of entrepreneurial tendencies within the transitional justice movement, in which the telling of the victims' 'story' is

> usually the entry point towards reconstituting victims as hapless, disempowered, and lacking in any rational thought or action. 'The story' is also the central device in sustaining the transitional justice industry … entrepreneurs theorize the field; set the agenda … and ultimately not only represent and speak for victims but also 'produce' the victim.

Thus the responsibility for the 'story', who 'owns' it, and indeed who writes it, are called into question. As a consequence, our attention is drawn to the underside of transitional justice in which the *politics* of victimhood, who acquires the label 'victim' and is subsequently recognised as such and who does not, is a significant feature of the policy process. Following Quinney (1972), conceptions of victimhood may not only be given by those in power, they may also be arbitrary.

To summarize: it is evident that whilst transitional justice seems to have become the accepted means by which societies endeavour to deal with post-conflict situations, what shape that response takes, how it is implemented, and what assumptions pertaining to the recognition of victimhood become embedded in the process are all subject to debate. The evidence in the examples cited here suggests that transitional justice can also suffer from being comprised of top-down initiatives that either fail to resonate with the victim who is constituted by them or miss the mark entirely. In the space afforded by such top-down processes, inclusionary and exclusionary understandings of the victim can create a hierarchy of victimhood infused with concepts of innocence, blame and legitimacy, which in turn can fuel the politics of victimhood. Thus transitional justice becomes the means by which the problems faced by victims in more conventional justice settings are recreated. In addition, however, there is another layer to transitional justice commented on by Robbins (2012). That layer explicitly connects the discussion here with the discussion in Chapter 6 on therapeutic jurisprudence. Robbins (2012: 104) observes that this ethic 'has become the driving concept of global approaches to transitional justice' but had no resonance with the findings of his study in Timor-Leste. This kind of observation connects the empirical work of Robins (2012) with that of Madlingozi (2014). Taken together they point to a deeply embedded 'global apartheid' (Madlingozi, 2014: 185). In this version of apartheid there are assumptions not only about the nature of victims and victimhood but also about what might count as reconciliation, both of which understandings can deny what is locally meaningful and doable.

The discussion above has also pointed to challenges to global transitional justice in the form of memorialisation practices in Sebrenica, burial rituals in Timor-Leste and what Nicolic-Ristanovic (2006) calls the 'third way' in Serbia. These 'movements' comprise locally constituted acts of remembrance through the construction of memorials, museums and sometimes more impromptu acts, as depicted in the cover image of this book (which we will address in Chapter 8). Such practices of resistance can and do exist outside of domestic and international calls for justice, as was documented in Chapter 5.

Conclusion: towards a political economy of reconciliation?

This chapter has explored the possibilities for reconciliation in the aftermath of mass victimisation. In so doing it has focused attention on the different ways in which the development of the International Criminal Court, the introduction of *truth and reconciliation commissions*, and a more general orientation towards *transitional justice* afford the opportunity for reconciliation for the victim. First, this discussion has illuminated the contested nature of reconciliation. As a concept it is vague, fuzzy and elastic. As a practice it is multifaceted and multilayered. Efforts to introduce mechanisms to facilitate reconciliation can fall foul of a failure to take account of its multifaceted and multilayered nature and, as top-down initiatives, can fundamentally miss the mark from the point of view of the victim. Second, in the implementation processes associated with reconciliation as discussed here, the space can also be created for the perpetuation of a hierarchy of victimisation in which some victims are made visible, others are rendered invisible, and notions of an 'ideal victim' can be sustained. It is at this juncture that it is possible to discern what might be called a moral economy of reconciliation (not overly dissimilar to the moral economy of trauma commented on by Fassin and Rechtman, 2009) in which the 'regime of reconciliation' (Verdoolaege, 2008) promotes 'good' victims and neglects those considered to be 'bad'. However, there is another layer to add to this understanding of reconciliation.

The drive for reconciliation, and the shape and form that it takes, can be connected to the wider emergence of therapeutic jurisprudence commented on in Chapter 6. In this drive the search for 'emotionally intelligent' justice (Sherman, 2003) takes particular forms on the global stage. Coming with the badge of approval from international organisations, therapeutic jurisprudence has not only been increasingly dominated by legalism (McEvoy, 2007), it has also resulted in a situation in which, 'therapy provides the language through which suffering is acknowledged, trauma ameliorated, and the legitimacy of new states is founded' (Moon, 2009: 86). In this way, as she argues, it is possible to discern a new form of legitimation for states to aspire to. This form focuses on the state's capacity to deal with the traumatic condition of its populace. This is a capacity that has overtaken the centrality of the rule of law and adherence to human rights in favour of the delivery of humanitarian reason (Fassin, 2012).

In these circumstances, the reconciliation entrepreneur (Madlingozi, 2014) possesses significant formal and informal power. This is more than a moral economy of reconciliation: this is a political economy of reconciliation (qua the political economy of trauma observed in Chapters 2 and 3) and can result in the victim's voice being muted or erased rather than recognised. Meanwhile, victims, however constituted in policy, as human beings with agency, find their own way as either individuals or collectivities to work with their experiences. Sometimes this may be a result of reconciliation already being a culturally embedded value in their society (as, perhaps, the case study of Anders Breivik illustrates) or because in less structured and often impromptu ways, they give voice to their feelings.

Further reading

It is difficult to source specific books that cover all of the issues touched upon in this chapter that reflect a concern with the victims' perspective. There is, however, a special issue of the *European Journal of Criminology* on 'Atrocity crimes and transitional justice' edited by Karstedt and Parmentier (2012) that will provide a research-based flavour of some of the issues discussed here as they are being developed within victimology. A more substantial edited collection by Letschert, Haveman, De Brouwer and Pemberton (2011), *Victimological Approaches to International Crimes: Africa*, is a good source book, and the edited collection by Buss et al. (2014), *Sexual Violence in Conflict and Post-Conflict Societies: International Agendas and African Contexts*, adds an important gendered perspective in these issues that shortage of space limited the coverage of here.

References

Androff, D. (2010) '"To not hate": reconciliation among victims of violence and participants of the Greensboro Truth and Reconciliation Commission', *Contemporary Justice Review*, 13(3): 269–85.
——(2012) 'Reconciliation in a community based restorative justice intervention', *Journal of Sociology and Social Welfare*, 39(4): 73–96.
Andrieu, K. (2010) 'Civilizing peacebuilding: transitional justice, civil society and the liberal paradigm', *Security Dialogue*, 41(5): 537–58.
Ame, R. K. and Alidu, S. E. (2010) 'Truth and reconciliation commissions, restorative justice, peacemaking criminology, and development', *Criminal Justice Studies: A Critical Journal of Crime, Law and Society*, 23(3): 253–68.
Asprem, E. (2011) 'The birth of counterjihadist terrorism: reflections on some unspoken dimensions of 22 July 2011'. *The Pomegranate*, 13(1): 17–32.
Braithwaite, J. (2011) 'Partial truth and reconciliation in the longue duree', *Contemporary Social Science: Journal of the Academy of Social Sciences,* 6(1): 129–46.
Buss, D., Lebert, J., Rutherford, B., Sharkey, D. and Aginam, O. (eds) (2014) *Sexual Violence in Conflict and Post-Conflict Societies: International Agendas and African Contexts*. London: Routledge.

Cairns, E. and Mallett, J. (2003) 'Who are the victims? Self-assessed victimhood and the Northern Irish conflict'. Northern Ireland Office Research and Statistical Series: Report No. 7.

Cameron, H. (2013) *Britain's Hidden Role in the Rwandan Genocide: The Cat's Paw*. London: Glasshouse Books.

Campbell, K. (2004) 'The trauma of justice: sexual violence, crimes against humanity and the International Criminal Tribunal for the former Yugoslavia', *Social and Legal Studies* 13(3): 329–50.

Christie, N. (1986) 'The ideal victim', in E. A. Fattah (ed.) *From Crime Policy to Victim Policy*. London: Macmillan. pp. 17–30.

Clark, N. (2011) 'Transitional justice, truth and reconciliation: an under-explored relationship', *International Criminal Law Review*, 11: 241–61.

——(2012) 'Reconciliation via truth? A study of South Africa's TRC', *Journal of Human Rights*, 11: 189–92.

Danieli, Y. (2006) 'Essential elements of healing after massive trauma: complex needs voiced by victims/survivors', in D. Sullivan and L. Tift (eds) *Routledge Handbook of Restorative Justice*. London: Routledge. pp. 343–54.

De Brouwer, A.-M. (2009) 'What the International Criminal Court has achieved and can achieve for victims/survivors of sexual violence', *International Review of Victimology*, 16: 183–209.

De Greiff, P. (2010) 'Theorising transitional justice', in S. M. Williams., R. Nagy and J. Esler (eds) *Transitional Justice*. New York: New York University Press. pp. 31–77.

Doak, J. (2011) 'The therapeutic dimensions of transitional justice: emotional repair and victim satisfaction in international trials and Truth Commissions', *International Criminal Law Review*, 11: 263–98.

Fassin, D. (2012) *Humanitarian Reason*. Berkeley and Los Angeles: University of California Press.

Fassin, D. and Rechtman, R. (2009) *The Empire of Trauma*. Princeton, NJ: Princeton University Press.

Garbett, C. (2013) 'The truth and the trial: victim participation, restorative justice and the International Criminal Court', *Contemporary Justice Review*, 16(2): 193–213.

Green, D. (2008) *When Children Kill: Penal Populism and Political Culture*. Oxford: Oxford University Press.

Groenhuijsen, M. (2014) 'The development of international policy in relation to victims of crime', *International Review of Victimology*, 20(1): 31–48.

Hamber, B. (2002) '"Ere their story die": truth, justice, and reconciliation in South Africa', *Race and Class*, 44(1): 61–79.

Hirsh, M. (2013) 'Ideational change and the emergence of the international norm of truth and reconciliation commissions', *European Journal of International Relations*, 20(3): 810–33.

Holgersen, S. (2012) 'Changing responses to terror: how Norway made sense of 22/7', *Environment and Planning D: Society and Space*, 30: 191–206.

Horne, F. (2013) 'Can personal narratives heal trauma? A consideration of testimonies given at the South African Truth and Reconciliation Commission', *Social Dynamics*, 39(3): 443–56.

Jones, N. A., Parmentier, S., and Weitekamp, E. G. M. (2012) 'Dealing with international crimes in post-war Bosnia: a look through the lens of the affected population', *European Journal of Criminology*, 9(5): 553–64.

Karstedt, S. and Parmentier, S. (eds) (2012) 'Atrocity crimes and transitional justice: Special Issue', *European Journal of Criminology*, 9(5).

Kashyap, R. (2009) 'Narrative and truth: a feminist critique of the South African Truth and Reconciliation Commission', *Contemporary Justice Review*, 12(4): 449–67.

Krever, T. (2014) 'Dispensing global justice', *New Left Review,* 85(Jan–Feb): 67–97.

Lestschert, R., Haveman, R., de Brouwer, A.-M. and Pemberton, A. (eds) (2011) *Victimological Approaches to International Crimes: Africa*. Cambridge: Intersentia.

McEvoy, K. (2007) 'Beyond legalism: towards a thicker understanding of transitional justice', *Journal of Law and Society,* 34(4): 411–40.

McEvoy, K. and Mallinder, L. (2012) 'Amnesties in transition: punishment, restoration, and the governance of mercy', *Journal of Law and Society,* 39(3): 410–40.

McEvoy, K. and McConnachie, K. (2012) 'Victimology in transitional justice: victimhood, innocence and hierarchy', *European Journal of Criminology,* 9(5): 527–38.

McEvoy, L., McEvoy, K., and McConnachie, K. (2006) 'Reconciliation as a dirty word: conflict, community relations and education in Northern Ireland', *Journal of International Affairs,* Fall/Winter, 60(1): 81–106.

Madlingozi, T. (2014) 'On transitional justice entrepreneurs and the production of victims', in D. Buss, J. Lebert, B. Rutherford, D. Sharkey, and O. Aginam (eds) *Sexual Violence in Conflict and Post-Conflict Societies: International Agendas and African Contexts*. London: Routledge. pp. 169–92.

Miers, D. (2004) 'Situating and researching restorative justice in Great Britain', *Punishment and Society,* 6(1): 23–46.

Moon, C, (2009) 'Healing past violence: traumatic assumptions and therapeutic interventions in war and reconciliation', *Journal of Human Rights,* 8: 71–91.

Nicolic-Ristanovic, V. (2006) 'Truth and reconciliation in Serbia', in D. Sullivan and L. Tift (eds) *Routledge Handbook of Restorative Justice*. London: Routledge. pp. 369–86.

Parmentier, S. and Sullo, P. (2011) 'Voices from the field: empirical data from post-war Bosnia and their relevance for Africa', in R. Letschert, R. Haveman, A.-M. de Brouwer and A. Pemberton (eds) *Victimological Approaches to International Crimes: Africa*. Cambridge: Intersentia. pp. 335–52.

Peacock, R. (2011) 'The South African truth and reconciliation commission: challenges in contributing to reconciliation', in R. Letschert, R. Haveman, A.-M. de Brouwer and A. Pemberton (eds) *Victimological Approaches to International Crimes: Africa*. Cambridge: Intersentia. pp. 315–33.

Pupavac, V. (2004) 'International therapeutic peace and justice in Bosnia', *Social and Legal Studies,* 13(3): 377–401.

Quinney, R. (1972) 'Who is the victim?', *Criminology,* 10(3) November: 309–29.

Robins, S. (2012) 'Challenging the therapeutic ethic: a victim-centred evaluation of transitional justice process in Timor-Leste', *International Journal of Transitional Justice,* 6(1): 83–105.

Rothe, D. (2014) 'Can an international criminal justice system address victims' needs?' in D. Rothe and D. Kauzlarich (eds) *Towards a Victimology of State Crime*. London: Routledge. pp. 238–49.

Schotsmans, M. (2011) 'Justice at the doorstep', in R. Letschert, R. Haveman, A.-M. de Brouwer, and A. Pemberton (eds) *Victimological Approaches to International Crimes: Africa*. Cambridge: Intersentia. pp. 353–84.

Sherman, L. W. (2003) 'Reason for emotion: reinventing justice with theories, innovations and research', *Criminology,* 41: 1–37.

Simic, O. and Daly, K. (2011) '"One pair of shoes, one life": steps towards accountability for genocide in Srebrenica', *The International Journal of Transitional Justice,* 5(10): 1–15.

Simonsen, K. (2012) 'Figuration of a cultural political crisis across Europe', *Environment and Planning D: Society and Space,* 30: 191–206.

Tavuchis, N. (1991) *Mea Culpa: A Sociology of Apology and Reconciliation.* Stanford: Stanford University Press.

Tutu, D. (1999) *No Truth without Forgiveness.* London: Rider Books, Ebury Press.

United Nations. (2010) 'Guidance note of the Secretary-General: United Nations approach to transitional justice'. United Nations, March.

Verdoolaege, A. (2008) *Reconciliation Discourse: The Case of the Truth and Reconciliation Commission.* Amsterdam, Netherlands: John Benjamins Publishing Company

Waldorf, L. (2006) 'Rwanda's failing experiment in restorative justice', in D. Sullivan and L. Tift (eds) *Routledge Handbook of Restorative Justice.* London: Routledge. pp. 422–34.

Wemmers, J. (2009) 'Victims and the International Criminal Court (ICC): evaluating the success of the ICC with respect to victims', *International Review of Victimology,* 16: 211–27.

de Ycaza, C. (2013) 'A search for truth: a critical analysis of the Liberian Truth and Reconciliation Commission', *Human Rights Review,* 14: 189–212.

Chapter 8

Towards a cultural victimology?

Introduction

Here we return to where this book began, with the work of Young (2011). He concluded,

> Above all we must constantly be aware of the inherent creativity of human culture and of the rush to emotions and feelings which characterizes the human condition and the capacity for imagination which this demands and engenders.
>
> (Young, 2011: 225)

Sat amongst the wide variety of social science disciplines, victimology also has the capacity to engender these sentiments. Indeed as Spencer (2010: 48) observes, 'there is always a politics of victimology research', a politics that is de facto engaged with emotions inherent within the human condition following *trauma*. It has been argued here that tapping into how people feel about and make sense of their experiences of victimisation is to think of them in terms of *testimony*. This can be articulated in a variety of ways, from the sterile presentation of victim-impact statements and violent incidents of self-immolation to collective campaigns for victim 'rights'. Thinking about how these experiences might be understood in the pursuit of *justice* requires the 'bogus of positivism' (qua Young, 2011) to be consumed creatively by victimology. We have endeavoured to do this by following three lines of inquiry throughout the course of this book: trauma, testimony and justice.

In Chapter 1 the different ways in which the term 'victim' has been constituted within victimology was discussed across four theoretical perspectives: *positivist, radical, critical* and, as we see it, the emergent *cultural*. Each perspective provides different ways of arranging the issues of power relations, suffering and choice for the victim. This discussion presented a fundamental problem for victimology: the dominance of positivist victimology. This is a perspective which removes the role of 'choice' from both individual and collective victims, and does not permit a grasp on how the concept of 'victim' is produced and reproduced over time and in different contexts. Radical victimology draws power and power relations into victimological debate. It is a perspective that opens up the scope of who and what can be considered to be harmful, and under what circumstances victimisation can be rendered (in)visible. Identifying the 'powerful' and the state as central concerns is not new, but radical victimology is a marginalised practice. However, rendering choice as a redundant facet of the experience of victimisation is, in some respects, perpetuated in the radical perspective too. Radical victimology encourages a broadening of the remit of victimological work to address victimisation as experienced by collectivities. However, even here what counts as suffering, whether for the individual or the collectivity, can fall foul of the problem of inclusion and exclusion. A critical victimology provides the capacity to understand victims' experiences as being affected by power relations, for their suffering to be addressed or ignored in the policy process, and for victims themselves to be players in some of the choices they make as 'victims'. This is a perspective influenced by feminism, a position that has also influenced the acknowledgement of power within radical victimology and thrown the narrow focus of positivist victimology into stark relief. Taken together, this first chapter offers a slightly different reading of the three main victimological perspectives and looks to add something more by positing the emergent perspective of cultural victimology.

In arranging these theoretical perspectives in relation to issues of power, choice and suffering, this chapter provided the key terms and reference points returned to as touchstones of victimological knowledge throughout the chapters that followed, organised across the three overarching themes of trauma (Chapters 2 and 3) testimony (Chapters 4 and 5) and justice (Chapters 6 and 7).

Trauma

In Chapter 2 we reconceptualised the ways in which the experiences of being a victim might be considered. Here it has been suggested that in considering the impact of crime on victims there are two narratives with which to arrange the different victim labels used to make sense of (criminal) victimisation (i.e. primary/direct, secondary and indirect victimisation). The first of these can be connected to the agenda of positivist, conventional victimology that draws attention to a 'victim narrative' via criminal victimisation surveys, the effectiveness of victim policy and the inclusion of the victims' point of view. Embedded within this narrative are gendered forms of victimisation that reinforce what we know, or think we know, about victimisation based on assumptions of the ideal victim: women are ostensibly vulnerable and susceptible to victimisation; men are not. This is challenged by a second narrative, emerging out of parallel, but frequently disassociated, concerns with the emotional and psychological consequences of victimisation: the 'trauma narrative'. This narrative usefully connects with, and in some ways supplants, notions of primary victimisation with that of 'trauma', a term which, in its use, also encapsulates secondary and indirect victimisation. By allowing the harmful to include emotional and psychological traumatic experiences, this offers access to a wider collectivity of victims within victimology, yet at the same time remains very much centered on the individual experience of harm and victimisation. When coupled with victim movements, the rise of the trauma narrative gives way to spaces where the victim's voice can be heard in all of its complexity, and offers a challenge to the narrow ways in which victims had been previously imagined.

Chapter 3 graduates the trauma narrative from the individual to the collectivity. This chapter sits alongside Chapter 2 as an applied exercise in how we might think of victimisation. To make this case, victimisation is illustrated as operating on two parallel continuums; the first being from the individual to the collective, the second being from conventional street crime to crimes committed by the state. Using hate crime as the framing device, in this chapter we demonstrated that the occurrence of victimisation both in terms of interpersonal (individual) victimisation and acts of war (collective) is often undergirded, and indeed connected, by essentialism. This facilitates victimisation, but placing the 'other' in positions where they are only understood in subhuman terms permits violence and victimisation to take place, both individually and collectively. Thus the core part of the trauma narrative is indeed the imbalance of power relations between the collective victim and the state, just the same as it is between the individual offender and the victim. In this chapter one crucial difference is that the state has the agency and influence to render its victimisation of collectivities 'legitimate', particularly when committing acts of 'war' and/or mass murder (i.e. genocide). In either circumstance the victim is rendered choice-less. The discussion within this chapter purposefully redirects the collective notion of suffering back to the individual in order to turn attention to our second theme: testimony.

Testimony

Although criminological work has indeed had various engagements with biographical research, the same cannot be said for victimology. In victimology there has been a myriad of research employing a wide spectrum of qualitative, quantitative and mixed methods but for the most part this research has been hamstrung by positivism. Chapter 4 interjected into victimological research methods by presenting a way of reading individual personal testimonies as sources of data. Learning about the embedded rather than abstracted experiences of victimisation is of value to victimology and the use of *testimonio* offers this to the discipline. The use of testimonio, as applied to personal testimony, facilitates a reading of victims' experiences as having choices for themselves, or having them systematically removed from their lives. It also engages victimological research with first-hand accounts of suffering in both mundane and extraordinary ways.

Victim personal testimony does not just reside with the individual. During the progression of victim policy in the US, UK and across Europe in particular, the victim found a 'voice' within the criminal justice process. However these voices were only those which were formally recognised by state judicial processes, prescribed a set of 'needs' and afforded claims to have them catered for as 'rights' provided by the state. What of those who were harmed outwith the criminal justice system? Victimology in particular has been complicit in paying less than adequate attention to state and corporate victimisation, but this does not mean that victims have not been striving to have their voices heard. In Chapter 5 the role of victim movements was illustrated as large and influential groups that seek to bring the suffering of victims of corporate and state violence into public view and maintain them on political agendas. The voices of traumatised collectivities are unsurprisingly less popular with state-based interests as they frequently represent less than politically neutral concepts of the victim, and are certainly not passive in their interests. This chapter makes clear that not only has corporate victimisation become marginalised in victimological work, it is also frequently hidden in plain sight in the public and political arena. Victim movements represent efforts to reclaim choice in the face of suffering, suffering that is indeed known about and recognised as harmful by the 'victim', but so often is subjugated by the powerful and as a result goes without recognition and/or validation. Here the implications and questions raised by experiences in the 'Global South' are more than evident for a victimological imagination.

Justice

The final theme of 'justice' looked to take up some of the issues raised in Chapters 4 and 5 relating to the 'voice' of the victim. Chapter 6 began by addressing two prominent debates within victimological work: victim impact statements and restorative justice. These two offerings are core to how criminal-justice agencies in many parts of the developed world seek to afford victims not only 'justice', but justice as a form of therapy following their experiences of crime. Despite the intentions of the former to place the victim's 'voice' at the centre of the justice process, the experience of these kinds of interventions is at best anecdotal and at worst merely rhetorical for *some* victims of crime – diminishing their experiences of the justice process rather than enhancing it, and creating ripples within the concept of victimhood which rearranges secondary victimisation as 'trauma'. The latter concept of restorative justice has a more prominent role in representing victim-centred justice and can result in greater levels of victim satisfaction and validation through being invited into the justice processes via an emotional engagement with the law. However, this does not translate as easily and effectively as an apology from the offender, nor forgiveness from the victim. So some questions are left unanswered in terms of how justice can be achieved for victims in enhancing the presence of their voices in the judicial process.

Chapter 7 addressed the questionable efficacy of achieving justice through apology and forgiveness as a matter of reconciliation. This concept itself has multiple meanings for different people under different circumstances. The discussion of reconciliation in this chapter takes a similar form to that of restorative justice in Chapter 6, but here is concerned with crimes that are less routine and committed between states mediated through international justice mechanisms: *truth and reconciliation commissions*, the International Criminal Court, and practices associated with *transitional justice*. This final chapter avers that, when situated internationally, victimisation remains anchored to the ideal victim: exposed to issues of hierarchical arrangement, (in)visibility, and multilayered approaches to justice that reflect assumptions about who is and is not a victim. Such international mechanisms also raise fundamental questions that probe whose interests are being served in the process of reconciliation and what does this term actually amount to, in real terms, if promising to deliver 'justice' by other means (i.e. 'truth'). There is perhaps more at stake for the inclusion of the victim's voice at this level of engagement too. In environments where mass victimisation and suffering have torn apart communities, ruined nation-states and continues to be embedded within the fabric of some post-conflict societies, the promise of reconciliation, facilitated via the voice of victims, is a precarious platform to situate justice. Truth can and does take many forms in the process of reconciliation, and peace building has become an assumed part of post-conflict restoration. The pursuit of 'truth' as 'justice' in these terms isolates innocence as an assumed part of victimhood. It becomes a category not only arbitrarily defined but also infused with blame and legitimacy.

In conclusion, we do not propose that this is all that is to be said on these matters, nor that it is an entirely simple agenda for others to follow. Indeed there is, in many cases, too much to be said about each of the issues that we have raised here and we are acutely aware of some of the limitations of what has been presented throughout this book. However we consider our arrangement of these debates to have demonstrated that there is another conversation waiting to be had within victimology: one that sets aside the 'bogus of positivism' (qua Young, 2011) and its implicit conventional victimology, and connects with a wider body of literature, methodology and creativity. This is not a tidy business – in this respect all that we can perhaps hope for is to have arranged our ideas into neat enough pillars that others may choose to build upon or knock down. For now, we wish to return to the concept of cultural victimology, alluded to throughout this book, to offer some further thoughts as to what this might entail.

Towards a cultural victimology?

It is notable that victimology played only a small cameo role within Ferrell et al.'s (2008: 190–91) 'invitation' to take cultural criminology seriously as a substantive area of study. Thus we see this as an opportune moment to offer an invitation of our own by developing what we have already started to outline loosely elsewhere (see Walklate et al., 2011; Walklate et al., 2014). We do this by reiterating some of our previous ideas and looking to add something further to what we envision the capacity of the discipline to achieve by way of a 'cultural' engagement.

The phrase 'cultural victimology' was originally termed by our friend and colleague Gabe Mythen (2007: 464) as relating to 'a victimology attuned to human agency, symbolic display, and shared emotion'; particularly concerned with an engagement with, and deconstruction of visual materials as a means of engaging critically with the study of victims (Ferrell et al., 2008). Such a 'cultural' engagement within victimology is constituted in several layers.

Victimisation is frequently the result of violence of different sorts. Violence(s) that present often unexpected experiences of individual or collective trauma engage various forms of victim personal testimony, and offer different ways of pursuing and achieving justice. When captured and communicated from the personal to the public, the ways in which these elements are represented, commentated on and outlined frequently occur via the national/global media, criminal-justice mechanisms, or public platforms (Ferrell et al., 2008). These are key imperatives for rendering different forms of victimisation either visible or invisible within the public psyche. The result of this visibility or invisibility frequently dictates the ways in which the state and its attendant services respond positively (or not) to certain types of harm (Mythen, 2007). There are, of course, further approaches with which to think of victimology in culturally informed ways, beyond the nuances of critical victimology implicit in this explanation, as this alone does not constitute a complete 'cultural' reading of victimological material. Most notably, as O'Brien (2005) has rightly questioned of criminology, it is important to ask more fully what is actually *'cultural'* about the strand of victimology being illustrated here? We do not intend to fully explicate an answer to this question here, but for now will explore our ideas in the presentation of a final case study: the victimologist as witness.

The victimologist as witness

Some time ago now Vincenzo Ruggiero (1992) suggested that those involved in social science research, particularly criminology, should include themselves as a site of analysis in their work. Leaning on the recognition of an inherent *double hermeneutic* in social science research proposed by Giddens (1976), Ruggiero (1992) suggested that criminologists are frequently exposed to the vagaries of the subject matter that they study and can often be guided by their past experiences into what they choose to research. The same could be said for victimologists, particularly given that victimology has been said to be the only discipline dedicated to the harms experienced by others (see Rock, 1994), and, as stated above, it is de facto engaged with emotional aspects of the human condition. These emotions are not just those of the victim (nor those of the offender, for that matter), and it should be remembered that social scientists are not automatons in what they do either. Returning to C. Wright Mills (1959), for whom the study of society begins with the self 'as minute points of the intersections of biography and history within society', he proposes that,

> contemporary man's self-conscious view of himself as an outsider, if not a permanent stranger, rests upon an absorbed realization of social relativity and of the transformative power of history. The sociological imagination is the most fruitful of the self-conscious.
>
> (Mills, 1959: 7)

Notwithstanding the gendered nature of the language with which *The Sociological Imagination* is written, the questions remain as to what this is taken to mean and why it is relevant to a cultural engagement within victimology. Our answer to this is quite simple; it is to question 'Who am I?', or perhaps more appropriately for our purposes 'Who are *we?*' While it is not our intention to indulge in needless personal accounts of our lives, we consider it a necessary part of a wider cultural engagement with the discipline to provide a brief insight into who we are in relation to the subject matter of our social science: victimology. We consider doing so as a platform to offer the reader a *double hermeneutic* reading of the material we have covered in this book, why we consider it to be important, and how we have arrived at these intersecting victimological interests from quite different avenues.

Reflecting on 9/11

Early in the afternoon during September 2001 the first author received a phone call whilst walking through a high street in the south of England. The message was simple: 'Get to a television!' Finding refuge in the first electrical store I could, I found myself amongst people who had presumably all received similar instructions from friends and loved ones. Like millions of people all over the world, this collective group of strangers were silently watching the events of 9/11 unfold live. As a young serviceman at the time, less than 24 hours later I arrived for duty in a leafy, rural area in the south of England, donning a combat uniform rather than shirt and trousers. Two months later I arrived in Kuwait for a four-month tour of duty, during which I watched preparation for the 2003 war in Iraq gather pace. Once back in the UK I remember uncomfortably watching the 'shock and awe' campaign in Iraq unfold. Soon after, I found myself at university studying criminology, with my academic interests informed by experiences that I was determined to learn from, but frustrated at having little literature to draw upon within the discipline. Some time later I completed a PhD in victimology (see McGarry, 2012), having found my way into a debate relating to the military but feeling infinitely restricted by the discipline's lack of *imagination*. During this time I was also employed by the civilian police, working with crime data, experiencing first hand the 'bogus of positivism' (Young, 2011) and the unreflexive, administrative nature of the criminological enterprise. These collective experiences had forced me to consider social events as globally interconnected; violence in Manhattan during 2001 had been felt as far away as the leafy corners of the UK, and continues to this day to be felt across the Middle East.

Experiencing these things first hand it is impossible not to think of them reflexively, seeing the world as fragile, intriguing and constantly changing. How victimisation is studied and measured, however – be it at the level of individual street crime or the collective level of widespread state, industrial or corporate harm – can and does place restrictive criteria on who and what we, as social scientists, include and exclude as a core part of our victimological imaginations. Part of our task within this book has been to open out the agenda of victimology so it might more readily consider such issues as a core part of its concerns.

The second author's reflections on 9/11 are somewhat more distanced in time and place. I was returning from holiday on a ferry from Northern Spain where it took some time for the collected travelers to absorb the images on the television screens of the Twin Towers ablaze. For many of the English people the first response was to think that this was a return to the bombing campaigns associated with the problems in Northern Ireland, and for the Spanish it reminded them of similar images associated with their own internal 'terrorist' issue: ETA. Neither group paid that much detailed attention at first. However, the enormity of these events slowly infiltrated the passengers and what had been in the past a lighthearted ferry journey became somewhat more somber. On returning home, the frequent practice night flights of bomb-laden jets from RAF Valley based in Anglesey, North Wales, were a clear indicator of what was to come long before any invasion force was announced publically. Since that time events have unfolded in the ways documented in Chapter 3 though it is easy to forget that, even within our Western-centric world view, such events are not responded to in the same way everywhere. As it happens I was also on the same street, at more or less the same time, when the car bomb exploded in Stockholm, Sweden in December 2011, almost 10 years later. This event, though not as 'big' as 9/11 or the London bombings of 2005 (discussed in Chapter 4), was dealt with in a very different way in that country. The refusal to be driven by the international media into a frenzied fear of the 'other' was almost tangible. Sweden, of course, having declared itself a multi-cultural society in the 1970s, rather like Norway (discussed in Chapter 7), had a different cultural take on this event.

Having been engaged in victim-oriented work since the early 1980s, both as a researcher and as an activist (see Walklate, 2008), I was already deeply embroiled in the conceptual and policy debates generated by victimology. I was engaged because I cared. Now that point of caring reached a height of passion fueled by the illegality of the warfare that followed 9/11 and the myopic response that both victimology and criminology seemed to have to these events.

My critical gaze has become sharpened and attuned to the presumptions of the Western world as I have been increasingly privileged to teach and work in other places. This book reflects some of that thinking, jointly produced and delivered.

By no means do we consider these experiences to give complete legitimacy to the intellectual work that we have presented here. We do however recognise our own 'self-consciousness' as social scientists (qua Mills, 1959) as being an important part of how we have engaged with our victimological imaginations in what we consider to be critically informed and creatively practiced ways. However, if this is who we are and what has brought us to discuss these interests in victimology then our next task is to ask, in what ways have we been observing them as victimologists? To answer this we look to the work of Richard Quinney (1998), who believes that 'the criminologist' has an unwitting role as a 'witness', but not in the orthodox way found in criminal courts. Quinney (1998) avers that if we are to endeavor to observe suffering and violence across a wide variety of crimes and victimisation as part of our day-to-day activities,

> Criminologists, for instruction on the bearing of witness, can become familiar with the many kinds of witnessing that are evident in a host of sources. Journalists, photographers, artists, social scientists, and many other writers report the sufferings throughout the world.
>
> (Quinney, 1998: 59)

As such, Quinney (1998) considers that as social scientists, with an interest in harm and victimisation, we are compelled as 'moral entrepreneurs' to 'see' an ethical commitment in our scholarly work. This is achievable in many different mediums, including books, literature, photography and social research, to name but a few. By engaging with what Peters (2001) refers to as 'baggage', as witnesses we are afforded a moral and cultural force that sees law and atrocity bound by notions of life, death, justice, trauma and suffering. Therefore as academic victimologists we *witness*. The issues presented throughout the pages of this book stand as a testament to our own interpretation of this witnessing, combining theory, case studies, photographs and personal testimony to highlight some of the 'traumas of our time' (qua Quinney, 1998).

Through witnessing what we consider to be important social issues for victimology to address, we can shed light on a variety of further harms, injustices, structural violence and vulnerability. Moreover – if we choose to – our non-violent action of witnessing can let us take a stand against forms of human wrongdoing that stretch from interpersonal violence to state and corporate victimisation (Quinney, 1998). These observations of 'witnessing' are made mindful of Elias' (1986) advice that a rights-based approach to victimology (as discussed in Chapter 5) can make complimentary use of two resources for a critical appraisal of victimisation. First, thinking about human rights offers the victimologist a wider imagination of what constitutes harm, and second, victimology can provide a depth of analysis to investigate what human rights uncover (Elias, 1986). However, it is the third pursuit of creativity and imagination within victimological work that we want to mobilise. This is what Peters (2001) refers to as 'active' rather than 'passive' witnessing. The active witness is someone who is at first passive, but becomes the privileged possessor and *producer* of knowledge to make visible what they have seen (Peters, 2001). As such *we* are indeed active witnesses to harm and victimisation, and as Ruggiero (1992) usefully points out, certainly not neutral observers of what we have presented throughout this book.

Witnessing and bearing witness to victimology

There is something to delineate further here: the distinction between 'witnessing' and 'bearing witness'. Spencer (2010) has previously advocated for a victimology that bears witness to the 'event' of victimisation of the self, the harms experienced by others, and the process of witnessing as a practice. We have advocated elsewhere for a similar view of victimological work that distinguishes between 'witnessing' what we 'see', and 'bearing witness' to see beyond what we 'see':

> It is important to set apart the complexities of the 'witness' from the simple onlooker. That is to differentiate 'witnessing' from 'bearing witness'. The former is what we 'see' (such as the symbolic and figurative observations of victims and their experiences), and the latter involves 'seeing beyond what we see' (including the State's political reaction to victimising events such as terrorist attacks). In doing so 'witnessing' becomes an integral methodological tool for a visual victimology.
>
> (Walklate et al., 2014: 265)

Let us now return to the image displayed on the front of this book, to add some further meaning to our role as witnesses in this regard, and to help bring these thoughts to a conclusion.

Witnessing: what we 'see'

As stated in the introduction, this image was taken by the first author of *The All Souls Altar of Remembrance*, within Trinity Church, Manhattan during late October 2013 (see Trinity Church, 2013 for further details and images not taken by the author). The building itself stands on Broadway and Wall Street, within half a mile from ground zero, the resting place of the collapsed Twin Towers of the World Trade Center following the terrorist attacks on 9/11. As Ryan Campbell (cited in Trinity Church, 2013), chairperson of the Trinity's Visual Arts Committee observes, this scene,

Figure 8.1 The All Souls Altar of Remembrance, Trinity Church, Manhattan

from its initial humble beginning a few years ago … has grown into a space that grasps the attention of the numerous tourists passing through Trinity's doors hourly. People of all types photograph it and organically contribute. It has become quite a conceptual piece of art, an installation that captures the imagination.

When displayed in colour this image is a vibrant mix of pinks, greens, yellows and blues (see Trinity Church, 2013), from the notes littered across a messy scene of jumbled paper, seemingly placed without care. When presented in the way seen here it takes a different form. Removing these colours renders it as a looming image, almost gaunt in its appearance, and although situated in a building (re)constructed of gothic revival architecture, this is not a gothic scene. It is a peaceful, public space of reflection and remembrance for loved ones lost.

Drawing the eye to the centre of the image we can see several branches emanating from the jumble of paper depicting a tree of life. Each of the small shipping tags affixed by string denotes messages with sentiments of love and thoughts of loved ones past and present. The fullness of these branches appear to have given way to some innovations: messages written on sticky notes placed around and in between the branches, stuck on to the altar behind and below. The sheer volume of these messages suggests a large footfall of visitors within this area of Manhattan, placed by a variety of people from all over the world, indicated by the assortment of languages with which each note has been written. There are further innovations to this space too. Just below the centre mass of the image there are more traditional symbols of remembrance – flowers wrapped in paper lie amongst the debris, and a font filled with sand holds a message and several glowing votive candles. To the right of the font there is a mask, halved, looking up at the jumble of paper, staring expressionless at a hand-drawn heart hanging from the lip of the altar. This is certainly a public space that we are meant to 'see', with messages and items placed for others to view as public displays of affection, remembrance and mourning. It is perhaps no accident that this scene caught the imagination, as suggested, particularly given Trinity's proximity to the collapse of the World Trade Center, by the poignancy of this public space, coupled with the first author's reflexive note above. However, in what ways does this image encourage us to bear witness, to see beyond what we are presented with?

Bearing witness: seeing beyond what we 'see'

As indicated above, undertaking victimological work, as advocated here, is indeed to engage with one's own biographical position. Moreover, Spencer (2010) avers that victimological work is also historical work, meaning victimological research is, by default, entwined with C. Wright Mills' (1959) own notions of *imagination*. Spencer (2010: 49) continues,

> the work of the researcher is always a work of mourning. If memory testifies to the fact that we can never fully recollect the past, then mourning affirms that we are never finished with the past: that the task of comprehending the past always lies ahead of us.

Bearing witness therefore means to transgress what is presented to us, to think of it in social, historical and cultural terms as C. Wright Mills (1959) had encouraged. We are therefore compelled to use this image as a point of reflection as well as observation, to consider what can be 'seen' beyond the image.

The terrorist attacks in the US on 9/11 have been a key focal point for much criminological work since 2001, and have in many ways been a point of orientation for this book. The altar in the image we have used here is not constructed as a memorial to 9/11, but its proximity to the collapse of the Twin Towers of the World Trade Center encourages us to make some associated connections. The altar is a space of memorial and remembrance for loved ones who have passed, a space for people to reflect, offer sentiments of affection, and to display mourning in a variety of ways. We may speculate that some of the feelings expressed in this way are perhaps encouraged by its temporal and geographical proximity to ground zero, suggesting that what was once a site of trauma and tragedy has been transformed into a public space of memorial. A space to remember loved ones lost personally, but also to remember in solidarity the trauma experienced by other individuals and collectivities. Throughout the past decade alone we can observe similar collective traumas, from the devastation of war experienced in Afghanistan and Iraq, ethnic conflict in Sudan, violent geopolitics in Russia and Ukraine, the spread of the Ebola virus across West Africa in Guinea, Liberia and Sierra Leone, to the disappearance of commercial aircraft in South East Asia. Each speaks of collective and individual traumas caused by imbalances of power, poverty and global inequalities in economics, health and justice.

The displays of personal testimony in this image are silent, respectful and peaceful. They have been made individually, but when gathered together on the altar present a striking display of collective testimony. Similar acts of silent personal testimony in action have been demonstrated by collectivities in the aftermath of 9/11. In the UK the town of Royal Wootton Bassett in Wiltshire and Highway 401 (the 'Highway of Heroes') in Canada have both previously become sites of public mourning for fallen military personnel who died following service in Afghanistan and Iraq. However, testimony is not always subdued, as recent events following the 2011 riots across the UK and public unrest in Ferguson, Missouri, in the US during 2014 have demonstrated. Both events were sparked by the fatal shootings of young black males by white police officers on both sides of the Atlantic. The Arab Spring in 2010 further illustrates the power of personal testimony in action to destabilise political corruption and kleptocracy and draw political attention to unemployment and human rights violations across the Arab world. More recently in Hong Kong protests staged by the Umbrella Movement in reaction to electoral reforms from Beijing demonstrated other voices demanding to be heard through political acts of defiance. Finally, the Occupy Wall Street movement against corporate influence, financial inequality and political corruption returns us to the surrounding geography of our image. Each of these acts of collective personal testimony has different goals, but they share the same purpose: the pursuit of *justice*. They are illustrative of the isolation felt by individuals from the political process and the distance forming between governments and their electorate; these are voices that feel they can only be heard if mustered to speak collectively against power. As such this image encourages us to see beyond what we 'see' – in Spencer's (2010) terms, the altar is a space to think of the past but also to ponder the future.

References

Elias, R. (1986) *The Politics of Victimisation: Victims, Victimology, and Human Rights*. Oxford: Oxford University Press.

Ferrell, J., Hayward, K., and Young, J. (2008) *Cultural Criminology: An Invitation*. London: SAGE.

Giddens, A. (1976) *New Rules of Sociological Method*. London: Hutchinson.

McGarry, S. R. (2012) 'Developing a victimological imagination: an auto/biographical study of British military veterans'. Unpublished PhD thesis, Liverpool Hope University.

Mills, C. W. (1959) *The Sociological Imagination*. Oxford: Oxford University Press.

Mythen, G. (2007) 'Cultural victimology: "Are we all victims now?" in S. Walklate. (ed.) *Handbook of Victims and Victimology*. Cullompton, Devon: Willan. pp. 464–83.

O'Brien, M. (2005) 'What is *cultural* about cultural criminology?', *British Journal of Criminology*, 45(5): 599–612.

Peters, J. D. (2001) 'Witnessing', *Media, Culture and Society*, 23: 707–23.

Quinney, R. (1998) 'Criminology as moral philosophy, criminologist as witness', *Contemporary Justice Review*, 1: 347–64.

Rock, P. (ed.) (1994) *Victimology*. Aldershot: Dartmouth Publishing.

Ruggiero, V. (1992) 'Realist criminology: a critique', in J. Young and R. Matthews (eds) *Rethinking Criminology: The Realist Debate*. London: SAGE. pp. 123–40.

Spencer, D. (2010) 'Event and victimisation', *Criminal Law and Philosophy*, 5(1): 39–52.

Trinity Church. (2013) 'Altar of Remembrance'. Available at https://www.trinitywallstreet.org/galleries/altar-remembrance.

Walklate, S. (1989) *Victimology: The Victim and the Criminal Justice Process*. Oxon: Routledge.

——(2008) 'Researching victims', in R. D. King and E. Wincup (eds) *Doing Research on Crime and Justice* (2nd edition). Oxford: Oxford University Press. pp. 183–204.

Walklate, S., Mythen, G., and McGarry, R. (2011) 'Witnessing Wootton Bassett: an exploration in cultural victimology', *Crime, Media, Culture*, 7(2): 149–66.

Walklate, S., McGarry, R. and Mythen, G. (2014) 'Trauma, visual victimology, and the poetics of justice', in M. H. Jacobsen (ed.) *The Poetics of Crime: Understanding and Researching Crime and Deviance through Creative Sources*. Surrey: Ashgate. pp. 263–83.

Young, J. (2011) *The Criminological Imagination*. Cambridge: Polity.

Index